*The Unknown Soldier*

## BOOKS BY JAMES LEASOR

*General*

The Sea Wolves
Author by Profession
The Monday Story
Wheels to Fortune
The Serjeant Major
The Red Fort
The One That Got Away (with Kendal Burt)
The Millionth Chance
War at the Top
Conspiracy of Silence (with Peter Eton)
The Plague and the Fire
The Uninvited Envoy
Singapore: The Battle that Changed the World
Green Beach
Boarding Party
Code Name Nimrod
The Marine from Mandalay
The Clock with Four Hands

*Fiction*

Not Such a Bad Day
The Strong Delusion
NTR—Nothing to Report
They Don't Make Them Like That Any More
Never Had a Spanner on Her
Follow the Drum
Host of Extras
Mandarin-Gold
The Chinese Widow
Jade Gate

*The Dr. Jason Love Case Histories of Suspense*

Passport to Oblivion
Passport to Peril
Passport in Suspense
Passport for a Pilgrim
A Week of Love
Love-all
Love and the Land Beyond
Frozen Assets: Return of the Intrepid Dr. Love

# The Unknown Soldier

## The Allies' Greatest Deception in the Days Before D-Day

## James Leasor

THE LYONS PRESS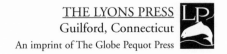
Guilford, Connecticut
An imprint of The Globe Pequot Press

The Lyons Press is an imprint of The Globe Pequot Press

10  9  8  7  6  5  4  3  2  1

Printed in the United States of America


Library of Congress Cataloging-in-Publication Data

Leasor, James.
        [Unknown warrior]
The Unknown soldier: the Allies' greatest deception in the days before D-Day
/ James Leasor.
p. cm.
Originally published: Unknown Warrior. London : Heinemann, 1980.
Includes bibliographical references.
ISBN 1-59228-418-3
1. World War, 1939-1945—Secret service—Great Britain.  2. World War,
1939-1945—Military intelligence—Great Britain.  I. Title.

D810.S7L36 2004
                                                          2004048305

Dedicated to the memory
of
Admiral of the Fleet the Earl Mountbatten of Burma,
KG, PC, GCB, OM, GCSI, GCIE, GCVO, DSO;
who formed X-Troop,

and to Colonel Sir Ronald Wingate, Bt.,
CB, CMG, CIE, OBE,
who told me the story on which
this book is based.

It is also for 'Stephen Rigby',
and all who served in X-Troop.


★   ★   ★


'He either fears his fate too much
Or his deserts are small
That does not put it to the touch
To gain or lose it all.

James Graham,
Marquis of Montrose,
1612 - 1650

'It is indeed remarkable that the vast long-planned assault fell on the enemy as a surprise both in time and place . . .

'There had been much argument about which front the Allies would attack. Rundstedt had consistently believed that our main blow would be launched across the Straits of Dover, as that was the shortest sea route and gave the best access to the heart of Germany. Rommel for long agreed with him. Hitler and his staff however appear to have had reports indicating that Normandy would be the principal battleground. Even after we had landed, uncertainties continued. Hitler lost a whole critical day in making up his mind to release the two nearest Panzer divisions to reinforce the front . . .

'Thus it was not until the third week in July, six weeks after D Day, that reserves from the Fifteenth Army were sent south from the Pas de Calais to join the battle. Our deception measures both before and after D Day had aimed at creating this confused thinking. Their success was admirable and had far-reaching results on the battles.'

> Winston S. Churchill,
> *The Second World War*, Vol V1.
> Triumph and Tragedy

'Hitler never believed that any operation, however outrageous, was not feasible, and his own career and the successes of the first year of the war, achieved often in defiance of the more cautious advice of his professional staff, gave him an unshakable belief in the rightness of his powers of imagination. How lucky this was for us . . . !'

> Sir Ronald Wingate, Bt.
> *Not in the Limelight.*

# Contents

# *Preface*

The Second World War, more than any other conflict before or since, attracted large numbers of men and women who willingly volunteered for particularly hazardous operations, which, even if successful, often offered little hope of their own survival. Of these volunteers, few could approach the dedication of the men who served in the British Army's most secret unit of totally unknown warriors, frequently called "X-Troop."

For reasons to be explained, virtually no documentation about them exists. They lived—and many died—under completely false names, with totally fictitious backgrounds. Their real names do not appear on any roll of honor or war memorial, but their courage, dedication, and resourcefulness played a huge and always anonymous part in the complex mosaic of Allied victory.

Most were Jews from European countries under Nazi domination. Many, perhaps most, had lost relations and friends in the concentration camps. In Britain in 1940, when a German invasion seemed imminent, many foreigners were interned because their political sympathies were unknown. As the threat of invasion diminished, they were released, and these men willingly put aside their real identities to volunteer for this unique and dedicated unit.

After the war, many became British subjects, often keeping the names they had been given when they joined X-Troop. Some stayed in Britain, others immigrated to the United States, to Canada, to Australia. All began completely new lives.

Every former member of X-Troop, whom I met during research for this book, enjoyed a successful career. Often, women they married—and later, their families—had not the slightest idea of their real background.

One former member, with whom I became friendly partly because of a shared interest in 1930s American cars, joined the British Security Service. One of his tasks, in that early postwar period in Germany, was to cultivate a relationship with a Russian, who was said to be eager to strengthen his contacts with the West. They would meet once a fortnight in a remote clearing in a forest. The Russian did not ask for money but did want a pair of new waterproof boots to replace his old shoddy shoes. This was arranged, but with some difficulty. All clothes and footwear were strictly rationed in Britain then, only available in exchange for coupons—and how to explain to some clerk the need in this special case?

The two men met regularly for several months. As the Russian's information became more and more important, my friend handed over the assignment to a more senior agent, and their meetings stopped.

"Did you ever meet him again?" I asked once.

"No," he replied, "But I saw him regularly. Whenever I watched the TV news showing Communist leaders taking the salute as the Russian troops and missiles passed by during the annual march in Moscow, there was my old informant, standing on the platform next to the most senior Party members."

This book tells the story of some who served in X-Troop, and like them all, steadfastly followed the aim of their leader: "To do something during my life which will make the world a better place after I have gone."

James Leasor
January 15, 2004

# Chapter One

The Army dispatch rider stopped outside the detached house on the outskirts of Eastbourne, pulled his Norton motorcycle up on its stand and walked in through the open front door.

'For the officer commanding, sir,' he said, saluting.

Captain Bryan Hilton-Jones opened the buff envelope, noted the date, in May 1944, and read the typed message.

A volunteer was urgently required for a secret assignment of the highest priority. He must be of non-Jewish appearance, speak German perfectly, and preferably have a German or Austrian background. A good knowledge of French on a conversational level was also desirable.

This volunteer should have a calm disposition, be a competent parachutist, and ideally would have undertaken pre-war technical or professional training; an academic qualification or degree was not essential.

This man would be required to work in dangerous circumstances, totally on his own.

'No reply,' said Hilton-Jones briefly.

The dispatch rider saluted and went out of the house. Hilton-Jones listened as the beat of his engine died away and then reread the message. For weeks, similar requests had arrived, addressed to him, or to the adjutant of No. 10 (Inter-Allied) Commando, seeking volunteers for unspecified military tasks. Sometimes the requirements seemed bizarre: the candidate must be a chemist, or be able to drive a Rumanian railway locomotive. But such unusual requests did not surprise him, for Hilton-Jones commanded what was arguably the strangest, most individualistic and most secret unit to wear uniform in any Allied army. Even its title was unusual: X-Troop.

1

Hilton-Jones was in his twenties, and because of his natural gift of leadership, members of X-Troop nicknamed him The Skipper. He had been born in Caernarvon, where his father was a doctor. His mother's family owned a large drapery business in Egypt. His parents separated when he was a boy, and his mother returned to Cairo, leaving him with his father and a strict housekeeper.

When Bryan Hilton-Jones was ten, his father died. His mother returned to Wales, bought a large house outside Caernarvon and proceeded to transform her son's hitherto quiet life. She took him on a visit to Egypt and the United States, and on his return, Hilton-Jones entered a preparatory school, then went on to Rugby and to Cambridge. In June 1937, he took a first-class degree in modern languages intending to go into the Foreign Office that autumn. Instead, he joined the Army. By 1942, Hilton-Jones was a lieutenant, serving in Scotland with No. 4 Commando. One morning he received orders to proceed to Harlech to take command of X-Troop, shortly after its formation by Lord Louis Mountbatten.

When Mountbatten became Chief of Combined Operations in that year, he decided to use the talents and abilities of young men who had come to Britain from countries occupied by the Nazis. Many were eager to join the Commandos, but no opportunity existed for foreign nationals to do so. Mountbatten changed this by forming No. 10 (Inter-Allied) Commando, with Troops of Free French, Dutch, Norwegians, Poles and Italian-speaking Yugoslavs. Each Troop consisted of up to ninety men with four officers. They had specialised knowledge of beaches, language and areas which he knew could prove of great value in operations on the continent.

The first commanding officer was Colonel Dudley Lister, a regular soldier who had previously commanded No. 4 Commando. Lister was a very big man, and a physical fitness fanatic. He had won the Military Cross in 1918 and received a mention in despatches for his part in the Lofoten Islands raid in 1941. He was also a former British amateur heavyweight boxing champion – one of only three army officers to hold this title since the 1800's – and had been Army heavyweight champion.

Major Peter Laycock was his second in command. He was a brother of Robert Laycock and an immensely popular officer.

As No. 10 Commando took shape, the question arose how best to deal with German sentries encountered, and prisoners captured on Commando raids.

For this, Mountbatten needed men who could speak colloquial German, read German documents and interrogate German prisoners. They must also understand German psychology, so he suggested to Mr. Churchill that he should form a further Troop of anti-Nazi German, Hungarian and Austrian volunteers. They were all technically enemy aliens and, understandably, were almost all Jewish. Although they detested the Nazi regime and Hitler, they had been interned in Britain, largely in 1940, when a German invasion was feared.

Nothing like this had ever been proposed before. Many senior officers felt that such a Commando Troop could not possibly succeed. Mr. Churchill thought otherwise and agreed enthusiastically that Mountbatten should go ahead with his plans.

'Because they will all be unknown warriors,' Churchill pointed out, 'they must perforce be considered an unknown quantity. Since the algebraic symbol for the unknown is X, let us call them X-Troop.'

Possibly Mountbatten was eager to enlist these men because he vividly recalled the tragic experiences of his father, Prince Louis of Battenberg, during the 1914-18 war.

Prince Louis came to Britain as a boy, accepted British nationality, and joined the Royal Navy at fourteen as a cadet. He rose to be First Sea Lord, the highest rank a serving naval officer could obtain, and with Churchill as First Lord of the Admiralty, he revolutionised naval training and equipment. But his German birth and background finally ruined his career.

During the First World War, Prince Louis became the victim of a campaign of virulent Press hostility simply because of his German origins. Fearing that this might eventually harm the Royal Navy, which he had served so outstandingly for nearly half a century, he resigned from the service. His great abilities were thus denied to the country he had adopted as his own at the moment that Britain stood in the greatest need of them.

Mountbatten realised that many young men from Germany, Austria and Hungary had escaped from the Nazis, and would be equally as loyal to Britain, as his father had been. Because of their 'enemy alien' backgrounds they had been removed from British universities, sometimes on the eve of sitting for degrees, or arrested in offices and factories, and sent out to internment camps in Canada and Australia.

3

Now they would be asked to volunteer for a fighting unit and if they did so, they would be given British names – the name Mountbatten was, of course, simply an English translation of Battenberg.

'The best method of security is not to put *anything* on paper,' ordered Mountbatten, and so all Troop records were kept to an irreducible minimum. Some felt that the title X-Troop could have sinister connotations, so the Troop came to be referred to as No. 3 Troop of No. 10 (Inter-Allied) Commando; or, ironically, to differentiate it from the other foreign Troops, as 'the *British* Troop.'

So close was its cover that even Charles Breese, the officer responsible for equipping the whole Commando, did not know of its existence.

'X-Troop was certainly kept secret from me,' he wrote years later. 'It was obviously kept firmly in the "need to know" category and quite rightly, too.'

The British Security Service, M15, investigated the background of every volunteer. Only when a man was declared 'clean' would Hilton-Jones interview him and explain the very grave risks he ran in case of capture. If the volunteer agreed to accept them, he signed a form which began simply, 'I understand the risks . . .'

Lord Louis Mountbatten ordered that in addition to a new British-sounding name, foreign members of X-Troop should also be given a totally fictitious, believable – and checkable – British background of family, friends and associations.

Before the Allied invasion of Sicily a British submarine had deposited a corpse in the uniform of a Royal Marines major off the Spanish coast, a deceptive scheme known as Operation Mincemeat. Documents and letters that 'Major Martin' carried in his briefcase suggested that Greece and Sardinia were the prime targets for landings. Hitler, disregarding the advice of his Intelligence experts, accepted this information as genuine and at once ordered reinforcements to Greece and Sardinia. Sicily was thus less heavily defended than it would otherwise have been. Mountbatten had written one of these letters of deception and afterwards, when anyone mentioned this scheme, he would say jocularly that 'Major Martin' was 'the best Royal Marines officer I ever had on my staff.'

Because an unknown corpse had been successfully supplied with an identity which deceived the German High Command, the OKW, (Oberkommando der Wehramacht) Mountbatten insisted that equally believable aliases must be given to every X-Troop volunteer. This was essential, because some were stateless. Others had left families or close relations in Germany when they came to Britain before the war. Many of their real backgrounds were known to the Gestapo, and if they were captured and identified, those of German nationality could have been arraigned for treason, with fearful results to them and any relations still in Germany.

If a member of X-Troop was captured, and gave his name as Jim Jones from Dartford in Kent, for example, he must know that town well enough to answer detailed questions about The Bull Hotel or the Heath, the State cinema or the Grammar School. If he claimed to be from Stockport in Lancashire, then he must know the names of the main cotton mills in the area, where and when the last trams ran, and which local herbalist sold the best sarsaparilla. Members of X-Troop could never risk appearing as Germans in British uniform; they must always seem as British as the flag.

After the Sicily campaign, Lord Mountbatten visited Brigadier Robert Laycock who had succeeded him as Chief of Combined Operations, and Laycock mentioned the excellent work of one member of X-Troop who had taken part in the landing.

'I would like to talk to him,' said Mountbatten. When the young man arrived, Mountbatten asked him whether he was satisfied with his new identity.

'Absolutely, sir. I know that if I am unlucky enough to be captured, they will never guess I am a German.' Then he paused.

'May I ask you a question, sir?'

'Of course,' replied Mountbatten.

'I was at school in Salem for a year with Prince Philip of Greece, before he went on to Gordonstoun. Where is he now?'

'You see that destroyer?' asked Mountbatten, pointing to the warship *Wallace*, which lay off-shore. 'He is a Lieutenant aboard her.'

The irony of this meeting was that the man from X-Troop could not pass on his good wishes to Prince Philip – because this would mean revealing his true identity. Indeed only one man, a senior civil servant in the Casualty Department of the War Office, evacuated to Liverpool, held the two parallel lists of names, true and false, locked in his safe. He was billeted with a local family, the Clelands, who for some reason gave him the nickname, 'Blossom.'

They had shown great kindness to a member of X-Troop, Colin

Anson, and he gave the name of their daughter Pat Cleland as his next of kin. When Anson was severely wounded in Sicily, news reached 'Blossom' in his official capacity, but so strict was all security surrounding X-Troop, that several weeks passed before the Clelands could be officially informed – although he was living in their house.

Every X-Troop volunteer was 'adopted' by English, Scottish and Welsh families, with whom they sometimes spent leaves, and whose photographs or letters they frequently carried in their battledress pockets. All mail addressed to X-Troopers under their old German names was intercepted by a special team in the Army postal service and readdressed. This scale of deception, with false Army numbers, names and requirements, had to be kept totally secret from the normal Army pay and records offices, but without disturbing the usual administrative routines.

Just how convincingly British the members of X-Troop did become was proved by Harry Nomburg, who had been born in Coburg, a small town in central Germany, and seat of the Dukes of Saxe-Coburg-Gotha. His family moved to Berlin, where he went to school. He came to Britain in May, 1939, and lived in Whittingehame, the former house of Lord Balfour, twenty miles south of Edinburgh, which had been converted into a farm school for refugee children. At sixteen, he was interned for three months as an enemy alien at Lingfield Racecourse in Surrey, then he joined the Pioneer Corps and, finally, X-Troop. At nineteen, he was its youngest member.

Apart from No. 10, he also served with 12, 6 and 3 Commandos in North West Europe, and early in 1945, after weeks of front-line duty in the south of Holland, spent a week-end on leave in Brussels which had just been liberated. In an attempt to smarten up, Nomburg decided to have his hair cut. A prosperous midle-aged burgher in the next chair in the barber's saloon invited him to his house for dinner. Nomburg was pleased to accept. The meal was served by a uniformed maid, on a table covered by a white linen cloth, set with silver – a welcome change from active service conditions.

Conversation was in English, and Nomburg's host related the experiences of a friend who had recently invited an American soldier home to dinner. Half way through the meal, the American asked him: 'Do you know Aachen (Aix-la-Chapelle)?'

'Of course,' the Belgian replied.

'Then you know Kaiser Street in Aachen?'

'Yes, I do. But why are you so interested in Aachen?'

The American explained that he had been born and raised in Aachen, and only emigrated to the United States just before the war.

'Imagine that,' said Nomburg's host gloomily. 'My poor friend, believing he had invited an Allied liberator to dine with him, had actually taken a *German* into his house. You can see, my friend, that is why I shy away from Americans. You can never be sure where they are from or who they are. This simply cannot happen with a *British* soldier. They are *all* British. No doubt whatever about that. And for this reason I picked you to dine with me tonight...'

Hilton-Jones stood up, crossed the room and looked out through the window at the sea. Lengths of railway line, encrusted with shellfish and raw with rust, sprouted from the shining shingle on the beach. Shreds of seaweed fluttered like tiny pennants from coils of rusty barbed wire, set up years before when the threat of a German invasion was at its height. That night, leading a raiding party, called 'Hiltforce' after him, he would discover what the shore defences looked like on the other side of the Channel, for he had to carry out a pre-invasion reconnaissance on the French coast to investigate a new type of barrier being built on the beaches, known as Element C.

With him would go Lieutenant George Lane, who, like him, had joined X-Troop on its formation in Harlech, and had since become the first officer to be commissioned from its ranks. Lane, a Hungarian, was married to Dr. Miriam Rothschild. Before the war, he had represented Hungary at water polo.

He was an undergraduate at Christ Church, Oxford, when war was declared. Shortly afterwards, he spent a week-end with Commander Sir Harold Campbell, an equerry to King George VI, and his family at their house in Kent. Lane told Campbell how anxious he was to join one of the services, but as a foreigner he did not know how best to go about this. Sir Harold asked him many questions about his family and background, and then the most important question of all: '*Why* do you want to fight?'

Lane had already turned down a civilian job with the BBC, as well as one in the United States, and his answer came readily.

'First, I want to fight *against* the Nazis and all they stand for, and second, I want to fight *for* England because I have found so much to

7

love and admire during the short time I have been living here.'

This reply satisfied Sir Harold, who arranged an interview for him with Colonel Mark Maitland, then commanding the Grenadier Guards. As a result of this, Lane was instructed to join the Training Battalion at Pirbright. These welcome orders were suddenly cancelled because a Home Office ruling stated that friendly aliens should leave the country.

Refugees from Germany and occupied countries were obviously not able to do this, but as an Hungarian, who had come to England to complete his education, the officials considered that Lane had no further reason to remain and so issued him with a deportation order.

Lane's friends rallied to help him stay. The deportation order was finally rescinded, on the combined recommendations of Anthony Eden (later Lord Avon), David Margesson, M.P. (later Lord Margesson) and another M.P., Jim Thomas (later Lord Cilcynnin) and George Lane was allowed to join not the Grenadiers, but the Alien Pioneer Corps.

'I must admit quite frankly,' Lane wrote later, 'that there were times, when I was standing knee deep in mud, mixing concrete for building camps, assembling Nissen huts and loading Army supplies, when I could not help wondering if I made the right decision or not.'

When Lane was promoted to sergeant, his section contained doctors, lawyers, university professors, engineeers, authors and former directors of large companies.

After many applications for a more active role and ten refusals, he was finally allowed to transfer to the Commandos. Then he was posted to Harlech as a sergeant to help organise X-Troop.

Both he and Hilton-Jones remembered those early days very clearly. Lane visited the local police station in Harlech the day he arrived to seek their help in finding billets. He was provided with a list of landladies who had let rooms to summer visitors before the war, and explained to them how he required accommodation and meals for a newly formed Commando. Some landladies appeared unenthusiastic at this prospect.

'How much are we going to be paid?' one asked him suspiciously.

'Not very much. About £2 a week for each man.'

This provoked the response that it would be difficult to feed any man properly on such a sum, let alone a Commando. But finally, and with obvious reluctance, several agreed to accept a soldier as a lodger.

On the day after X-Troop arrived, when they had all settled into their new homes, several landladies came out into the street with joyful faces to greet Lane.

'We didn't want them because we thought they were *English*', they explained. 'Why didn't you tell us they were foreigners? We would have been delighted to have them for nothing!'

Most of the landladies, however, were pleased to take the Commandos as lodgers. Many had members of their own families in one or other of the services and they treated the new arrivals as one of their family.

From Harlech, X-Troop moved to new billets in Aberdovey, a seaside resort about 45 miles south. Here, behind The Dovey Inn, and the covered market where they would keep their arms in a locked and guarded strongroom, they formed up on arrival in a square facing the Welsh Bethel.

After roll-call, they filed into the market hall and Hilton-Jones explained what the future held for them.

'You are starting a new life in a new unit,' he began. 'In this Commando, we have No. 1 Troop, the French; No. 2 Troop, the Dutch; and you in X or No. 3, are to be known as the British Troop. So the first thing you all need now are new names that sound British – even if you can't pronounce them.

'There are many distinguished precedents for changing a name. The former War Minister, Mr. Horeb Elisha, is now better known as Mr. Hore-Belisha. Sam Goldwyn was once Sam Goldfish. I suggest you choose new names that start – like his – with the same letters as your real names, in case you have initials sewn on handkerchieves, and so on.

'To everyone you meet here in Wales, and anywhere else while there's a war on, you will be Brown, Jones, Smith, Jackson, or whatever name you choose. If you have a thick accent, then it's because you've lived abroad – as far away from Britain as you like. Borneo, Burma. Somewhere like that. And remember, the less you tell *anyone*, the safer it will be. For you – and for everyone else.

'Good security, keep your mouth shut. Good health, keep your bowels open. Now report back here to me with your new names in exactly one hour. Dis-miss!'

Across the road, and nearer to the Penhelig Arms, where Hilton-Jones was billeted, and the English Presbyterian Church of Wales, stood a long, low building facing the estuary of the River Dovey. This had been a 19th century bath-house, but now with bow-windows overlooking a terrace and flag pole, it looked more like a yachting club-house. This was the Aberdovey Literary Institute and Library, and inside it the new arrivals queued for copies of *Burke's Peerage and Landed Gentry*, *Who's Who*, *The Tatler* and *The Sphere*, searching for suitably aristocratic and English names. They returned determined to call themselves Berkeley-Tremayne, Charrington-ffrench, Dalrymple-Grosvenor, and so on.

Bryan Hilton-Jones listened patiently to these proposed new names chosen by men, some of whom pronounced them with thick German or Jewish accents.

'You *must* have a name you can remember easily and pronounce well,' he pointed out patiently. George Lane explained how when called upon to change his own name, he decided to call himself Smith.

'Don't be a bloody fool,' his then commanding officer had told him brusquely. 'You can't even *pronounce* it properly.'

'I thought my English was pretty good, sir,' replied Lane stiffly.

'It is, but not your accent. Your real name is Lanyi, so why not be Lane? But not English – Welsh.'

One volunteer admired Nelson sufficiently to take that admiral's name as his own. Private Finckelstein decided on Ferguson, and then chose Findlay. When Hilton-Jones asked him why, Finckelstein replied in his new English accent: 'From time to time, sir, strangers will be bound to ask me what my name was before I changed it to Findlay. Now, I can always answer, Ferguson.'

And there was Private Tischler, who decided to become Thistle-thwaite. But since no-one seemed able to pronounce this new name correctly, he finally settled for Thompson.

Several men had decided on their new names and identities before they arrived in Wales. One was Colin Anson who, as Claus Leopold Octavio Ascher, had been serving in the 87th Company of the Pioneer Corps. After being accepted by X-Troop, he reported with several others to the Pioneer Corps depot in Bradford to await a posting.

Hilton-Jones arrived with new paybooks to be made out in their new names. Ascher thought first of becoming Andrews or Anderson, but several friends also had the same idea. As he was considering the matter, an Avro Anson training aircraft flew overhead. On impulse, he

10

decided he would choose Anson, with Colin to counter the Claus, for his handkerchieves were already embroidered with his initials. Afterwards, he always maintained that Avro Anson was his godmother.

Hanns-Guenter Engel, the son of a Breslau lawyer, originally thought of calling himself Hiller, a slight variation on his mother's name of Hillel. Then he changed his mind and decided on Envers. His original initials were the same as those of H.G. Wells, so he became Herbert George Envers, usually known as 'H.G.' or 'John.'

He had arrived in England from Berlin in 1938. An uncle was already in London, practising as a dentist, and John went to Richmond House School in Cliftonville, Margate. After a time, he heard that there was no more money to spend on his education, so he had to take what work he could find. His jobs included washing bottles for a cosmetics company in the Balls Pond Road, Islington, and working for Norman Hartnell Perfumes. He had the idea that one day he might qualify as a chemist, but in the early days of the war was actually out of work and drawing unemployment pay. He was interned in a camp in Huyton near Liverpool and then released to join the Pioneer Corps, and X-Troop.

One of the few who did not keep to names with his original initials was Ludwig Blumenfeld. In 1938, on behalf of his widowed mother and himself, he had applied to the Nazi authorities for the special permission necessary before Jews could leave Germany. Fortunately, he gave the date of their departure as three days later. In fact, they were booked to fly from Tempelhof that same afternoon, and did so – only hours before the S.S., advised of their intentions, arrived to arrest them.

Blumenfeld joined the Pioneer Corps, served in France in 1940, returned to England and volunteered for X-Troop. For his new English-sounding name, he chose Michael Merton simply because it was easy to pronounce and remember – in any language.

Manfred Jacobus – Fred Jackson – was born in Berlin in 1921. His younger brother left Germany in 1938 with the help of a scheme to resettle German Jewish children in England, and Manfred followed him in August, 1939.

The authorities would allow him to bring out only 10 marks – about £1 – from Germany. At the frontier, S.S. officials opened his suitcase, took out his neck-ties and deliberately cut each one into shreds with scissors, on the pretext that they had to be certain he was not attempting to smuggle out any bank notes inside them.

On the train from Dover to London, Jackson shared a compartment with an elderly man and a young woman. They soon realised that he was a refugee, and the woman walked through the train collecting money from other passengers; she raised about £7 for him.

His mother received permission to leave Germany, but was turned back at the border on the Sunday war broke out. She was sent to Auschwitz and eventually killed there with his other relations.

A Hungarian volunteer named Sauer, who had served in the Foreign Legion, bought a detective novel by Dorothy L. Sayers to read on the way to Aberdovey. He became Private Sayers.

An Austrian, Peter Arany, thought of becoming Arlen, after Michael Arlen, but a colleague, Dicky Abramovitz, who was called in before The Skipper in front of him, took this name instead. Arany, who had served in 246 Company of the Pioneer Corps, commanded by a Major Master, became Peter Masters. The 's' at the end of the name was a mistake, but he stayed with it. He came from Vienna; his father had been born in Hungary, and was decorated in the Austro-Hungarian Army during the First World War, when he served on the Russian Front as an infantry lieutenant. Peter Masters' grandfather on his mother's side was a goldsmith and jeweller, who had made tiaras for the Hapsburg family. He went to Antwerp as a refugee, but when the Nazis invaded Holland they deported him and killed him. He had often talked of ranching in South America and it was suggested that Peter should gain some experience with a view to emigrating there. With this intention, Peter Masters came to England and worked on a farm in Berkshire for 18 months. He had to leave when the land was declared a defence area prohibited to aliens shortly after the war began. He moved to a London art school which closed after two months, during the 1940 invasion scare. The day after it shut down he was interned at Lingfield Race Course, living in the stables. Here he met Harry Nomburg and his father.

Peter Masters' parents were divorced, and he had no idea that his father had also been interned only a few days before him, and was living in vastly superior quarters in the members' enclosure grandstand.

'The stables are no good,' he said grandly, and managed to have his son moved in with him.

Later, Peter Masters was transferred to the Isle of Man, and to

Huyton. His mother deliberately underwent minor surgery so that he could be released briefly on compassionate grounds to visit her. He arrived in London at the time of the air raids.

A Scotland Yard detective came to their home in Hampstead to check whether Mrs. Arany had recovered sufficiently to allow her son to be re-interned. Their discussion was interrupted while all three sheltered under the dining room table as the bombs began to fall. Afterwards, the policeman shared a brandy with them.

'I can see you are not well enough for your son to leave you yet, m'am,' he told Mrs. Arany. Peter explained that he had just volunteered for the army.

'Well, we can't intern one of His Majesty's soldiers, now, can we?' replied the policeman.

Tommy Swinton, formerly Schwitzer, who could trace his family back to 1602, came from Budapest, where he and George Lane had belonged to the same swimming club. In 1934, Swinton was picked to be in a frame to represent Hungary at the Olympic Games in 1940 in Tokyo. Although the Berlin Olympics were only two years away, the Hungarians were already training their contenders for the games to follow. Swinton's father had been educated in England, and sent his son on a special course of business studies and English for foreigners at the City of London College.

He went on to the London School of Economics and then volunteered for the Pioneer Corps. He was posted to a Royal Engineers depot in Warwickshire, concerned with earth-moving equipment.

When Hilton-Jones interviewed Swinton as a possible candidate for X-Troop, he asked him whether he could jump down from the height of the ceiling of the room. Schwitzer replied that he could, but added that he would not be able to pick himself up, because his right leg had been strapped up with an elastic bandage for the past few days. He had cracked a bone in this leg in an accident with a Ransome-Rapier crane.

This honesty impressed Hilton-Jones, who immediately accepted him, but insisted characteristically that Swinton must be fit and ready for parachute jumping within three months.

# Chapter Two

When X-Troop went on parade in Aberdovey for the first time under their new names, some found it difficult to respond to them. When a man has grown used to being Gródzinsky for 25 years, he does not immediately answer to Graham or Goodfellow. But gradually they grew accustomed to this, and so began the most physically strenuous time of their lives, and also one of the most enjoyable.

For the first time for most of them since war began, they were living in civilian houses, without the restrictions of internment or barracks. And they felt exhilarated at the prospect of taking an active part against the Nazi regime which had forced so many of them to flee from the countries where they had been born.

But some found difficulty in understanding the local accent. George Lane, for instance, enjoying the luxury of a hot bath after a long route march, noticed one night that his landlady's fourteen year-old daughter was standing in the doorway, regarding his reclining body through the steam.

'Surely a man's bathroom should be a private place?' he remarked to the girl's mother.

'Oh, don't worry about *her*,' the mother replied reassuringly. 'She's only a little tart.'

At least, that is what Lane thought she said. What the girl's mother had said, in a strong Welsh accent was, 'She's only a little *tot*.'

Although Colonel Dudley Lister was in his early forties, he could keep up with men nearly half his age on forced marches. He was also a very stern disciplinarian. Once, he noticed a member of the French Troop relieving himself on sentry duty, and ordered that the man should be returned to his unit immediately. The French officer commanding the Troop protested that this was one of his best men. Lister remained unimpressed. The man had to go. Lister was, however, very fair, and when one member of X-Troop accidentally shot another, he accepted his explanation that it was an accident, and allowed him to soldier on.

Hilton-Jones was an equally good disciplinarian, but with a different style. Some of his men likened him to T.E. Lawrence. He was slim, of athletic build, with the shyness of the intellectual. There was also a certain dash and bravura about him that appealed. In a blue M.G. sports car he had bought as an undergraduate, he would dash from the French Troop in Criccieth, to the Dutch at Portmadoc; from the Belgians in Abersoc to the Norwegians in Nevin, and the Poles in Barmouth.

He was always enthusiastic and seemingly tireless. He made great demands of his men, but he never ordered anyone to do what he would not first do himself – and invariably better than those who came after him. He would lead, and the other officers and men followed in strict order of seniority.

One of these officers was James Monahan, who had been a reporter and ballet critic with *The Manchester Guardian* and had also worked for the BBC. He drew the admiration of members of X-Troop because although, like Hilton-Jones, he was not built in the accepted image of a Commando, he was extremely tough and dedicated.

Every day, before each lecture or parade, Hilton-Jones would take the Troop on a run up some local hill and down again. He realised that many of his men would have to parachute to their destinations, and so he made them jump out of the first floor windows of houses to grow accustomed to landing on hard ground.

Once, in the hills behind Aberdovey, Hilton-Jones showed X-Troop how to cross a deep abyss by rope. One who followed his lead had no head for heights. The man's face turned white, and he trembled before he reached the top of the rope.

'Look at that man,' said The Skipper, 'and you will see a perfect example of *nervous* exhaustion.' Thereafter, this member of his Troop conquered his fear of heights.

Hilton-Jones was fond of repeating Army aphorisms: 'Sweat saves blood, and brain saves both.' 'Time spent in reconnaissance is seldom wasted.' 'Everything's an attitude of mind.'

For parachute practice, X-Troop travelled to the parachute training

15

centre at Ringway near Manchester. He assured everyone that they did not *have* to jump. Only volunteers were required, and anyone who did not feel keen on parachuting would be excused. In fact, only two men did not jump. One had been a ballet dancer, and did not wish to risk breaking an ankle because he hoped to return to this career after the war. The other was extremely large and explained he was not built to jump; no single parachute could support his weight. On D-Day, these two men were the only members of X-Troop to drown during the landings.

The parachute course lasted for eight days and involved eight jumps from a balloon and an aircraft. After they completed seven jumps, they were told that no unit at Ringway had ever claimed a hundred per cent record – eight jumps by every member on the course. This was because one or more might be injured in a jump, or be unable to continue for other reasons.

One member of X-Troop, Corporal Jack Jones, broke two ribs on this seventh jump. But so keen was he that X-Troop should be the first totally successful unit that he had himself strapped up and completed the eighth jump with the rest of them.

At the Commando training centre at Achnacarry Castle in Scotland, a Scottish sergeant informed them dourly that they were among the first non-Scottish soldiers to live in the castle in 200 years.

'Do you object to that, sergeant?' someone asked him.

'Not at all,' he replied. 'After all, *it's not as if you are bloody English!*'

And it wasn't – although they all tried their best to appear so with their new names, identities and carefully practised English accents.

The men in X-Troop learned fieldcraft, and camouflage; how to read a map in French, German and English; how to march by the compass. They undertook speed marches, covered assault courses with live ammunition, trained with British and German weapons, practising how to dismantle and reassemble them in darkness as well as by day.

They became experts in picking locks, in laying demolition charges, in swimming long distances in full battle order. They were taught how to deal with hidden underwater obstacles on a beach at night; how to drive continental locomotives; how to climb rocks and cliff faces, how to fall, and how to kill or incapacitate in a dozen different ways, all with speed and silence. And because they were individualists, Hilton-Jones noted that they worked far better in small groups or on their own than they did as a complete Troop.

16

Captain John Coates, the Commando's Intelligence Officer, gave them lectures on German order of battle, on tactics, strategy and security. Everyone had to pass strict tests on German weapons, German psychology and the German army's different badges, uniforms and weapons.

Unlike the men he instructed, Coates had come to No. 10 Commando purely by chance. He had been educated at Abbotsholme in Staffordshire, a school that maintained an exchange system with the German Hermann Lietz schools, Buchenau and Bieberstein, and a similar French school, L'Ecole des Roches in Verneuil-sur-Avre, and at Cambridge Coates read French and German.

As a conscientious objector, he joined the Royal Army Medical Corps, but after Dunkirk transferred to a more active corps and was commissioned. While awaiting a posting to 61 Division in Northern Ireland, he decided to visit London, and shared a compartment on the train with an older man. They began a casual conversation that soon developed into a serious discussion on comparative Indo-European philology.

'I must introduce you to Dickie Mountbatten,' his companion told him as they reached London. He then introduced himself as Peter Murphy on the staff of Combined Operations Headquarters as Liaison Officer with the Political Warfare Executive. He had held a commission in the Irish Guards during the First War, and had been a personal friend of Lord Louis Mountbatten for many years.

When Murphy learned that Coates had not booked overnight accommodation in London, he suggested he should stay at his flat, and next morning he would take him to meet Lord Mountbatten.

They arrived early, when Mountbatten had just emerged from his bath and was dressing. Coates, as a very newly commissioned second-lieutenant, did not know how to greet a naval officer of such seniority and eminence in these circumstances, and therefore decided to go strictly by the book. He put on his gloves and cap, tucked his cane under his left arm and saluted smartly as though on a parade ground. When the interview – little more than a friendly chat – was over, Mountbatten turned to Peter Murphy with mock gravity.

'If you *ever* bring any more pongos to my flat and tell them to salute me, I'll shoot you,' he told him.

Shortly after this, Coates' appointment as No. 10 Commando Intelligence Officer was confirmed.

After training in Wales, X-Troop moved south to Sussex. The hour of their departure was supposed to be secret, but they had made so many friends among Welsh families in Aberdovey that the little station was crowded. Many women were weeping, believing that these men with English, Scottish and Welsh names, but thick foreign accents, were going into action immediately.

On the south coast, they were billeted in private houses around headquarters in Eastbourne.

One morning in the early days, when Jack Langley, now commissioned, ran the company office, he saluted Hilton-Jones on parade and then announced in a stage whisper: 'The pigeons have arrived, sir.'

Langley was referring to carrier pigeons which some members of X-Troop carried in wicker baskets. Each bird had a tiny canister fixed to one leg in which a message could be inserted. Once, on a raid in Northern France, an X-Trooper parachuted down on to a cliff top with a carrier pigeon in its basket strapped to his body. He made his reconnaissance, wrote his message, fixed this in its tiny container to the pigeon's leg, and released the bird. But instead of winging back across the Channel, the pigeon wheeled once and alighted on a promontory – where it promptly went to sleep.

Langley's words, 'The pigeons have arrived,' became a kind of catchphrase for X-Troop, meaning, '*This is it.*' Now the pigeons were about to arrive for an Aryan-seeming German or Austrian, who must be of calm disposition, thrived on working alone, doing he would not yet be told what, except that it was dangerous and important.

When men were being interviewed for specialised tasks like this, they would sometimes be instructed to report to a certain room in the War Office building in Whitehall. The number of this room changed from time to time, so that many believed that it was as fictitious as Room 504 in the popular song of that name.

These men might return to their billets after several days, or a week, or longer. They did not say where they had been or what they had done, and no-one asked them. They might have taken part in a Commando raid, made a parachute drop or crossed the Channel disguised as French civilians to land secretly on the far shore and undertake some assignment for which special professional or technical qualifications were required. The less anyone knew about anyone else's business the safer it was for everyone.

Those who were left, who watched the Troop diminish week by

week by such postings or more orthodox attachments as interpreters, wondered when the pigeons would arrive for them. Many had been training from the earliest days in Harlech – and for what?

They had volunteered eagerly, expecting instant action, and instead they had waited for years. One said he felt like someone playing Russian roulette. The cylinder of the revolver spun and he would squeeze the trigger. But which of the six chambers held the bullet? Would they be attached to another Commando, or would they be chosen to visit that numbered room at the War Office about which a lance corporal, lately of Heidelberg University and Trinity College, Oxford, quoted Homer in the saloon bar of The Dovey: 'And not a man appears to tell their fate?'

Hilton-Jones glanced at his watch; he must telephone his wife Edwina in Wales before lunch time. They had known each other since their teens, and she had been in the WRNS attached to HMS *Glendower*, a naval shore establishment near Pwllheli, when he was stationed in Aberdovey. At their wedding in the Aberdovey church, men from X-Troop provided a guard of honour with their Commando knives. When the Troop moved south, Hilton-Jones and his wife rented a semi-basement flat in Eastbourne; she had returned to Bangor some time earlier to have their first baby.

Usually, he telephoned her each evening. A morning telephone call was his means of obliquely informing her, without giving her any details, that he was about to leave on a special assignment and so would not be able to call her at the usual time that evening.

But first he must find a volunteer for this unknown task. Through the window he could see X-Troopers doubling along the promenade in battledress, their webbing packs strapped tightly on their backs, rifles at the trail.

The unit was nearly down to half strength, for many had been posted on other individual missions or attached to Commandos over-seas in North Africa, Sicily, Italy.

Paul Streeten could have been a candidate for this latest mission. Before the war, he was a student at Aberdeen University, and had at once volunteered for the RAF. He was turned down because of his nationality, but then, through some administrative muddle, calling-up papers arrived for him when he was in an internment camp. Although he would have been delighted to accept this invitation to join the RAF, as an alien, he could not.

19

He was interned in Britain and Canada, volunteered for the Pioneers, returned to Britain to join 251 Pioneer Company, and served in Cheltenham, Cirencester, Oxford and Bristol, mostly digging trenches. He felt that his talents were wasted there, and when he was selected for X-Troop, said that it was not his intellectual abilities that had influenced his selectors, but his athletic prowess. He was an excellent runner, and had represented the Pioneer Corps to good account in a number of athletic events.

In X-Troop, he chose the name of Streeten, because two maiden ladies of that name had been kind to him before the war and during university vacations. But Streeten was unavailable for this new assignment: in the previous year he had served in Sicily and Italy, where he had been severely wounded.

There could have been Konrad Goldschmidt, who had been reading law at Cambridge when the war began. He was interned in a tented camp at Bury St. Edmunds and in due course released to join the Pioneer Corps. He transferred to the Royal Army Ordnance Corps and spent weeks painting tanks khaki at Donington Racecourse, until he was able to volunteer for X-Troop. He took the name of Brian Groves to commemorate a friend killed in action earlier in the war. But now he also had been severely wounded in Italy, serving with a Royal Marine Commando.

Max Moody – formerly Mayer – a pre-war middle-distance champion runner for the Jewish athletic club, Maccabi, in Germany, would have been a possible choice, but he was already marked for another special task on D-Day: to infiltrate the German lines with a Royal Naval signaller, and direct the fire from Allied battleships off the Normandy coast to particular targets.

A short time earlier, Moody had jumped by parachute in an exercise on Salisbury Plain, and in landing had torn muscles in his groin and right arm so badly that it was thought he would be discharged from the Army on medical grounds.

He was taken to a hospital specialising in such accidents. Here, almost incredibly, the surgeon turned out to be his father, Professor Mayer. When he saw that the patient was his own son, he felt unable to operate, and the operation took place under his guidance, but with another surgeon.

Moody reported back to Eastbourne and was so keen for action that he assured The Skipper he was perfectly fit. Privately, however, he admitted to his friends that he still could not raise his right arm high enough to give the Heil Hitler salute.

George Lane would also have been a good candidate, for he did not panic or become flustered in a dangerous situation and could also find humour in adversity.

Once, Lord Louis Mountbatten personally briefed Lane about what appeared to be a new type of German mine being laid in shallow water on the French beaches. A sample was required immediately so that it could be examined and evaluated.

The urgency arose because the pilot of a United States Mustang, shooting up German coastal batteries near Calais, saw that some of his rockets were falling short of their target into the sea. Aerial photographs revealed an unusual pattern of underwater explosions that these rockets had started.

Professor J D Bernal, one of Britain's foremost physicists, examined enlargements. The rockets had detonated sunken mines in the vicinity, but why should these explode without any direct contact? Were they fitted with some new device sensitive to the noise of aircraft engines, or to any disturbance of the water in which they were laid?

The task for Lane's party had been to bring back as many sample mines as they could find so that they could be dismantled and examined. He set off with three others in a motor torpedo boat. Two miles off the French coast they transferred to a small dory and approached the shore. If sighted by German sentries, they hoped to be taken for local fishermen. They discovered a number of mines in the sand and others attached to stakes in shallow water, and returned with them.

Professor Bernal examined them all and reported that they did not possess any new sophisticated actuating mechanism that could be set off through the sound waves of an aircraft engine or the shock waves of a rocket landing near them in the sea. They were simply old mines originally intended for use on land. The salt water had eaten into their thin metal cases. When the Mustang's rockets had exploded in the sea, the sudden unexpected pressure had set off these corroded canisters.

On another occasion, Lane had gone to France with a sergeant-major and one other man to try and capture a German prisoner for interrogation. They had to cross a minefield, and unrolled a length of white tape behind them to show them the safe way out should they have to leave quickly.

Suddenly, a German patrol opened fire and the three members of X-Troop raced for the shore. When they reached the minefield the third man, a fairly new recruit, refused to follow the tape.

'I'm going straight through on my own,' he said. 'It's quicker.'

'Don't be a bloody fool,' retorted the sergeant-major. 'You'll blow yourself up. Follow us.'

The man made as though to run, so the sergeant-major knocked him out, threw him over his shoulder and carried him back to their boat.

When they were safely at sea, Lane asked why he had done this.

'He's my brother-in-law and an idiot,' the sergeant-major explained. 'I promised my sister I'd look after him. I had to hit him like that to save his life!'

All these recollections, and more, ran through Hilton-Jones's mind as he watched X-Troop form up outside the house and dismiss to their billets. As they turned away, he saw his man, in the third row: above medium height, well-built, dark-haired. Hilton-Jones knew that he was half Jewish, but with his blue eyes he could pass as Aryan. He spoke German perfectly, as one would expect, and he could also conduct a conversation well enough in French. He was a Bachelor of Science from London University, and had lived for much of his life in England. For some reason that Hilton-Jones did not know, he had never become a British subject; otherwise, of course, he would not be in X-Troop.

At thirty-one, this man was older than some of his colleagues, but his age meant he was level-headed, quiet and more self-sufficient. He was also a bachelor.

Hilton-Jones wrote down his name: Stephen Rigby. Then he glanced once more at his watch, relieved he had made his choice so quickly.

He would just have time to ring his wife in Wales before he invited Rigby to volunteer for a very dangerous task about which he could tell him nothing at all – because he knew nothing whatever about it to tell him.

# Chapter Three

Mr. Churchill stood by the side of the Humber staff car, shading his eyes against the sun. He wore a dark suit, his familiar spotted blue bow tie and square-crowned bowler. Smoke from his cigar drifted towards the rows of tanks that stretched in khaki rows against the green of the Suffolk fields.

The Prime Minister turned to his two colleagues, Major General Leslie Hollis, Senior Military Assistant Secretary of the War Cabinet and the Chiefs of Staff Committee, and Colonel Ronald Wingate, of the Cabinet Joint Planning Staff. Together, and in step, the three men began to walk slowly towards the first line of tanks.

'A most impressive display of armour,' said the Prime Minister approvingly. Then he drew on his cigar and smiled impishly.

'Yet, so you assure me, Hollis, each of these huge tanks could be vanquished by a bow and arrow, or even by a boy with a bowie knife?'

'That is so, Prime Minister,' Hollis agreed. 'A farmer in one village reported to the local commander that his bull got into a field of these tanks and charged one. He was amazed when the bull's horns ran right through the side, and the whole tank collapsed. The farmer simply couldn't understand it.'

'I trust you did not enlighten him?'

'We explained they were life-size inflatable rubber models, purely for training purposes, Prime Minister.'

'And though they may never move an inch from these fields, they will all prove as useful to us as several divisions of real tanks?'

'In fact, sir, they will probably be even more valuable. We have other groups farther along the south-east coast and around the Thames Estuary and the Kent coast. They all look particularly impressive from the air.'

This was, of course, the intention. These dummy tanks were part of *Fortitude*, an immensely complex plan to delude the German High Command about the time and place of the imminent Allied invasion. One of its most important ploys, code-named *Quicksilver* was to persuade them that the main Allied landings would not be in Normandy, but elsewhere along the French coast, principally in the Pas de Calais. There might be other landings elsewhere along that coast, but these would be diversions or subsidiary attacks.

If they could convince the Germans of this, then casualties would be greatly reduced, because Normandy would be relatively lightly defended, and this, in turn, could appreciably shorten the war.

The German High Command – OKW – realised that the long awaited Allied invasion must come some time that summer, but they could only guess where or when. Certain considerations, of course, influenced their thinking. For one thing, they believed that the Allies would need to capture a large port in Northern France to disembark troops and tanks and stores. They had no inkling that the invaders would bring floating Mulberry harbours with them, and so could land on open beaches. Nor did they imagine that the Allies would lay a pipe-line under the Channel to pump fuel from England to France.

The most likely port seemed to be Calais, for in addition to its harbour and docks, Calais stood at the narrowest part of the English Channel; to reach it would therefore involve the allies in the shortest sea crossing. Calais was also near the German V-weapon launching bases, and was the nearest large French sea port to the German frontier. The OKW therefore considered that, on balance, Calais was the most likely choice for the invasion, and accordingly had reinforced its already heavy defences.

For months, a dedicated team of British officers, founded by Mr. Churchill and known for security reasons under the innocuous title of the London Controlling Section, had assiduously and energetically encouraged this belief by a wide variety of means. Under the direction of Colonel John Bevan, a pre-war stockbroker with a distinguished service record in the First World War, when he had been awarded the Military Cross, the LCS created a vast and phantom army, apparently involving thousands of British, American and Canadian troops, in the south east of England from where their destination could only be Calais. If it had been intended to land in Normandy or Brittany, then surely these troops would be encamped farther west – where, in fact,

24

the real invasion forces were already gathered.

Twenty acres of Army tents stretched within sight of the English Channel. Every tent was empty and their canvas sides flapped like huge drum skins in the early summer wind. But from the chimneys of field kitchens, (equally deserted, and incapable even of boiling an egg) smoke poured thickly every day, as though phantom cooks had regiments of ghosts to feed.

Trucks, staff cars and ambulances with huge red crosses painted on their roofs to help identify them easily from the air, moved in convoys around the area, past enormous dumps of jerry-cans and piles of ammunition boxes ringed with barbed wire fences. Four hundred landing craft lay moored in rivers and creeks from Lowestoft south to the Thames Estuary. From the air these appeared to be fleets of invasion barges, built to transport this fictitious force, but none would ever put to sea. They were simply skeletons of tubular scaffold poles welded together in the shape of ships covered by grey canvas, and floating on empty oil drums. Some of these imaginary ships even had crews who, contrary to naval orders, strung washing from the rigging. Viewed from the air, this added authenticity; the ships must obviously be manned and ready to sail.

At Dover, nearly three square miles of foreshore had been cleared to provide the site for what from the skies appeared to be an oil storage depot of immense capacity, no doubt to service the Allied armies once they had landed in and around Calais. Basil Spence, Professor of Architecture at the Royal Academy, had designed this fictitious installation, using miles of sewage pipes and scaffolding, unwanted oil tanks, huts and broken-down jetties in its construction. A wind machine from a film studio blew clouds of dust across the scene so that – again from the air – it seemed that work was proceeding at a furious pace to expand the huge installation with one intention: to supply the fuel needs of an Army about to cross the Channel to Calais.

The RAF maintained regular fighter patrols above these sites and many other equally bogus establishments along the south and east coasts. The pilots were under orders to allow occasional German reconnaissance planes through to photograph these preparations for invasion, but never below 30,000 feet. Above this altitude, fake barges, inflatable tanks, trucks and guns, empty camps and make-believe convoys appeared totally genuine; below it, German cameras might expose the illusion.

25

Photographs of General Montgomery leaving the heavily guarded gates of the oil depot in Dover appeared in local newspapers. General Eisenhower spoke at a widely reported local dinner in the White Cliffs Hotel. At this celebration, the Mayor of Dover said how pleased he was at the opening of a new installation, the precise nature of which, he said, 'must remain secret until the war is over, but which will bring the borough material benefits of consequence.'

During the previous months local newspapers had published many letters, apparently from retired vicars and schoolmasters, who deplored the decline in morals since the arrival of so many foreign troops in Suffolk (or Essex or Kent). Other residents (whose addresses German Intelligence could check from street directories) wrote protesting about the lack of courtesy that some foreign tank drivers showed to other road-users in these areas. Did they imagine they were still back in the wide open spaces of the Middle West, or the Canadian prairies instead of in East Anglian/Kentish/Essex lanes? Copies of newspapers containing these items, and others like them, were flown to Lisbon where Axis agents forwarded them to their controllers in Germany.

*Fortitude* was in two parts, *North* and *South*. The Northern plan dealt with the supposed activities of a combined British and American force assembled in Scotland. With an equally fictitious Russian army, they were preparing to attack Norway. Hitler personally believed that Norway was of the highest strategic importance to the defence of the continent. Since the German occupation in 1940, he had kept a garrison of 380,000 troops, with Panzers and aircraft and 1,500 coastal defence guns in that country. *Fortitude North* intended to ensure that these men and guns stayed there instead of moving south to France before D-Day, when their presence could be crucial.

In the south of England, the fictitious First United States Army Group (FUSAG) under command of the flamboyant American General George S. Patton, was meanwhile apparently assembling in a wide area from Dover to Cambridge to Kings Lynn. Jeeps and other vehicles regularly patrolled roads within this wide triangle. They carried radio transmitters, whose operators sent messages, either in easily breakable codes or *en clair*, to fictitious divisions, brigades and battalions, giving the impression that huge numbers of troops were being assembled here from other parts of the country.

Across the Channel, along the northern coast of France, German radio operators diligently intercepted these signals, which were added to the other rapidly growing files on Allied intentions.

To corroborate these aerial photographs and radio-messages, and other pieces in this huge and brilliant mosaic of deceit, German agents, working under British control in England, were also supplying a constant stream of misinformation to their German masters.

Since 1939, more than 100 German agents had been captured on arrival in Britain by parachute or from U-boats and given the choice of full collaboration with the British or summary trial and execution. Those who chose the first alternative now worked under strict guard and control. They supplied details of real regiments, giving their heraldic Divisional and Corps signs so that German Intelligence officers could check on their existence – but not their real locations. That the German OKW believed what they were being told was proved by intercepting and decoding their radio messages to their agents. They were convinced that the fake oil dock at Dover was genuine, and German long-range coastal guns at Cap Gris Nez regularly shelled it. The shells did little damage because the site was a wasteland, but a team of British soldiers on duty there lit sodium flares after each bombardment to simulate fires caused by direct hits.

But just how deeply convincing were the other items that the planners had devised? Did the OKW believe *all* the lies – or could any of their members guess the truth?

Military and logistic preparations for *Overlord* had already occupied nearly three and a half years. Such was the great residual strength of Germany, despite retreats and defeats in North Africa, in Russia and Italy, that even the combined forces of the Allies, backed by the immense industrial resources of the United States, could not be certain of success in the D-Day landings.

Much – perhaps all – would depend on the speed with which Allied troops gained a foothold in France. If they failed to do so swiftly or were thrown back, the whole invasion might have to be postponed for weeks, perhaps even for that year. Allied intentions would have been revealed, and German defences in Normandy would instantly increase. There might then have to be a completely new plan – and how long would that take to formulate?

It was imperative that the Germans totally accepted the deception plans as genuine, for the success of *Overlord* was inextricably bound up with this acceptance. From 1941, British deception schemes had proved of great value during the North African desert campaigns, and in subsequent landings in North Africa and the invasion of Sicily. But the D-Day invasion was infinitely the most important.

If the landings were lightly opposed, casualties on both sides would be low. If the landings were heavily opposed, ultimate victory would not be put in jeopardy, but it could be postponed indefinitely, with needless death and suffering in a pointlessly prolonged campaign. If they were successfully opposed and prevented, then the military and political consequences would be incalculable. A small number of men thus bore a weight of responsibility quite out of proportion to their military rank. To their efforts could be laid much of the praise for victory, or the blame for setback.

This was the background to the visit the Prime Minister had paid to one of these phantom regiments.

Mr. Churchill and his companions finished their inspection and climbed into the back of the car. Hollis sat on his right, and Wingate on a folding seat behind the driver's partition.

Hollis was a cheerful, imperturbable man, who had joined the Royal Marines Light Infantry in 1914 at the age of eighteen. In 1936, as a major, he was appointed Assistant Secretary to the Committee of Imperial Defence and then had taken over his present role. His ebullience had already been much tested during the war, when, working in Mr. Churchill's underground headquarters deep below Whitehall, he had attended, on average, three meetings of the War Cabinet and Chiefs of Staff Committee every day. Sometimes his hours of work were so prolonged that he had no free time whatever, and so he engaged a masseur to pummel him for an hour at seven o'clock each morning to keep him fit. Even during these sessions Hollis dictated to a secretary.

The subterranean headquarters, which he had helped to site and design, was known unofficially as 'The Hole in the Ground' and contained more than 150 rooms. Here, in his office, Hollis also acted as link-man between the War Cabinet and Chiefs of Staff Committee and the secret agencies and organisations that had proliferated during the war.

It was best that as few people as possible knew of certain of their activities or, in some cases, even of their existence. Thus Hollis might see the Political Warfare Executive representative at three o'clock in the afternoon; a Special Operations Executive officer at half past three,

28

and perhaps Ronald Wingate from the London Controlling Section half an hour later. Because so many secret organisations existed, liaison between them was sometimes poor. Hollis vividly recalled one such instance earlier in the war when German U-boats were decimating Allied convoys in the Mediterranean. It was believed that the German commanders learned of the imminent arrival of convoys when pilots of Luftwaffe reconnaissance planes reported that protecting British submarines had left their depot ships.

Someone therefore proposed that dummy British submarines should be constructed from rubber to replace the real ones when they left on patrol. One day, the pilot of an RAF aircraft flying from Alexandria, and knowing nothing of this plan, reported that he had sighted several unknown submarines in the Red Sea. This was desperate news. The Red Sea, more than 1,000 miles long, was immediately closed from end to end, and all Allied ships ordered to make for the nearest port while a bomber strike was arranged.

Deception teams were hard at work, constructing their monster toy submarines of rubber and metal tubing when they saw the bombers approaching and realised their danger. With no place to hide, their only hope of survival lay in convincing the RAF pilots that they were British.

They therefore tore off their shirts and trousers and waved them frantically. The pilots had not expected this reaction, and decided that these leaping near-naked men were not German. They returned to base for further orders without carrying out their mission. Disaster had been averted, but by such a narrow margin that it was some time before the matter could be safely discussed in the presence of the Navy.

Ronald Wingate, a slim figure, wearing spectacles, might appear old at fifty-five still to be a lieutenant colonel, but his military rank bore no relationship to his importance, or to his contribution to the war machine. After all, even John Bevan, the head of this supremely important Section, was only a colonel.

Wingate's quiet, diffident manner concealed a brilliant mind. His father had been created a baronet for being largely instrumental in making the Sudan a condominium of the British and French governments. 'Wingate of the Sudan', as he became known, had been Director of Military Intelligence in Egypt, and had fought at Omdurman, an action in which Winston Churchill also took part.

Ronald Wingate, partly through his father, enjoyed the widest range of friends and acquaintances. He took a first at Oxford, and subsequently held several important political offices in the Government of India, and later became Political Agent and Consul in Muscat and Oman. He had served in the Army during the First World War, and rejoined in 1939. He was a distant cousin of General Orde Wingate, the Chindit leader in Burma.

As their car moved along the high-hedged lanes towards the main London road, Mr. Churchill took a black silk bandage from his jacket pocket and, as was his custom, wrapped this around his eyes and leaned back against his seat. He dozed for a time and then sat up, visibly refreshed. He removed the bandage.

'Have you any further thoughts on this, Hollis?' he asked, as though there had been no break in their conversation.

'I repeat that these rubber tanks, and indeed all the deception plans, are extremely impressive.'

'But will they impress the Germans?' Churchill asked him. 'They are the principal audience to whom this play-acting is directed, not us. What do you think, Wingate?'

Colonel Wingate paused for a moment, looking out at the patchwork of fields between which the car was travelling.

'From all our intercepts, Prime Minister, the general concensus of opinion in the German High Command is that the main landing will be in the Pas de Calais. Rundstedt certainly holds that view. Rommel is perhaps not so convinced, but he still feels it is likely.'

'And Hitler?'

'Undecided, Prime Minster.'

'Then we must make up his mind for him.'

This diversity of military opinion ran deep between Hitler, Rommel and Field Marshal Gerd von Rundstedt, the German Commander-in-Chief in the West, a lean-faced man of sixty-eight, old in the service and cautious with age. The front for which he held ultimate responsibility extended for about 3,000 miles, from Amsterdam in the north to the Spanish border in the south, and then along the south coast of France to the Italian frontier.

To defend this, he had sixty divisions, which meant that each division had to 'cover' a front of roughly fifty miles. In the First World War, the Germans had calculated that the maximum front a single division could defend against strong attack was only three miles, so he was dangerously extended – unless he could accurately discover the area of Allied intentions, and concentrate his forces accordingly. Hitler had complicated the situation by personally putting Field Marshal Rommel in charge of all coast defences. To minimise friction between the two commanders, Rommel held the rather nebulous title of Inspector of Atlantic Coastal Defences.

Rommel was fifteen years younger than Rundstedt, and, because of his early victories in North Africa, far more widely known to the German public. Both men were highly professional soldiers who did not minimise the threat an Allied landing would present, but they did not entirely agree on where it would come or how it could best be contained.

Rommel knew from experience the important part that aerial superiority played when the British defeated his armies in North Africa, and he realised that in the coming invasion the German Luftwaffe would be totally outgunned and outnumbered by the Allied air forces. He therefore wanted to crush the invasion with overwhelming force before beach-heads could be properly established and consolidated.

Rundstedt also accepted the risks inherent from Allied air supremacy, but feared that airborne landings might take place inland, and particularly around Paris. For this reason, he did not wish to commit too many of his troops close to the coast.

Hitler, who would always disregard expert military counsel and any number of irrefutable facts in favour of what he claimed was his intuition, did not wholly agree with either view. He feared a third danger: strong Allied attack from the Mediterranean. To increase these fears, and also widen the gulf between his generals, who did not agree with Hitler, the deception planners had mounted an imaginative scheme earlier in the year.

A middle-aged actor, M.E. Clifton James, then a lieutenant in the Royal Army Pay Corps, had once appeared in an army amateur show as General Montgomery. The resemblance was so remarkable, that after coaching Clifton James in Montgomery's way of walking and talking, the LCS gave him the chance of a second and more important performance in this role. Clifton James flew to Gibraltar as General Montgomery with no attempt at concealing the visit. He dined with the governor – who had been through Sandhurst with the real General Montgomery – then went on to Algiers to meet the British commander. German agents reported both these visits of 'General Montgomery,' and as a result, on Hitler's orders, the OKW prepared immediate contingency plans to repel an Allied landing from the Mediterranean.

Now the rift was growing between the Führer and his generals over the best use to make of the Panzer divisions. With such a long front to defend, their presence at the right place and time could be crucial. Hitler had never appreciated the principles of mobile warfare and personally kept complete control of all Panzer dispositions. Neither Rundstedt nor Rommel could move any Panzer division in France without the Führer's approval and authority.

Allied Intelligence calculated the whereabouts of these divisions by radio intercepts and aerial reconnaissance, backed up by an ingenious ploy of the French Resistance, some of whose agents worked in local laundries. They arranged that prices for the German army's washing were always exceptionally reasonable, and so bound to attract custom.

When a unit was moved elsewhere, these agents would deliberately mislay some of their parcels of laundry. The German quartermaster concerned would therefore give the laundry clerk a forwarding address. Within the hour, the unit's new location would be on its way to England by radio or pigeon.

The OKW had 10 Panzer and Panzergrenadier divisions in France to meet the awaited invasion. Each division contained several hundred tanks, with other armed vehicles, plus a full complement of infantry and artillery. Hitler had ordered that they should be placed to counter attacks to the North or South of France, which meant that their strength was pointlessly dispersed. Three divisions were deployed to counter any landing from the Mediterranean; the 2nd SS Panzer Division, Das Reich, between Montauban and Toulouse; the 9th Panzer Division within the triangle of Avignon, Nîmes and Arles, and the 11th Panzer Division in Bordeaux.

Of the remaining seven divisions, the 1st SS Panzer Division Leibstandarte 'Adolf Hitler' was in the north, at Beverloo in Belgium; the 2nd Panzer Division between Amiens and Abbeville; the 16th, east of Rouen, north of the Seine, and the 12th SS Panzer Division 'Hitler Jugend' in Lisieux, south of the Seine.

Farther west, the 21st Panzer Division had its headquarters in Caen, with the Panzer-Lehr Division in the triangle of Le Mans, Orleans and

Chartres. The 17th Panzergrenadier Division was stationed between Saumur, Niort and Poitiers.

The deception planners in London knew how vital it was to keep all these Panzer divisions, in addition to the seven other divisions already stationed north of the Seine, where they were for as long as possible after the Normandy landings. Every day, even every hour, would be vital; a week would be invaluable. For the past few months, members of the French Resistance had been systematically destroying railway junctions and rolling stock, while the RAF carried out a deliberate bombing programme on railway bridges and tunnel mouths to hinder their movement towards Normandy.

Now Mr. Churchill asked a question that the Chiefs of Staff had also asked Hollis many times: 'Have we any evidence that the Panzers may be about to move?'

'There are conflicting reports, Prime Minister,' Hollis replied. 'Rommel urgently wants the Panzers to be as near the north coast as possible, but Rundstedt cannot agree. Of course, Hitler has the final word. What will happen, whether they move or whether they stay, depends absolutely on him, sir, and who has his ear.'

'Over this matter, gentlemen,' replied Churchill, 'it is imperative that we reserve that privilege for ourselves.'

They sat in silence as the car moved swiftly along the almost deserted roads, considering the impact that the Panzer divisions could have if they did move west before the invasion. Their immense fire-power, coupled with their mobility and the daring way in which Rommel would undoubtedly use them, could thwart the initial Allied landings. This would be extremely serious for the occupied countries, and could produce political implications with Russia. It was not impossible that such a setback, coming on the eve of the United States Presidential election, could even make the Americans decide to treat the Pacific area as the major priority, with the European invasion relegated to secondary importance.

Churchill was the first to speak.

'There must be some way in which we can persuade Hitler not to move the Panzers, and the other divisions east of the Seine, no matter what Rommel or Rundstedt or anyone else may advise. I am thinking of some dramatic ploy that will touch his heart and imagination, perhaps in a totally irrational manner. We do not need long, gentlemen. Even two or three days would suffice. Anything after the landing will be a bonus. Movement then will be exceedingly dangerous because of our air strikes.

'Have you and your colleagues given full thought to this matter, Wingate? We need one last push to tilt the balance of the Führer's opinion in our favour, however briefly.'

'With the very limited time at our disposal, Prime Minister, and indeed, even if we had several more weeks, it would be difficult now to do anything more on a wide canvas of deception. But as an artist, sir, you may agree that when the authenticity of a painting is in doubt, the matter can be resolved if the signature is proved genuine?'

'I take that point. Have you any specific scheme in mind?'

'I have mentioned one idea to General Morgan, Prime Minister,' Wingate admitted.

General Frederick Morgan was the British Chief of Staff to General Eisenhower, the Supreme Commander of the Allied Expeditionary Force. In this capacity, Morgan held overall responsibility for all planning for the invasion, actual and deceptive. He was a considerable tactician, but he did not always agree with Colonel Bevan's imaginative proposals for deception schemes. Some he disliked largely because he did not fully appreciate how the German mind would work in a projected situation. Nor did he always recognise the subtle difference between 'black' propaganda, as practised by the Political Warfare Executive and intended for general German consumption, and the London Controlling Section's Machiavellian attempts to deceive the professionals in the OKW over Allied strategic intentions. As a result, relations between General Morgan and the Section were sometimes formal. Wingate knew Morgan well; they had first met in Baluchistan years before the war.

'And what did Morgan say?' Churchill asked him now.

'He did not think my proposition entirely feasible, Prime Minister.'

'Let me judge that. Pray proceed.'

'My proposal is to send over to Germany one of the German agents we have working for us here. We have already sent one or two of them to Lisbon, to meet their German colleagues, where they carried out their assignments admirably, and returned to England as agreed.

'We would select the most trustworthy and he would go back, ostensibly on Hitler's business, but really, of course, on ours. He would carry papers that would confirm all we wish to confirm. In my view, such a venture might *just* swing the balance of belief in our favour – at least long enough for us to take advantage of it.'

'A dramatic proposal indeed, Wingate. But to my mind one that presents too many grave risks, and would provoke too many questions.

'Let us for a moment put ourselves in Hitler's position. Why should this man so suddenly and fortuitously arrive with all this valuable information? Indeed, why should we ever believe he will? He has changed his allegiance once to save his skin. Is it not possible – nay, probable – that he will do so again? A trip to Lisbon is one thing, to Berlin quite another. Or even if he does remain trustworthy, would not the temptation be great for him to hide somewhere until the invasion takes place, and then he could join up with our people – or simply disappear to his own devices?'

'Our intercepts of German radio traffic should tell us whether he had carried out the assignment, sir.'

'Agreed. But they could not make him do so. Nor could anyone else, for we would have no influence whatever over him or his actions. So long as these German agents are here in this island, they are our creatures. Once our of our control, he would become his own man. And what is to prevent such a person from telling the Germans not the plausible story we might give him, but the truth?'

'I agree, Prime Minister,' said General Hollis firmly. 'The risk is too great to consider sending back a turncoat. I personally feel extremely dubious that Hitler, despite his so-called intuition – let alone professionals like Rundstedt or Rommel – would accept for one moment whatever such a man might have to say, no matter how well it was dolled up with forged documents. Would *we* in these circumstances?'

'The information he took, sir, would of course be corroborated by wireless messages from German agents over here, people in whom they have implicit faith,' continued Wingate. 'They trust one so highly that they have recently awarded him the Iron Cross!'

'As the son of a clergyman, Hollis,' said Churchill, 'you will pardon me if I repeat the parable of Lazarus and Dives, which I feel is not without relevance in this present situation.

'Dives, you may recall, was a rich but ungodly man who fared sumptuously every day. Lazarus was the poor man at his gate, who had to be content to eat the crumbs that fell from the rich man's table.

'Both men died. But while angels carried Lazarus up into heaven, Dives went down to hell. In his misery, he saw Lazarus and Abraham in paradise, and implored them to help him, which they explained they could not do. So Dives asked permission to return to earth to warn his five brothers of the sombre fate that would await them if they did not change their evil ways. Abraham refused this request. He said that if Dives' brothers did not listen to Moses and the prophets, then they would certainly not be persuaded, even if a man was raised from the dead.

'If a dead man coming back to life would not be accepted, gentlemen, why should the words of a messenger lacking this dramatic resurrection be believed?'

'I agree, Prime Minister,' replied Hollis, 'but, with your permission, if I might play the Devil's advocate, the message of a dead man has already been believed by the enemy in this war. Operation Mincemeat.'

'True,' admitted Churchill.

'And, if I may make the point, Prime Minister,' added Wingate. 'The Bible story only reported Abraham's *opinion*. The matter was never actually put to the test. If we send someone back now, the Germans would be advised in advance by their most trusted agents here that he was bringing Intelligence of the greatest importance. They would know when and where he was arriving, and so could meet him and treat him with the respect to which they would believe he was entitled. They would, in fact, already be part persuaded. It would not in any sense be what I understand is known in the insurance world as "a cold canvas." '

'In insurance terms the risk is too great,' replied the Prime Minister. 'Both to our plans and to this man. Two alternatives only concern us – his success or his failure. Either way, he is concerned with simple survival. So let us assume for a moment that the Germans *are* inclined to believe what he says. They will then keep him under surveillance, or maybe even as a prisoner, until his message is proved true or false. Since indeed it must very speedily be proved palpably false, what is *his* future? At the best, a quick death. At the worst, a slow one. If they do not accept his story at all, then he will face these alternatives fates all the sooner. Not a very attractive prospect for our messenger.'

'We would be deliberately sending a man to his death, Prime Minister,' said Hollis.

'In war that happens every day. What makes this different is that he would know right from the beginning how slim are his chances of survival.'

'We could offer him a large sum of money, or at least take care of his family, if he did not come back, sir,' suggested Wingate.

Churchill shook his head disparagingly.

'I do not think the man we need would be influenced by any financial inducement, gentlemen. He would do this as a matter of honour, as a personal challenge on the highest level, an opportunity to attempt something no-one else is qualified to do – with risk and glory in equal proportions. But where could we find such a volunteer, with the right German background, in whom we would have complete confidence?'

Churchill paused, chewing his cigar, his brow corrugated with thought. Then he began to speak softly, as though he was thinking aloud.

'There *is* just one possibility, gentlemen. When I appointed Mountbatten Chief of Combined Operations two years ago, you know how he immediately raised a new Inter-Allied Commando of Norwegians, Dutch, Hungarians and French, men who had common cause with us. He would even have included a Troop of Americans, but they already had their Rangers. Then he went on to form a troop of unknown warriors with unknown potential – X-Troop.

'Might someone for your purpose be found here? They are all brave young men of spirit and education. Highly trained and fighting fit. Many have lost relatives, even entire families, at the hands of the Gestapo, so they know what they are fighting for. And, like Cromwell's Ironsides, they love what they know. All have willingly volunteered for hazardous service of any kind, fully accepting the risks they run if they are captured. And whoever undertakes such a mission as you propose must be a volunteer. This is not for any pressed man.'

Churchill stubbed out his cigar.

'Such an individual,' he went on, musing on the prospect, 'would indeed hold history in his hands. And such a man, very possibly a Jew, would be spurred and emboldened by the knowledge that his success would not only save the lives of thousands of other men of his age, but would speed comfort and succour to millions of his own race and religion who, like Lazarus, have suffered grievously.

'I suggest that, if you wish to proceed with this idea, you first instigate tentative enquiries on this basis, Wingate. Success or failure will depend largely on the calibre of the man you send. And whatever you decide, pray keep me informed.'

'Thank you, Prime Minister,' said Wingate gratefully.

He did not think it necessary to explain that before he left London that morning, he had already instructed his Army liaison officer to request that the officer commanding X-Troop provide a volunteer for what he could only describe with deliberate vagueness as an unspecified task of the highest importance and danger.

# Chapter Four

Rigby took out the key on the imitation gold chain that Elena had given him and opened the door of the house in Carlisle Road, Eastbourne.

The road ran at an angle to Grand Parade and the sea. Before the war, several houses here, with names such as Belle Vue, Belvedere, and Braemar, had been guesthouses where, for two weeks every summer, year by year, families from London's less fashionable suburbs, like Peckham, Willesden and Sidcup returned to them with loyal regularity. Then damp bathing costumes hung from washing lines in back gardens, while shrimping nets and metal buckets decorated with pictures of starfish and jolly fishermen smoking clay pipes littered the halls.

Now, many houses stood empty and forlorn, curtains drawn, with 'For Sale' notices outside, but some, as in this case, were still occupied, and the owner had taken in soldiers. Other members of X-Troop were billeted in similar houses in Eastbourne and along the coast to Seaford and beyond. Some were on good terms with landladies, whose husbands or sons and daughters were in the Forces. Others, willingly or not, were on even more intimate terms, and conducted affairs with their landladies, as they had done in Harlech and Aberdovey. One of Rigby's colleagues was reluctantly involved with his middleaged landlady, and he would remark ruefully to his friends when they returned from a route march: 'It's all right for you lot, you can get some kip. Soon as *I* get in – there's my landlady waiting for me in her birthday suit!'

Rigby closed the front door behind him. A grandfather clock ticked importantly in the narrow hall. He called: 'Elena? Elena?'

Elena was his landlady's married daughter. Her husband had been killed during the disastrous Norway campaign early in the war. She was in her early twenties, a cheerful girl with fair hair and a pert nose. Rigby had never seen her surly; she possessed what her mother called 'a sunny disposition.'

Now she was on duty with a local unit of the National Fire Service and this week usually returned home at about one o'clock, for she was on the early-morning shift. Generally, an appetising smell of cooking greeted Rigby when he came in; either Elena or her mother liked to have a meal ready for him. He did not know how they managed so well on their meagre rations, but they always prepared something that smelled good and tasted better.

Rigby had never thought he would feel warmly towards a woman like Elena, almost to the extent of depending on her, and missing her when she was not there. She was several years younger than him, and of totally different background. Perhaps this accounted for some of the attraction they had for each other. Her father had worked for the local council and died relatively young; he had been gassed in the first world war. He left an insurance policy worth several hundred pounds, and with this her mother bought the house to run as a summer boarding house, with occasional lets during the winter.

Rigby had known other girls before he met Elena, but none had affected him in the same way. She was the only one with whom he never felt bored after an evening at the pictures, or a walk across the downs. There seemed so much to discuss; more indeed than they ever had time for.

Elena found him an equally agreeable companion. Her husband had been quiet, reserved, almost taciturn. She appreciated Rigby's conversation and his enquiring, educated mind. She knew he had lived abroad, but he did not say where, for this was against all orders.

To Elena 'abroad' could be anywhere: India, Peru, the South Pole. She had only once been out of England as a little girl, when she went with her parents on a day trip to Dieppe. The fact that Rigby had lived in another country accounted in her mind for his ability to speak German and French, for the slight accent that sometimes appeared when he was either tired or excited, and the fact that he occasionally uttered a German swear-word when he was angry.

'Elena?' he called again. He climbed the steep, narrow stairs to his bedroom. No other member of X-Troop was billeted here; he was fortunate to be the only lodger. He sat down on his bed, took off his boots and webbing gaiters and flexed his toes thankfully in his thick grey army socks. Then he slipped on a pair of old P.T. shoes which he used as slippers, and lit a cigarette.

The room was small. A marble-topped wash-stand with a jug of water, a basin and a soap dish stood in the bay window. A lithograph of Holman Hunt's painting, 'The Light of the World,' hung above the bedhead. Elena's mother was a leading member of the local Baptist church. She was shocked when Rigby told her about the artist's unorthodox life; she had not really believed him.

Rigby went into the next room, Elena's bedroom. Her bed was rumpled and the pillow dented. He saw a crumpled handkerchief on the bedside table and underneath it a blue envelope. There was something unusual about the envelope and also something familiar. It was not English in pattern and shape, but continental. It reminded him of Germany. He turned it over. On the back he read: From: Private Hargreaves, J.P. The Warwicks, and then the word STALAG and a number.

Hargreaves. Elena's married name. This must be from Jack, her husband. But how could it be when he had died four years ago? He looked at the front of the envelope; German stamps, a censorship number, and the date. It had been posted nearly six weeks earlier.

He opened the envelope, hardly conscious that he was prying into a part of somebody else's life, and no concern of his. He felt physically numb and cold, remote from his actions. The letter was written in pencil. The handwriting was large and round, with many misspellings. He only read the first few lines: 'My dear wife, thank you for yours of the 17th, just received. Well, not much has happened here . . .'

Rigby folded it up quickly. Not much might have happened to Private Hargreaves, but a whole world was crumbling for Private Rigby. He had read enough; he had read too much.

He thought at first that her husband, who she had told him was dead, must suddenly have been discovered in a prisoner-of-war camp. But this was wishful thinking. The fact that he acknowledged her letter showed clearly that she had known at least from March the 17th – or maybe it was February the 17th? He did not know and it did not matter. What did matter was that Elena had lied to him over something of supreme importance when a lie had been unnecessary. If he could not trust her about that, could he ever trust her again? Did he even want to?

Rigby walked out of the bedroom and closed the door silently. Although the house was empty, he did not wish to make any noise. It was as though her husband Jack was now under the same roof and he needed to avoid him. To advertise his presence would be to invite discovery.

He walked downstairs to the kitchen. The whistling kettle on the gas stove was beginning to hum. Elena must have left the house for only a few minutes; 'popped out' was the expression she used. He had told her that this made her sound like a cork leaving a bottle. She had laughed at that; Elena laughed easily.

Her canary fluttered yellow wings of welcome in the cage above the sink and then tucked its beak beneath its feathers. Rigby turned down the gas and stubbed out his cigarette on an ashtray stamped 'A present from Eastbourne.' He and Elena would joke about this, and he would tell her, '*You* are my present from Eastbourne.' And she would laugh at this, too, and then her smile would slowly fade and she would look at him and move towards him and put her arms around his shoulders, standing on tip-toe so that her hair was against his face, her heart beating against his. The room was full of memories that now he wished he could forget.

The back door opened. Elena came in, carrying a parcel wrapped in old newspapers. She put it down on the draining board of the sink.

'I just popped out,' she explained, as Rigby knew she would. 'Heard they'd got some fish in on the corner. Didn't want to miss that.'

She smiled at him, and then saw his face, not cheerful, as he usually appeared, but with the skin tight on his cheekbones as though he had aged years since she had last seen him earlier that morning.

'What's the matter?' she asked him. 'You ill or something?'

'I went upstairs,' Rigby explained, not looking at her eyes, but at the parcel. 'Your door was open. Thought you might be asleep, so I went in. I saw a letter.'

'Oh.'

The word was neither an exclamation or a question, simply an acceptance.

'Did you read it?' she asked.

Her voice was very small and thin, not above a whisper.

'Only the first few lines. I shouldn't have done that, but I saw the name on the back and I thought you must have heard he was alive. But – you knew all along?'

Elena began to unwrap the newspaper very carefully, as though this was important and had to be done immediately. The fish looked grey and uninviting; it was one of a type that the Ministry of Food had taken to praising. Before the war, it would have been thrown back into the sea. Elena put it on a plate, and the plate on a shelf in the larder. The canary cheeped again, fluttered its wings briefly and went back to sleep. Elena took out a packet of tea from the cupboard, a tea-pot with a red rubber extension on its spout, then two cups and saucers, a paper bag of sugar, a half empty tin of condensed milk.

'How long have you known?' Rigby asked her again. Still she did not answer. Rigby guessed that she had known about her husband before she met him.

'Why didn't you tell me?'

'I meant to,' she replied quietly. 'You must believe me. I meant to. And then I began to like you, and I thought it wouldn't matter. And then I loved you, and it didn't matter at all.'

'Have you told him – Jack – about me?'

'No. What good would that do? Poor devil's been a P.O.W. for four years.'

'The war can't last for ever. What happens when it ends?'

'I know what I want to happen,' she said, but somehow her words lacked conviction. Rigby looked at her, meeting her gaze, but in a different way, a more critical way than he had ever looked at her before. She had lied to him, deliberately misled him. It was one thing making love to a widow; quite another to the wife of a prisoner-of-war, a man he had been told was dead.

'It doesn't make any difference to us,' Elena said fiercely, as though trying to convince herself.

'I don't love Jack. I never loved him, not really. Not like I feel for you. I knew that the moment I met you. But I didn't before. Can't you see?'

He hardly heard the words. Of course it made a difference; it altered everything. Then his rational mind forced him to admit that he had not been totally frank with Elena. She did not imagine he was really a German Jew; that his name was not Rigby but Rosenberg. She would never suspect that none of his friends in X-Troop were who they seemed to be, but like him were men with false names and fake backgrounds, as unreal as actors in make-up and costume playing parts; in this case, Englishmen. What would she say if she knew this?

He told Elena he had been born in Salford, not in Frankfurt. She knew nothing about him except what he had chosen to tell her; and that was mostly lies, make believe, false as his English accent, his English name, his English next-of-kin. They had trusted each other and deceived each other, for reasons that had seemed important at the time. And now?

'Have a cup of tea,' Elena said. 'You'll feel better then.'

This remark would normally have amused Rigby, almost touched him. Now, it irritated. A cup of tea was the easy English panacea for everything. They sat, elbows on the oilcloth-covered table, sipping the warm, sweet tea, making pointless conversation, deliberately avoiding the subject both knew they should be discussing.

The front door bell rang. Elena started up to cross the kitchen. Rigby gripped her arm.

'I'll go,' he said roughly, for this gave him an excuse to leave her, to be on his own.

A clerk from X-Troop office stood on the front step.

'Skipper wants to see you,' he announced importantly. 'Company office. Now.'

'Now?'

'Yes. Something's come up.'

'What?'

The man shook his head.

'He didn't say, but a DR's been with a message. Perhaps it's to do with that.'

Rigby ran up the stairs to his room, put on his boots and gaiters, came downstairs to the hall. He half turned to call to Elena, to tell her he would be back. Then he changed his mind. There was no need for that. He was his own man now.

He shut the door quietly behind him and walked with the orderly down the road, along Grand Parade to the company office. The sun had retreated behind clouds. The sea seemed grey and sombre as his mood.

Rigby did not talk to the clerk. He did not know the man well – he was a relatively new arrival – and this did not seem the best time to engage him in conversation. Rigby thought about his mother in Montreal, wondering how she was coping with what was still to her a new world, a new language, an entirely new culture. His mother could not understand why she had to write to him under his new name, and he had never found a convincing reason – or at least one that convinced her – for he could not tell her the truth.

Was he ashamed of his old name? Surely he could not feel ashamed of his background?

His parents had brought him to England just before the First World War as a baby only weeks old. His father worked for a watch-maker in Manchester who imported German and Swiss watches and alarm clocks, and needed an assistant who could write and speak French and German. They had taken lodgings in a terraced house with a Mr. and Mrs. Rigby in Salford, under the shadow of the chimney of the cotton mill where Mr. Rigby worked as an engineer.

When the First World War broke out, Stefan – he was Stefan then – had a high temperature and sore throat. The doctor diagnosed diphtheria. Stefan's parents had to leave immediately for Germany with other enemy aliens, but Stefan could not be moved because he was too ill and suffering from a contagious disease. His parents had therefore no option but to leave him behind.

'Don't worry,' the doctor said reassuringly. 'This war will be over by Christmas. Everyone says so. Stefan will be well and strong by then, and waiting for you here.'

His father left ten gold sovereigns with Mrs. Rigby for Stefan's keep until Christmas; he would have given her more, but this was all he had. When the money was spent, the Rigbys, with two children of their own, had a third to feed and care for. They considered farming Stefan out, but in the end they kept him, dressing him in hand-me-downs and making him feel in a dozen different if sometimes unintentional ways that he was alien, unwanted, not one of the family.

Looking back, Rigby realised that money must have been very short and he was simply an extra, unwanted mouth to feed, but as a child he did not know this. His parents had gone before he was old enough to remember them. The Rigbys to him were his father and mother.

He started school in September, 1918. Bigger boys picked fights he could not win and called him 'dirty German Jew'. He could not understand why, for he was neither German nor a Jew; nor was he even dirty.

Early in 1919, the Rigby's son Ralph came home from school complaining of a bad headache. Within days he was dead, victim of the influenza epidemic that swept across Europe in that first year of peace,

45

deadly as the Black Death of the Middle Ages.

The doctor who called to fill in the death certificate was a stranger. Stefan, listening outside the bedroom door, overheard him say, 'How sad the little German boy died just when the war was over.'

But Ralph was not 'the little German boy,' and Stefan could not understand what the doctor meant. How could he ask, for that would have revealed he had been eavesdropping on grown-up conversation?

After Ralph's funeral, the family moved to Wolverhampton; Mr. Rigby had found a new job with A.J.S. Motorcycles.

'We have lost a son and gained one,' Mrs. Rigby kept telling Stefan, but he did not understand what she meant. Even so, he felt happier, for now she bought him new clothes, and called him Stephen instead of Stefan.

'We like the sound of it better,' Mrs. Rigby explained. 'It's more English.'

He did not understand this either, but again did not ask why. A.J.S. Motorcycles fell into financial difficulties, were taken over by another firm, Matchless Motor Cycles, and they moved again, this time to Plumstead, south east of London, where Matchless had their factory.

Stephen went to the local county school, and having a gift for music, travelled twice a week on the top deck of an open General omnibus over Bostall Heath to Upper Belvedere for private music lessons. After each lesson the teacher, Mr. Werner, gave him a cup of tea and a Bath Oliver biscuit, and then the boy would wait for the return bus by the Eardley Arms public house. One evening, he saw a German newspaper in Mr. Werner's kitchen as he sat having tea. Mr. Werner told him that he was German, and had actually fought with the German army in Flanders. How extraordinary and even exciting to be talking to an ex-enemy! Yet he did not appear to be an enemy, but seemed very friendly. He even showed Stephen a medal he had won; an Iron Cross, second class.

Stephen explained how he had been baited at school in Manchester as a German Jew. A faint shadow touched Mr. Werner's face and then was gone, but Stephen saw it and wondered what it meant, although he did not like to ask. Had he offended him in some way only adults recognised?

'You must learn German,' Mr. Werner told him. 'Then you can answer them back in a tongue they will not understand. You can be as rude as you like.'

46

'I start next term,' replied Stephen proudly.

'Then I will help you,' Mr. Werner promised. And at no cost he gave Stephen an hour's tuition in German every time he called. The more Stephen spoke the language and the more he read about Germany, the greater dissatisfaction did he begin to feel with his own suburban life. He found that he liked precision and punctuality, and despised procrastination, especially as practised by Mr. Rigby who found difficulty in making up his mind about the simplest things.

Stephen, given encouragement for the first time in his life, discovered he had an unusual gift for languages and also for science. When he was fourteen he built a five valve radio that would bring in such unlikely stations as Bremen, Hilversum and even Schenectady. He won a form prize for an essay in German two years running, and after he matriculated, he was apprenticed to a local electrical firm and then took a job with a company building wireless sets in West London. On two evenings a week he took classes in German and French at Woolwich Polytechnic; Mr. Werner introduced him to other Germans, living in the area. Soon he could speak German as well as he spoke English.

On Stephen's 21st birthday, Mr. Rigby called him into the front parlour and handed him an envelope. It contained a cheque for £200, an insurance which Mr. Rigby explained he had taken out to mature when he came of age.

'There is also something I have to tell you,' Mr. Rigby went on in a rather strained voice. 'Something we should have told you years ago. But we kept putting it off, the wife and I. You are not our real son. When Ralph died, we told the doctor that the German boy had died. We could not bear to lose the two of you. We have done our best by you ever since.'

He explained how the situation had arisen.

'Didn't my parents come back for me after the war?' Stephen asked him.

'Yes. But your name was on the death certificate. So officially you were dead.'

'What is my real name?'

'Stefan Rosenberg.'

'So I *am* a German Jew?'

'Yes.'

Mr. Rigby produced an old sepia tinted photograph; Stephen sat on a woman's knee, wrapped in a white woollen shawl. A man, grave and bearded, stood behind their chair.

Stephen hurried to tell Mr. Werner the news. Mr. Werner listened sympathetically.

'What an amazing thing,' he said. 'Of course, it explains your interest in our country.'

He gave slight emphasis to 'our'.

'Now I must find my real parents, if they are still alive,' Rigby told him.

'Of course. And you must tell me all about your trip. But unfortunately, Stephen, you will have to write to me. I am leaving this house. I have got a job as a sales representative in West London.'

'But your music?'

'This is a very poor livelihood. I have barely kept body and soul together. At least this will mean a regular salary.'

'Have you an address where I can write?'

'We will keep in touch, I assure you,' said Mr. Werner. 'Now, I don't want to rush you, but I have another student due in ten minutes . . .'

Stephen wrote to his parents at the only address Mr. Rigby had for them in Frankfurt. He did not receive a reply, so he added two days of his annual holiday to the Easter weekend and travelled to Frankfurt. He went to the address, a block of flats; a young man opened the door.

'The Rosenbergs?' Stephen asked him in German.

'They've gone. They are Jews, you know. They owe you money, or something?'

'Something,' agreed Stephen. 'Have you any address?'

'Here's where they say they are.'

He produced a piece of paper with an address in Vienna. Stephen copied it and caught the next train.

The address was a block of flats near the Kaernterstrasse. A uniformed porter escorted him up in the lift to the third floor, and pressed the door bell. A woman opened the door. She had greying hair and a pale, sad face. She bent down to hold a small dog by its jewelled collar.

'Gentleman to see you,' the porter told her, and left them together.

Stephen produced the photograph Mr. Rigby had given to him. She looked at it in silence and then at him more closely.

'Who are you?' she asked suspiciously.

'That little boy in the picture, grown up. Your son.'

'You can't be. He died. The Embassy told us.'

'No. You were wrongly informed.'

'Come inside,' said Mrs. Rosenberg. 'Meet my husband.'

Stephen's father was of middle height, with greying hair. To Stephen, the flat seemed over-furnished and over-heated after the Rigbys' spartan detached house. The carpet was too thick, the curtains too heavy; altogether too much gilt and ormolu and plush. He handed the photograph to Mr. Rosenberg. He examined it in silence and then looked closely at Stephen.

'Where did we live?' he asked at last.

'Arnold Street, Salford.'

He explained how Ralph Rigby had died, why the death certificate was in his name.

'We made enquiries through our Embassy after the war,' said Rosenberg. 'They told us you were dead. All this time . . .'

Words faded and he wept.

The Rosenbergs accepted him then, still scarcely able to believe that, like the prodigal son, he had returned; he who was dead was alive again. At first the atmosphere was stilted, then slowly it thawed and relaxed. Years of parting began to dissolve.

'Now I have found you, I want to come back to Germany,' Stephen told them. 'It is my country.'

'That would be unwise,' said Rosenberg. 'There is much feeling against us, you know. Your mother is a Catholic, but I am Jewish. It is not a good time to be a Jew in Germany.'

'I read about that, but surely it's all greatly exaggerated?'

'Quite the reverse,' his mother said grimly. 'That is why we moved from Frankfurt. But the Nazis are strong here, too. I think that Hitler will seize Austria – as he has always said he would. Then there will be even more trouble.'

'Why do you stay on then?' asked Stephen.

'Where is there to go? I have built up a good business. It is late now to take up roots. One has hope, one lives in faith.'

'I still want to try my luck in Germany,' Stephen insisted.

Austria to him seemed a chocolate box country; Gemütlichkeit, Strauss, the blue Danube, whipped-cream cakes. This was not for him. Germany was where he had been born, where he belonged. He stayed with his parents for the rest of the holiday, but their defeatist attitude irritated him almost as much as the English casual approach to life. He could neither explain nor understand their sad acceptance of persecution.

'Father was in the First World War,' he told his mother. 'He served Germany, he was wounded. Yet now you are in fear. Why? I cannot believe it.'

'But it is true, my son.'

Stephen Rigby travelled back to England, determined to do all he could to find a job in Germany. He visited the German Embassy and explained to an official that he was a German subject, although he had been brought up to believe he was English. He now wished to emigrate to Germany.

He was passed from one office to another, and finally told that someone would be in contact with him at his place of work. A week later he received a telephone call. A Mr. Duncan would make himself known in the saloon bar of The Goat and Compasses off Tottenham Court Road, London, at seven o'clock on the following evening.

Rigby arrived early. The bar was full of used-car dealers, who conducted their business on the pavements of Warren Street. None gave him more than the briefest glance; he was not one of them. Then the door opened and to his amazement in came Mr. Werner, his former piano teacher.

'My dear Stephen,' Werner said warmly, gripping his shoulders with both hands. 'Well met, my friend.'

'I am waiting for someone I don't know,' Rigby explained.

'Would it be Mr. Duncan?' asked Werner.

'Yes. How did you know?'

'As the English saying is, I am he, or it is I.'

'I don't understand,' said Rigby.

'I will explain,' replied Werner. 'In due course. But not here. It is unwise to discuss important matters in public places. Now let us forget Mr. Werner. He no longer exists. Let us drink to Mr. Duncan and to the future.'

They did so, and then walked up to Regent's Park and stood by the side of the boating lake.

'I wrote to you several times,' said Stephen. 'But you didn't reply.'

'I was away on other business. I am sorry. That is why I have changed my name. A new profession demands a new identity.'

'So you are not a sales rep any more?'

'No. But it was a useful means of meeting people who could be useful in different ways. I am now attached to our Embassy. We have checked your background in England and Germany and we are satisfied you are German.'

'But I told you that in Belvedere.'

'We like to check things for ourselves,' explained Duncan pompously. 'Now, you wish to work for Germany?'

'I want to work *in* Germany,' corrected Rigby.

'That is not an easy matter to arrange. The best help you can give our country now is by working outside it, but still for it. I must remind you that Germany has nearly three million unemployed. Things will get better, of course, under Herr Hitler and National Socialism. But this will take time. Stay here in England. Take a university degree. As our Führer has so often stated, the future belongs to men with trained minds.'

'I could not afford the fees.'

'We could help you. I believe you are eligible for a place at – say – London University to read electrical engineering – and German? You must be able to read German scientific books – and also to translate English manuals into our language.'

'But how can I help Germany at the university?'

'We will discuss that when the time comes. Not now.'

They walked in silence past beds ablaze with flowers. The colour and richness reminded Stephen of his parents' flat in Vienna and, by contrast, his father's gloom.

'What about the Jews?' he asked. 'My father's Jewish.'

He did not add that his mother was Catholic, but this Mr. Duncan already knew; indeed, he seemed to know a great deal about Stephen's background.

'There are members of the Nazi Party on the highest level, who have Jewish blood.'

'But the Nazis are persecuting the Jews.'

'Nonsense. We are of course antipathetic to Jewish profiteers, as indeed we are to all who take advantage of our economic situation. The fact that some happen to be Jewish is purely coincidental. They could as well be Bavarian or Austrian or Berliners.

'You know, I am sure, that in the Great War, our Führer was twice proposed for the Iron Cross, first class? But do you also know that when he received this honour – one of the highest decorations a

51

German soldier can win – his sponsor was Captain Gutman?'

'No. Is that important?'

'Of the highest importance, my friend. *Because Captain Gutman was a Jew.* You will not find facts like that in the British newspapers, now, will you? They are very heavily biased against us, for they have much to lose. We, on the other hand, have everything to gain.'

As Mr. Duncan spoke, his face became flushed and his voice rose, as though he had been addressing a crowd and not just one other person in an almost empty park. His enthusiasm surprised Stephen, but his sincerity impressed him. He decided to take his advice and drew out his savings from the Post Office to become a student at the Imperial College of Science, with regular evening classes in spoken and written German. At least once a term, he would meet Mr. Duncan in a different public house; in Kew or Hampstead or Fulham, and once in Bray. Mr. Duncan would hand him an envelope that contained some used pound notes to pay for Stephen's lodgings. The number of notes was rarely the same; sometimes he received twelve or fifteen, and once seventeen. Stephen wondered – but quickly put the ungrateful thought from his mind – whether there might originally have been twenty pound notes in the envelope and Mr. Duncan had removed several for his own use.

He appeared interested in Stephen's academic progress and when Stephen took his degree, told him of a vacancy with a radio-manu-facturing firm in North London until a suitable opening might arise for him in Germany.

Stephen spent some time with his parents in Vienna during univer-sity vacations, and on each visit he became uneasily aware that his father's gloomy prophesies were coming true. The Nazi Party grew steadily stronger in Austria, and to be a Jew became more and more unpleasant.

Stephen now began to feel concern for his parents' welfare, even for their survival. The idea of working in Germany no longer seemed quite so attractive. He asked Mr. Duncan for his advice, and his help. But Mr. Duncan had his own worries and was not concerned with Rigby's. His superiors, he explained, were anxious to discuss details of a new radio set, to be known as 'The 38' that the British Army was shortly due to receive. Parts of this, if not all of it, were apparently being made by the radio company where Stephen worked. Could he obtain details?

'But I am not a spy,' Stephen protested. 'I wanted to live and work in Germany, but you persuaded me to stay here.'

'Of course. Because you could be more useful here with a scientific qualification.'

'But not by doing things like this. I wish to help my country in a positive and constructive way. Not by copying a circuit diagram or telling you how long high tension batteries will last, or things like that.'

'But can't you understand, that *is* helping us? That is precisely why we helped you to get a degree.'

But Stephen was unwilling to help Mr. Duncan, who in turn said coldly that he was quite unable to assist the Rosenbergs in any way.

'You owe us an obligation, a debt, if you like,' he said.

'I owe you nothing,' replied Rigby. 'All this arose simply because I wanted to work in the country where I was born. Now, I don't. They won't accept my parents even though my father served in the German Army in the war.'

'I cannot become involved in a political diatribe,' said Duncan. 'I will offer you a deal. You seem proud of being a Jew, and Jews like deals, don't they? So here is mine. I will do all I can to help your parents to leave Austria if you will find me every detail you can about the 38 set.'

They walked on for a moment in silence. Rigby considered the offer. Duncan, who had once appeared so friendly and helpful, was now not such a congenial companion. There was something arrogant, ruthless, disagreeable about him. More, he did not trust him. Rigby guessed that if he supplied even the most innocuous details about the set, Duncan could hold this over him as a lever; and then he would never be free of the man.

'I can't do it,' Rigby told him finally.

'You mean, you won't,' corrected Duncan.

'That's right. I won't,' said Rigby.

They parted that night without shaking hands.

Stephen travelled to Austria for Easter, 1938, arriving in Vienna on Thursday, March 10. On the following Sunday, the country faced a national plebiscite: should Austria stay independent, or become part of the greater Germany as Hitler had been demanding for the past three years?

Stephen knew that most Austrians had no wish whatever for Anschluss; they infinitely preferred their independence. This was despite a vast and comprehensive propaganda campaign the Nazis had organised to bully people into changing their minds. Nazi sympathisers daubed swastikas on walls and shop-windows. Overnight, they scattered millions of paper swastikas, the size of postage stamps, on the streets. They ran up illegal swastika banners on flag-poles outside public buildings, and laid piles of wood in the shape of huge swastikas in open spaces, soaked them with kerosene and lit them. After dark, these flaming, crooked crosses could be seen for miles. They secretly promised swift promotion and bonuses to Government officials and civil servants if they would publicly declare themselves in favour of Hitler. The German government even withdrew its subsidy for German tourists in Austria. But all to no purpose.

The Nazis then began to orchestrate a programme of violence and intimidation. They smuggled bombs into Austria to use against selected targets, and rifles and revolvers for an uprising against the Nationalists. But still the overwhelming majority of Austrians wished to keep their country's independence and freedom.

Tension grew, and on this particular Friday had reached its peak. Every road was crammed with people, some wearing Nazi badges, others with Nationalist emblems. Usually, political demonstrators marched to the open squares that faced the Votivkirche, the Town Hall, and the Parliament House, but today the local Nazis had deliberately led their supporters into the narrowest streets, past the German Tourist Office, where a gigantic portrait of Hitler blazed with floodlights. The police could not possibly control crowds in these confined spaces.

Nazis had also levered up paving stones in side roads, smashed them and set the pieces in piles, ready to use as missiles. Loudspeakers on lamp-posts relayed official announcements. Stephen heard fragments as he hurried through the streets.

'*The Chancellor . . . and the Council . . . cancel for the present moment the plebiscite of March 13.*'

So the Government was admitting defeat – before anyone had the opportunity to vote. As the crowds realised this, their chattering ceased. Nationalists prudently removed the badges from their coats and began to hurry away; they had no stomach for a fight. Mounted policemen also formed up and rode away smartly. Motorcycle police followed them, abandoning responsibility for keeping peace between the rival factions, leaving streets littered with stones, broken bottles,

54

sticks. The heavy and unhealthy silence was broken by shouts: 'Sieg Heil! Juden, raus!'

A group of young men with Nazi swastika armbands came round the corner and saw Stephen. They had been drinking and were unsteady on their feet. One hurled an empty lager bottle at him. Another, carrying a Nazi flag, lunged at him with the pole.

Rigby seized the end of the pole, pulled and pushed it sharply. The man fell over on his back, shouting that he was being attacked by Jews. The others ran towards Stephen. He dodged across the square. They followed him for about fifty yards and then fell back to beat up a young couple still unwisely wearing red and white Nationalist rosettes. As Rigby reached the block of flats where his parents lived, a loud-speaker boomed from the lamp-post opposite the front door; the Austrian Chancellor was speaking.

' ... *Thus I take my leave from the Austrian people in this hour with a heavy heart: 'God save Austria!'* '

God save all of us, thought Stephen. He rattled the main door impatiently. The porter opened it, taking his time. Now he wore a swastika badge on his lapel. The Rosenbergs waited at the window of their flat, looking down into the street through net curtains as though they did not want anyone to recognise them. They turned as Stephen came into the room; he saw that his father's face was a mass of bloodied bruises.

'Some Nazis caught him,' Stephen's mother explained. 'One recognised him. He'd been to the shop. Said he was a Jew.'

'I called the police,' said his father, 'but when they arrived they simply stood and watched.'

The German Army crossed the border and was in Vienna by evening. The manager of each block of flats in Vienna was ordered to provide lists of Jewish tenants, so that 'duties' could be assigned to them. Mr. Rosenberg's instructions were to scrub anti-Nazi slogans from walls and wash the streets with pails of diluted acid. No brushes were provided and he had to tear his jacket into strips to make cleaning rags. The acid burned his hands and knees as he knelt on the pavement. Then he and others were forced to clear out a blocked public urinal, using only their bare hands.

After four days of such treatment, the Rosenbergs realised they would have to try to escape while they had any chance of doing so successfully. Many of their friends had already disappeared. Shops owned by Jews had been looted or closed; some had suffered both fates, Rosenberg's among them.

'No Jews are being allowed to cross the frontier,' he reported grimly. 'Everyone has to have a special permit from the police to leave. We might manage something if we had any money to bribe the swine.'

But the bank accounts of Jews were sealed; they could not withdraw any money.

'We still have some silver in the flat and paintings. That would make it worth someone's while,' said Stephen.

'And trains are crossing into Switzerland,' his mother added hopefully; she telephoned the station every day.

They moved around the flat, selecting silver and ornaments small enough to carry. They filled suitcases and carried them down the service staircase into the underground garage. Rosenberg's Opel was parked in a corner. The Nazis had not seized this because they had not discovered that it was his. They piled the cases into the boot and Stephen drove to the main station; a train was leaving in half an hour.

A number of foreign journalists and newsreel cameramen had gathered on the Swiss side of the frontier to interview refugees, hoping for some dramatic scenes that would provide a 'story'. Nazi immigration and customs' officers had therefore been ordered to do or say nothing that could be photographed or reported overseas to the detriment of the Third Reich. Rosenberg had a brief, whispered conversation with a man in a leather overcoat. A suitcase changed hands. Other officials grudgingly allowed the Rosenbergs to cross into Switzerland.

In Geneva, Rosenberg collapsed. He had lost his home, his business, his savings. Now the realisation of his predicament produced its own reaction. He had saved his life, but lost the will to live. Stephen pawned all the silver they had brought with them to pay for medical treatment, but his father was beyond all human aid. Within days, he was dead.

Stephen used what was left of their money to bring his mother to England. She feared the coming war in which she believed the Nazis would be victorious. Then she was certain that they would seek out all who had so far eluded them. The greater distance she could put between herself and Nazi Germany, the safer she would feel. She decided to move to Canada; a widowed cousin in Montreal invited her to share her apartment and she accepted gratefully. Because of the war,

Stephen had not seen his mother since the day in August, 1939, when he waved goodbye to her at Southampton as she sailed west aboard the S.S. *Empress of Britain.*

# Chapter Five

Hilton-Jones looked up from his desk as Rigby entered the room and saluted.

'Stand at ease,' he told Rigby. 'Stand easy, and sit down. This isn't a company office matter. A special posting has just come in that could interest you, so I thought I'd have a word. As you know, I'm off myself tonight and I don't know when I'll be back.'

Hilton-Jones read out the requirements.

'You seem to fit the bill better than anyone else left in the Troop. Are you interested?'

'They say the sort of man they want, sir, but give no clue what he has to do.'

'That's usually the case with anything hush-hush. You'll have to take it on trust. But, of course, you don't *have* to take it at all, you know. The job requires a volunteer. Sorry I have no more details. It's not the routine sort of posting, like being attached to a Commando as an interpreter or something like that. It's something for an individualist, who likes being on his own. That's partly why I thought of you. You'll never be one of a crowd.'

'This posting doesn't offer much chance of changing that, sir.'

'But you will take it just the same?'

'Certainly, sir.'

No member of X-Troop ever refused a posting. All originally volunteered because of the prospect of action, despite the infinitely greater risks with their background. They would never quibble about the type of action proposed.

'Actually, I'll be glad of the chance of a move, sir. I have been in the Army for almost three years and I'm still here – training.'

'Perhaps this is what you've been training for,' said Hilton-Jones briskly. 'I hope so. Anyway, report here at 08.30 hours tomorrow for a rail warrant and movement order. And – good luck!'

'Good luck to you, sir.'

Both men stood up. They shook hands warmly across the desk. Then Rigby saluted and marched out. Neither realised they would never meet again.

Elena sat at the kitchen table, her tea long since cold. She lit a cigarette absently, but it tasted as bitter on her tongue as the previous three. She stubbed it out in the ashtray. She had feared, dreaded, that Stephen would one day discover Jack was still alive, and he had. But why today? Dear God, why had it to happen now, just when everything had been so wonderful between them?

Other women whose husbands were prisoners-of-war formed relationships with men and kept their secret. She knew of two in Eastbourne. Sometimes the lovers knew about their husbands and simply did not care. But Stephen was different. He was sensitive, thoughtful, not like Jack; not like other men she had known. She could imagine how she had hurt him, although she had not wanted to do so. That made the whole thing so much worse. She had kept silent in case she should hurt him, or more unthinkable still, lose him. Now she had failed on the first count, and could so easily fail on the second.

Elena knew that Stephen was as generous as he could be on his pay, for he made a regular allowance to his mother in Montreal. She also knew that his mother was Mrs. Rosenberg, for she had seen a letter from her once in Stephen's room. She had not liked to ask him about this, because to do so would involve admitting she had been in his room when he was not there. Elena had seen his few possessions that were not Army issue – a German silver cigarette case, an onyx lighter, a watch with a metal cage across its face, a pair of hair brushes – and felt a warm glow of affection because they were his, and had belonged to him before she knew him, before she had loved him.

Maybe his mother had remarried and Rosenberg was now her new name? Maybe Stephen had changed his name because he did not want to appear foreign? Did it matter, was it at all important? She thought not, but still she wondered. At the same time, she wished she had never met her husband. Many wives felt like that; perhaps most, if she could believe her friends.

They had married at the outbreak of the war, and almost immediately he was called up in the militia. He had been posted to France, returned to Britain, and then sailed for Norway. Since then he had been in a German P.O.W. camp. People said they would be strangers when they met again. But then they had been little more than strangers when they had said goodbye.

His love-making had been totally different from Stephen's: hesitant, unsure, unsatisfactory. Jack had simply sought an animal satisfaction. With Stephen, she felt emotion and experience shared. And now, was she once more to become a woman without a man; or worse, a woman tied by a legal and religious ceremony, by signatures witnessed, to the wrong man?

Elena heard the key turn in the front door lock. She hurriedly emptied the ashtray into the bin, poured away the cold tea, nervously patted her hair before Stephen came into the kitchen. His face was still sombre, but he had a different air about him. Sensing change and fearing it, she moved towards him. He stood in the doorway, not coming any closer, not acknowledging that she had moved.

'I am leaving,' he said tonelessly.

'What? This house? You are going somewhere else in Eastbourne?'

'No. I am being posted. Away.'

'Is it ... because ...?'

Her voice dwindled into an infinity of unspoken regret.

'Nothing to do with that at all,' Stephen replied quickly. 'The company office clerk came to fetch me. The Skipper had news for me. I'm going tomorrow. Oh-eight-thirty.'

'But – where? When will you be back?'

'I don't know,' he said. Then, as though this answered both her questions, and in a sense it did: 'I am taking all my kit.'

'But you must know where you are going? When your friends have been posted, they all know their new unit, what they're going to do.'

'No. Not all.'

'I am sorry,' Elena said clumsily, meaning about her husband and her deception, about Stephen's sudden departure, about all the loose ends in their lives that now seemed farther apart than ever.

'Never mind,' Stephen replied as brightly as he could. Despite his irritation with English attitudes, he relapsed instinctively into the soothing cliche.

He wanted to tell her that he had also deceived her. He was not who he seemed; he was not British but German; his name was not Rigby and never had been. But this was not a time for revelations; this was time to say goodbye. Maybe also time for a new beginning.

He took a step forward and put his arms around her. Often he had done this as a physical manifestation of his feelings. Now, it only seemed a muscular action. He wanted to tell her that he understood why she had lied to him; that when the moment of decision came, he would do whatever she wished – leave her life or stay in it, despite her husband. But his thoughts could not clothe themselves with words. He said nothing.

Elena sensed his feelings; she began to cry. Over her shoulder Stephen could see the canary fluff its wings, rattling the loose wire bars of the cage as though, like him, it was eager to be away.


Rigby threw his kitbag and pack up on the rack of the empty third-class compartment, sat down and lit a cigarette. Through the dirty window, edged with black paint to ensure a light-tight join when the curtain was pulled down after dark, he looked out at the fresh Sussex countryside.

Gradually, as the train trundled towards London, the view became more and more built-up. Soon, tenements, mean streets and vast areas flattened by bombs, stretched on both sides of the line. Here and there, trees sprouted from acres of bulldozed bricks; nettles and wild herbs covered piles of rubble. A few advertisement hoardings still stood defiantly. Outside a roofless public house he saw the deliberately ambiguous advice: Take Courage.

This was only the third time he had visited London since war began more than four and a half years earlier. The first visit was when he had come from work in the wireless factory to the one-room flat he rented in Hendon. Two Special Branch policemen were waiting for him; he was to be interned as an enemy alien.

He protested that his name was Rigby, but he had never applied for British citizenship and now, of course, it was too late. He was driven out by coach with other aliens to a camp hurriedly established in the grounds of Alexandra Palace, north of London, and then moved to a boarding house in Douglas, in the Isle of Man. A square of similar houses had been ringed with barbed wire to minimise chances of escape. Early in the following year, he travelled to Halifax in the hold of S.S. *Duchess of York* with 5,000 other young Germans, ironically listed on the manifest as 'friendly enemy aliens.' On the other side of a wire mesh screen lived less friendly enemy aliens, captured German sailors and rabid Nazis.

From Halifax, Stephen Rigby and his colleagues travelled by train to a camp outside Sherbrooke, a city about ninety-seven miles east of Montreal at the junction of the Magog and St. Francis rivers. Its early settlers included loyalists, who crossed into Canada from America after the War of Independence. One of them, Gilbert Hyatt, built a flour mill, and the little town that grew around it became Hyatt's Mill. In 1818, it was renamed Sherbrooke, after Sir John Coape Sherbrooke, then Governor-in-Chief of Canada.

This was an attractive and prosperous city, with facilities for fishing, sailing and golf. But such agreeable diversions were not for the new arrivals. The distinction between Nazis and Anti-Nazis dissolved on landing. So far as the authorities were concerned, they were all Krauts, and therefore all potentially dangerous.

They marched from the station to the camp, carrying suitcases that bore bright labels of faraway European hotels: Hotel Pupp, Carlsbad; Hotel Bristol, Wien; Hotel Vier Jahreszeiten, München. The Quebec Central Railway, a subsidiary of the Canadian Pacific, had its wagon repair shops at Newington, between Bowen Avenue South and the St. Francis River, roughly a mile south-east of downtown Sherbrooke. Now these old buildings were to be their home indefinitely.

As they tramped up the road towards this camp, they heard an unexpected roar of welcome from behind the wire. Rows of German prisoners began to sing the Horst Wessel Song, stamping their feet, while others shouted: 'Sieg Heil! Heil! Sieg Heil!' When these prisoners realised that the new arrivals were Jews and others who had fled from Germany, the singing stopped abruptly. The Nazis shouted abuse instead.

Some of the newcomers went on hunger strike in protest against being incarcerated with men whose politics had already hounded them from their homeland. As a result, they were segregated. The Canadians issued them with blue battledress uniforms with a big red patch on their back to mark them as enemy aliens should they ever manage to escape. Barbed wire ringed the camp, and armed sentries constantly patrolled the perimeter. At night, floodlights blazed around the whole area.

Few visitors were allowed inside. One of them was Lewis Rosen-

62

bloom, the manager of a local men's outfitters, Rosenbloom Limited. The camp adjutant, Major Alex Edmison, knew that the aliens would need new clothes from time to time, and for simplicity's sake chose one supplier. Lewis Rosenbloom would come into the camp and take orders for underpants, flannelette pyjamas and cheap fibre suitcases to hold their belongings.

One internee lay ill for weeks with a rare lung complaint, which bitterly cold weather made worse. He was a young German doctor, who hoped to specialise in cardiography, and who had already published three books on this subject in Germany. As he grew weaker, he was moved to Sherbrooke Hospital, where finally he died. A Canadian guard was posted in his room day and night. This man insisted on smoking although the patient explained politely to him the terrible pain that cigarette smoke caused to his ravaged lungs. When he died, Lewis Rosenbloom was called in to help make up the ritual Jewish quorum for his funeral.

During the spring of 1940, the internees started a university in the camp, and a sick bay for minor ailments. The aliens included professors, accountants, actors, company directors, doctors, dentists, lawyers and engineers, who gave lectures on their careers. One morning, a Canadian officer came in, tight-lipped, obviously having heard bad tidings. Someone asked him what had happened.

'Good news for *you*,' he replied bitterly, 'but bad news for us. Paris has fallen.'

To Rigby and to many others, this reply epitomised the official attitude to them; since they were German they must be hostile.

Weeks lengthened into months. Summer passed. Snow fell silently, day after day. Flakes froze as they fell and absorbed all sound, so that the men felt they were living in a perpetual Christmas card. Their huts had wood-burning stoves which they crammed with logs until the metal became incandescent. Even so, hard ice formed inside the windows, and when they went out, the cold dried the skin on their faces, and frost grew on their eyelids and around their mouths.

One morning, as Stephen Rigby stood at the window of his hut, looking out at the snow several feet deep, a corporal came into the room.

'Someone to see you,' he announced briefly. 'All the way from London.'

'London, Ontario?'

'No. London, England.'

The visitor was Sir Alexander Paterson, who was visiting intern-ment camps to interview possible candidates for the British Army. Paterson was a devout Quaker, a former Commissioner of Prisons and a dedicated advocate of reform in the penal system. He could not offer any enemy-born alien the opportunity for active service; the only unit they would be allowed to join would be the Pioneer Corps. Rigby and a number of others immediately volunteered; anything must be an improvement on internment in this frozen land.

Their first posting in Britain was to Bideford in North Devon. Here they learned to dig ditches and latrines, to lay foundations for military huts, to build roads. After this basic training, some were posted to clear bomb damage in Liverpool. Others went to fell forests in South Wales; to stack metal sections of bridges in the Midlands; to unload steel and drums of petrol in railway sidings in Yorkshire.

The work was hard and boring. Their only outward sign of individuality and education lay in the newspapers they read: *The Times*, *The Manchester Guardian* or *The Daily Telegraph* as opposed to Jane's escapades in *The Daily Mirror*. One of Rigby's colleagues was determined to continue his studies for an honours degree in English. As he worked with pick and shovel, he wore an elastic rubber band around his right wrist, which held small scraps of paper on which he jotted brief notes on items he wished to memorise in any break during his work.

One British officer commanding an Alien Pioneer Company realised how important the Jewish religion was to many of his new arrivals, and arranged for a complete set of cutlery, cooking utensils and an oven to be available so that they could properly observe the Passover.

Another C.O. changed the traditional pay-day from Friday to Thursday, so that zealous Jewish soldiers did not have to handle money on the eve of the Sabbath.

A third, less sympathetic, seeking to make a joke in front of his sergeant-major at the expense of a recruit who spoke English with a heavy accent, pointed his service revolver at the recruit across his desk in company office.

'What would you say if I shot you?' he asked suddenly.

'At this range, sir, I don't think I could say very much,' the recruit replied calmly.

64

The officer turned to his sergeant-major, much impressed.

'Damned sharp, these foreigners, eh?'

One morning, Rigby was ordered to see his own company commander; a chance had arisen for him to volunteer for more active service. With a handful of others he reported to the Great Central Hotel in Marylebone Road, which housed troops in transit through London. In a room on an upper floor Captain Hilton-Jones explained that a Commando Troop was being formed of men who were technically enemy aliens, but anti-Nazi. Were they interested in volunteering to join it?

'Can you tell me anything more about it, sir?' Rigby asked him.

'Nothing,' Hilton-Jones admitted bluntly. 'You will have to take it on trust. But I can assure you it will be worthwhile.'

Once more, Stephen Rigby had volunteered, and after a few weeks, during which the Security Service investigated his background, he was accepted.

So his second visit to London had ended with a conversation between Hilton-Jones and himself as unsatisfactory as the discussions that had preceded this visit. Now he was again volunteering for a posting about which Hilton-Jones could not – or would not – tell him anything. Maybe he should have followed the advice of old soldiers: Never volunteer for anything? But then if he had, he might still be behind the wire in Sherbrooke.

The sergeant clerk in the Movement Control office at Victoria Station examined Rigby's movement order, saw the reference to a Room 909 in the War Office and checked his name against a list pasted to a piece of hardboard.

'Car's out the back for you,' he told him.

'Where's it taking me, sarge?'

'You'll find out when you get there.'

Rigby walked out into the yard where the buses turned and taxis waited. A Ford station wagon was parked to one side, its windows sprayed khaki except for small peep-holes in the middle – to stop people looking out or in? The elaborate camouflage seemed only to call attention to the vehicle.

'This for Room 909?' Rigby asked the driver.

'Yes. Get in.'

They set off in silence and drove north around Hyde Park Corner and up Park Lane, where Rigby was surprised at the amount of bomb damage. They went along the Bayswater Road, through Shepherds Bush, to Western Avenue.

'Where are we going?' he asked.

'You'll see,' replied the driver in a tone that discouraged conversation.

A short distance beyond Beaconsfield he turned off the main road, between two stone gateposts, and drove down an overgrown drive. He stopped outside a large shabby Edwardian house. Several Jeeps and Austin pick-up vans were parked on what before the war had been a hard tennis court. Troops were billeted in the stable-block. Someone was whistling 'Amapola'. The house appeared almost derelict, with pieces of stucco missing from pillars. A sergeant clerk in shirtsleeves came down the steps to meet him.

'Rigby?'

'Yes, sarge.'

'Char and a wad in the room on the left, if you want 'em. Then have a wash and brush up. Captain's waiting.'

'What's this about, exactly?'

'He'll tell you.'

The captain sat behind a trestle table in a room that overlooked an orangery, now a sad mass of overgrown weeds, with most of the glass panes broken. In pre-war days this room had been the library. The bookshelves were empty now except for a set of telephone directories and a copy of King's Regulations.

The captain was about his own age. Rigby thought with a twinge of regret that he could have held that rank had he been born British – or even if he had been wise enough to become a British subject when he could have done.

'Sit down,' the captain told him. 'You've come a long way?'

'From Eastbourne, sir.'

'I meant before that.'

'From Canada. And long ago, from Frankfurt.'

The captain's cap lay on the table; it bore the badge of the Intelligence Corps, a floral heraldic device rudely described by members of other regiments as two pansies resting on their laurels.

'Any idea why you have come here, Rigby?'

'No, sir.'

'Well, let's fill you in as much as we can. You originally volunteered for X-Troop, or No.3 Troop, which you knew could involve unusual risks for you?'

66

'I understand the risks, sir. I signed a special form to that effect.'

'Of course you did. But this particular assignment involves rather more risk than any serving soldier – even a Commando, and especially a German-born Commando – should be expected to take in the usual call of duty. We need a volunteer with your background and training for a hazardous and individual task in France. It will be of the utmost importance to the success of the Second Front landings. And because of this, I must tell you that the dangers are proportionately high.'

'Why choose me, sir?'

'Captain Hilton-Jones selected you as a possible candidate. You speak German perfectly, of course, and you also speak French. You have a scientific degree, which will be useful in establishing a believable background for you.

'Next, you volunteered to fight for this country, not against the country of your birth but against the Nazis who control it. I must make clear that this is a very great difference, Rigby. We are fighting all Nazis, *not* all Germans. This job would give you a unique opportunity of striking a harder blow for your beliefs than most other individuals anywhere.

'And lastly, to be absolutely honest, because there is no point in pussy-footing about, we're right up against the clock on this and there are not that many suitable candidates.'

'Can you tell me anything at all about it?'

'Not until you agree to go, unfortunately. I know that sounds a chicken-and-egg situation, but there it is. No compulsion, of course, and if you say "no" then you return to your unit and await any other posting. I am a sort of first filter. If you don't want to go any further, then you won't. The car's outside. It could take you right back to Victoria, and by this evening you would be back in your billet. No hard feelings on either side.'

'And what would you do then, sir?'

'I'd try someone else. No other option. But no-one we know seems as suitable as you. That's not bull, but fact. And why Captain Hilton-Jones put you forward for it. Of course, we'll get *someone*. But if we are driven to use second or third best, then obviously we diminish the chances of success by the same ratio.'

Stephen stroked his chin. Was it for this vague and ominous-sounding assignment about which he would be told nothing until it was too late for him to withdraw, that he had waited in the Pioneers and then in the Commandos for so long? Perhaps, as The Skipper had

67

hinted, this was indeed the opportunity for which he had been training. There was only one way for him to find out.

'If it really is as important as you say, I'll go along with it, sir.'

'Good. I hoped you would say that.'

The captain pressed a button on his desk. The sergeant clerk appeared in the doorway.

'Private Rigby will need a car to take him to London. You know where.'

Rigby and the captain stood up. It was time to leave. Rigby saluted.

'I think that maybe, in all the circumstances, I should be the one who salutes you,' said the captain quietly, and did so.

# Chapter Six

As the three open cars turned off the road at Longues-sur-Mer, six kilometres from Bayeux and began to bump in convoy towards the Channel cliffs, the sun reflecting from the sea hit their occupants like a fist between the eyes.

'Stop here,' ordered Rommel. He jumped out of his Horch on to the sandy grass, a stocky figure wearing a Field-Marshal's leather greatcoat, and carrying his baton. Field glasses hung from a leather thong around his neck. He began to walk briskly towards a command post, perched on top of the cliffs. Admiral Friedrich Ruge, his naval liaison officer, fell into step with him.

The second car disgorged more staff officers; the third, three journalists. There would have been four but the fourth seat was piled high with concertinas. Rommel often took these with him on his tours of inspection of coastal defences. If he was satisfied with what he saw, and the way in which his orders had been interpreted, he would present a concertina to that unit for their entertainment. The journalists wrote accounts of the Field Marshal's visits. Sometimes, he asked them to emphasise points important to him, or what he considered important to Germans generally, such as the high degree of accord with the French on the Channel coast. On their own initiative, they would stress the impregnability of the German defences, the fine morale of all troops concerned and the general sophistication of their equipment.

The command post Rommel had come to see was dug forty feet down into the yellow sandstone of the clifftop and ringed with barbed wire. Its concrete roof was several feet thick, shaped like a huge mushroom and supported by concrete girders. The gap between the roof and the walls was only three or four inches wide; just enough for an observer to see out, and maybe to use a machine gun, but too narrow to allow a grenade to be lobbed inside. Small branches torn that morning from trees and bushes covered the entrance. The fronds of ferns stuck into camouflage netting trembled in the sea breeze.

From the command post, the cliff sloped down steeply to the sea. The tide was out, and rows of wood and steel stakes protruded from the damp sand like giant arrows. The nearest row of stakes was crowned with mines that high tide would conceal. They could blow a lethal hole in the hull of the largest landing craft.

A frontal assault on this command post – and hundreds like it along the coast – would be difficult and costly. Fifty yards behind it, four giant bunkers were concealed by mounds of earth as large as Saxon burial barrows. Through heavily shielded openings the long barrels of heavy artillery protruded from concrete emplacements six feet thick. These guns were mounted on circular bases that could be turned by electric motors, or manually if the current failed.

The guns had a range of 15 miles, could traverse through nearly 180 degrees, and were so heavily protected by concrete that even a direct hit from a shell would barely crack the outer surface. But Rommel realised that while the emplacement might be little damaged, the shock of an explosion as far as twenty yards away could stun or even concuss the gunners. It would not need a direct hit to put them out of action, and once their guns fell silent, determined attackers could scale the cliffs and sweep on inland past them.

This possibility was frequently in Rommel's thoughts but his face was impassive as he accepted the salute of the officer in charge of the post, and scanned the horizon through his binoculars. Nothing sailed on the shimmering sea. They were safe for another day at least; and no doubt for much longer than that. But soon – in weeks or at most, months – when moon and tide and weather were in accord, that stretch of sunlit sea would be thick with invasion craft. And if these attackers could pulverise the defences, then Germany would have lost the battle for Europe.

Once ashore in numbers, able to exploit their exceptional mobility and superior air cover, nothing could stop the Allies. In such a situation, these great gun emplacements would have as little relevance to the war as the ruined and ancient forts Rommel had seen in the baking deserts of North Africa; monuments to a failed strategic sense, concrete tombstones of defeat. It was therefore imperative to check the enemy before they could exploit their advantage. They *had* to be defeated in front of the guns: in the shallow waters of the sea and on the beaches.

Rommel had been the Führer's favourite during the successful Africa campaign, one of his youngest commanders, whose dash and audacity swiftly made him a national hero. His standing was so high that one of Montgomery's first tasks on assuming command of the Eighth Army was to destroy the legend that Rommel was invincible. Yet even Rommel's success and public popularity worked against him. The Führer distrusted too much success in his subordinates; he was the leader, the fount of honour and glory. Anyone who grew too high in public esteem must be considered a rival and therefore of potential danger.

After the Allied landing in Tunisia, Hitler moved Rommel to Italy to command German forces in the north. Here his relationship with Field Marshal Kesselring, Supreme Commander in the south, was delicate. Who was really in command? In the last analysis, if conflicting orders were given, whose orders should be obeyed? After the Armistice in Italy, Rommel expected an Allied landing to come in northern Italy. This did not materialise, but it was growing increasingly clear that the Allies must invade France within the near future, and Hitler moved Rommel to Northern France to organise defences along the coast, from Denmark in the north to the Spanish frontier in the south.

To do this Hitler gave Rommel command of Army Group 'B', but he had never clearly defined Rommel's actual position. He came under Hitler's personal orders and could – and regularly did – report direct to him. Rommel's title, Inspector of Atlantic Coastal Defences, was confusing and sometimes embarrassing; there could not be two commanders. The situation that had caused friction in Italy was in danger of being duplicated in France.

Field Marshal Gerd von Rundstedt was Commander-in-Chief in the West but Rommel did not come under his authority, although he was his junior in the army hierarchy. Rundstedt had never been close to Hitler, to whom he often referred as 'that Bohemian corporal'. He approved what the Nazis had done in expanding Germany's armed forces, but he did not subscribe to their political beliefs.

Because the German army in France did not know whose orders to obey should they receive contrary instructions, Rundstedt diplomatically suggested to Rommel that he should take charge of what could be the most important section of the coast – from the Dutch border in the North, to the Loire in the South.

This reduced the risk of discord between the two Field Marshals (and their staffs), but did nothing to resolve the deep and basic difference in their approach to repelling the Allies. This hinged largely on where the Panzer Divisions could best be employed, for these divisions held the key to success in defeating the invasion on the beaches, before the Allied troops could gain a foothold.

Rundstedt, old and cautious, controlling his forces from a château in St. Germain-en-Laye in the western suburbs of Paris, where Louis XIV was born, wished to keep the vital Panzer divisions, with their tanks and other armoured vehicles, in reserve, well back from the coast, to be deployed wherever they could be of most use.

In the background, hundreds of miles away, Hitler could not make up his mind as to Allied intentions and how best to counter them. He insisted that the Panzer divisions could only move on his express authority.

Hitler, in his fairytale castle at Berchtesgaden, overlooking the Alps, was retreating more and more into an illusory world of his own making. He kept declaring that new secret weapons would soon bring victory. Certainly, German scientists had many ingenious devices under development: the jet engine; a rocket plane that was even faster; a flying bomb controlled by radio from a distance of 100 miles; a missile capable of homing in on any enemy aircraft, attracted by the heat from its engine; and a torpedo with a controlling device sensitive to sound which could pursue a ship, attracted by the noise of its engines, so that any attempt to escape would be futile.

Even one of these devices could have helped bring victory to Germany – or at least greatly postpone defeat – despite Allied superiority in men and equipment, if they were fully exploited. But this did not happen. So far as Hitler was concerned, the fact that these weapons existed was sufficient. He did not appear to comprehend that they needed to be refined and manufactured in quantity.

One Panzer division was nominally under Rommel's command, the 21st, south of Caen. The rest remained technically under Rundstedt's orders. All, in fact, were subject to Hitler's whim.

The Führer did not visit the coastal defences in France. He had done so once four years earlier, when he inspected troops at Cap Gris Nez and looked across the Channel towards England, as Napoleon had also done before him. Recalling this, Rommel also remembered Napoleon's view that committees did not win wars. Neither, he thought, would compromise.

It was essential that he had the Panzers marshalled along the coast, tanks full, engines warm, crews on standby to go at once wherever the need was greatest. Time and again, he had urged the necessity to defeat the invasion forces on the coast when they were most vulnerable. Once they gained a bridgehead, however small, it could be enlarged under the protection of their overwhelming aerial superiority. The initial battle would be lost, and so would the war. But how to convince Hitler and Rundstedt of a fact that seemed to Rommel so self-evident and so crucial that there should be no need to convince anyone?

Earlier that year, General Heinz Guderian, acknowledged to be Germany's greatest exponent in the use of armoured troops, who had fought with brilliance in Poland and France and Russia and was now Inspector-General of Panzers, had visited Rommel to discuss strategy against the awaited Allied invasion.

He had agreed entirely with Rommel that it was absolutely essential to have Panzer units ready and available during the first hours of enemy landing. Guderian's views had greatly heartened Rommel; this was agreement from an expert whose views he respected above all others. Yet despite his eminence, Hitler had treated Guderian with exceptional harshness. When Guderian was commanding the 2nd Panzer Army in Russia, Hitler ordered him to report to his headquarters in East Prussia and explain the reasons for lack of progress on the Eastern Front.

Guderian described to the Führer the fearful conditions that German troops were experiencing in the bitter Russian climate. They could not dig weapon pits because the ground was frozen to a depth of five feet. The frost was so severe that they could not gouge out holes for posts to carry field telephone lines. Engines froze solid, horses died, transport was reduced to sledges. Many units did not even possess stoves on which troops could cook a meal. Hitler refused to accept this recital as fact. He accused Guderian of exaggerating and being defeatist. Guderian was dismissed and placed on the reserve list of officers. Here he stayed in virtual limbo until February, 1944, when Hitler again sent for him. The Führer explained that he had read

73

several of Guderian's pre-war articles on Panzer divisions and their use, and was greatly impressed. Conveniently ignoring the fact that he had dismissed Guderian a year before, he now appointed him Inspector-General of Armoured Troops. On such personal whims and odd chances of fortune German strategy now depended.

Rommel was experiencing the same furious frustration he had known in North Africa two years earlier. Then, he had been denied the supplies and reinforcements he needed. The Eastern Front in Russia had first priority, and long before the battle of El Alamein he had to accept the inevitability of British victory.

Now, lowering his binoculars and glancing at the faces of those in the bunker with him, he felt the same dull, bitter resentment against the Führer who would not, or simply could not, understand the urgency of his requirements. More than 1,700,000 mines had already been sown along the French coast, but he had asked for nearly three times as many. The munition factories could not supply enough; they were short of materials. And then the French Resistance was so active – blowing up sections of track, sabotaging trucks – that only a fraction of the mines and other weapons produced now reached their destination.

Underwater obstacles with mines attached to them, known as Czech hedgehogs, bristled beneath the surface of the sea in their thousands. But it was impossible to cover all the coast. The invaders might choose a section where the defenders had relied too much on natural obstacles, such as submerged rocks, and exploit their advantages. The more he saw, the more Rommel worried about the disposition of the Panzers. They held the balance between defeat and victory.

'Give this unit a concertina,' he ordered his A.D.C. 'They've done a very good job.'

And so they had, as static defenders. But what if the attackers simply passed them by?

An orderly brought the concertina from the car, and there was a moment of embarassment until someone was found who could play the instrument. Then a corporal began playing *Lili Marlene*, the song of the Afrika Korps. Rommel smiled approvingly and climbed into his Horch, next to the driver, where he always preferred to ride.

The little convoy set off back along the dunes, came down on to the main road and turned east towards his headquarters, thirty miles away in La Roche Guyon. The road was empty and the sun was hot. The drone of the car engines became soporific. Soon, Rommel ordered his driver to pull off the road under the shade of some trees. The other two cars stopped at a respectful distance behind him.

Their drivers opened the car boots and brought out hampers with packed lunches. Rommel was virtually teetotal. He did not smoke, and took little interest in his food. On a tour of inspection like this he was content with a vacuum flask of thin soup and some sandwiches, but sometimes, when his mind was elsewhere, he would even forget to eat these. Now he stood, hands behind his back, looking across the landscape.

On his orders, every open field where an aircraft or glider could land had been dug with trenches or dotted with cairns of stone. Long poles were driven vertically into the earth if there were no suitable stones. The troops called these posts 'Rommel's asparagus.' He was thinking now that the trenches would provide unintended but excellent protection for enemy paratroops. So many trees had been cut down, that several units had protested that their cover had been removed, and now they lay naked to air attack. One complication solved immediately produced another when time was also an enemy.

His driver approached him and saluted; lunch was ready. As they prepared to eat, they heard the distant, increasing noise of an approaching motorcycle. Perhaps this was a dispatch rider with an urgent message for the Field Marshal? The officers stood, watching a bend in the road behind them.

An army motorcycle and sidecar came into view, travelling fast. A corporal was in the saddle, and a young French girl in a summer frock sat in the sidecar, her hair streaming in the wind. The corporal saw with horror the array of generals ahead of him. He faltered, the machine slowed. He stopped in front of Rommel, dismounted and saluted smartly.

'Private Schmidt, Herr Field Marshal. Reporting to No. 78 Infantry Regiment with the regiment's laundress. *Sir.*'

He saluted again, was back on the machine and away before any one could ask him for his regimental number or indeed anything else.

The officers turned to each other, some with disapproval, others wishing they were young and single on a motor cycle with a pretty girl in the sidecar, instead of planning a defence which at best could only delay a terrible and ignominious defeat.

None of them thought for a moment that the corporal was telling the truth, which in fact he was. And even if they had believed him, they would never have imagined that not only was the girl in his sidecar a laundress, but she was also about to report to her friends in the French Resistance full details of a new posting for the corporal's regiment.

# Chapter Seven

A corporal clerk knocked respectfully on the heavily panelled door, waited for a moment, and then opened it.

'Private Rigby, sir,' he announced.

Rigby walked into a high-ceilinged room overlooking St. James's Park. Through tall windows he could see barrage balloons droop despondently in the afternoon sky. Two chairs were drawn up in front of a leather-topped desk. Behind this sat a middle-aged man in major's uniform. His hair was thin, and he wore first war medal ribbons on his service dress tunic. He motioned Rigby to a seat.

'I understand you have volunteered to do something about which you know nothing except that it will be important, dangerous and lonely – possibly in that order?' said the major. He spoke in a quiet voice. Before the war he had been a history don at Cambridge. He might now be discussing an abstract point at a tutorial.

'That is so, sir,' Rigby agreed.

'I can tell you a bit more about it. Smoke?'

He offered Rigby a Turkish cigarette from a gold case.

'As you and probably everyone else in the civilised world must be aware, Rigby, the Western Allies plan to land in France this year as the quickest way to advancing into Germany and bringing this war to an end. The coast of France possesses only a limited number of places suitable for this operation, and over the past few months, we have been endeavouring to persuade the Germans we will land in one area, whereas in fact we will land elsewhere. If we can induce them to believe what we are telling them, Panzer and infantry divisions will not be there to defend the area where and when we do land. This will mean that casualties on both sides will be greatly reduced, the invasion will be off to a good start, and victory brought that much nearer.

'As a result of our endeavours, German opinion as to our intentions is divided. Fortunately, the majority of the OKW, the German High Command, appear to believe we will land in the Pas de Calais, which we very much want them to think is our intention.'

The major stood up and pointed to a large scale map of Europe that hung on the wall behind his desk.

'Others, however, favour Cherbourg, here. Some think we will land at Le Havre, or on the west coast of France or even down south around Toulouse here. We have to convince them overwhelmingly that we will land in the Pas de Calais. Other landings, if any, will simply be for diversionary purposes. What is required now is a dramatic – even emotional – reason to convince the waverers that Calais is our main objective.'

'But how can I help, sir?' Rigby asked him. 'I know nothing whatever about strategy.'

'Some would argue that such an admission is in itself an excellent qualification for high command,' replied the major drily. 'You are not required to know anything about strategy. You are required to proceed to France by parachute or light aircraft, ostensibly as someone involved with the French Resistance. You will be supplied with papers as a French citizen and you will also carry other more secret documents which will back up what you have to tell the Germans.

'On arrival, you will approach the nearest German unit, explain to their Intelligence officer that you have been working here in Britain with the Abwehr, the German Secret Service, and ask to be taken to the highest possible military authority to whom you will show these documents and tell your story.'

'But will the Germans believe this, sir? It sounds too far fetched.'

'A lot has already happened in this war, Rigby, that is infinitely more far-fetched than this. Fiction, after all, is only a distorting mirror for truth, and often a dull and cloudy mirror. Obviously, if you simply arrived on your own, no-one would believe you. But over the past four years we have captured a number of German agents who landed in this country, and they are all working for us and not for the Abwehr. Their German masters, of course, do not know this and trust them implicitly. Far fetched, too. But absolutely true.

'They send back regular messages under our direction by all manner of means – wireless, photographs reduced to the size of a full-stop in a typed letter, the safe hand of a supposedly neutral diplomat, and so on.

'Several of these agents will mention you by your code-name as one of their most trustworthy suppliers of information. They will even inform their German controlling officers where you will land and possibly the date you expect to be there. You will thus be expected, and trusted.

'These agents will corroborate your story, of course. And remember that many in the German High Command already believe implicitly what you will have come to tell them. Your presence – with other measures that we will undertake here to substantiate your information – will reinforce their belief and should bring the doubters into line. That is the assignment, Rigby. Now, any questions?'

'Once I've told them my story, sir, what then?'

'I cannot answer in precise terms, obviously, but the Germans may keep you under surveillance – perhaps confined to a house – until the invasion. We will continue to give the Germans every reason to believe that our main landing, when it comes, is only a feint, and that the full force of the invasion will be in the Pas de Calais.

'Once the landing starts, then your job is over. You should get out of their sight as quickly and discreetly as you can. Hole up somewhere, possibly. Resistance groups in the north aren't so strong as elsewhere in France. Normandy farmers are rather like Lowland Scots. They don't care to become involved in other people's business – so long as no-one gets involved in theirs. So you may be best off on your own. But, remember, you've only to keep out of sight until the Allies reach you – which shouldn't be too long.'

'As I see it, sir, the job falls into three sections, each with their own particular risks. If I join the Resistance, I have somehow to leave them without arousing suspicion and join up with the Germans. I then have to persuade the Germans to believe a story I find myself difficult to accept. Assuming I succeed, I next have to give them the slip and either hide somewhere or try for the coast to meet our own troops as they advance.'

'No-one has ever claimed this was an easy assignment, Rigby. That is why a volunteer with your qualifications was needed. But think of the prizes to be won. First, you will help to save literally thousands of lives – on both sides. Of course, the Allies *will* win the war, whether you go or whether you stay, whether our deception plans are believed or whether they aren't. That is fact, for now, at last, the weight and muscle is all on our side. But victory could still be a long haul. The Germans are tough fighters. And it would shorten that haul immeasurably if the invasion is *not* met by the full force of the Wehrmacht. Which is where your contribution will be so important.'

'One final question, sir,' said Rigby. 'How will you know when – or even if – I do make contact?'

'We have our means,' the major replied guardedly. He did not intend to be drawn on this, because the way in which German radio messages were intercepted and decoded was possibly the most closely guarded secret of the war.

'I cannot go into details, but I assure you we will soon know whether you have succeeded, and probably even where you are. Now, any further questions? No?'

He stood up; they shook hands across his desk.

'Now I must wish you well and hand you over to my colleague, Captain Angus with whom you will work closely for the next few days.'

'You mentioned a code-name for me,' said Rigby.

'Ah, yes, I nearly forgot. It is Nimrod.'

'Nimrod,' repeated Rigby. 'The great hunter. The son of Cush who possessed the cities of Babel, Erech, Akkad, Erech and Calneh, in the land of Shinar or Babylonia. I regard that as a good omen for the whole enterprise, sir.'

'And I regard your erudition as an equal guarantee of success.'


To residents of Finchley Park Road in North London, Mr. Robert Frazer was a middle-aged widower who had worked for an oil company in Rangoon before the war and returned to England on the death of his wife.

It was assumed he had retired early on what neighbours called 'a good pension,' for he did not appear to have a regular job, or, indeed, any job at all. Some thought he had retired through ill health, and several wives in the road felt sorry for him. One or two, whose husbands were away in the Services, had invited him in for a cup of tea, but Mr. Frazer always declined such invitations.

Mr. Frazer employed a housekeeper, and a young man, thought to be his nephew, was sometimes seen walking with him. This younger man wore the uniform of a captain in the South Lancashire Regiment, and it was believed locally that he worked at the War Office. He was sometimes seen wearing glasses, and the general feeling was that, although of athletic build, bad eyesight must have kept him from more active service. Perhaps a strain of poor health ran in Mr. Frazer's family? Mr. Robert Frazer, however, was not to be drawn on this or any other subject. In the idiom of the area, he kept himself to himself. He would nod to neighbours civilly enough in response to their greetings in the street, but all attempts to make conversation were met with polite but brief replies.

'Bit quiet here after Rangoon, I expect?'

'Sometimes.'

'Better than being out there with the Japs, though, eh?'

'Yes.'

'Would you subscribe to our local Warship Week, Mr. Frazer?'

'Certainly.'

He would produce a ten shilling note from his wallet, and waving away any receipt or even thanks, he and his nephew would continue on their walk.

On most mornings, Mr. Frazer took a regular promenade around the town, and then came back home. Sometimes he and his nephew would have a beer at a public house before lunch, and then stroll home, always walking close together. It was as though Mr. Frazer did not wish to walk on his own; certainly no-one had ever seen him out alone.

In fact, Robert Frazer had never been to Rangoon, nor was the young officer his nephew. Both men were fit, but neither was who or what he seemed to be.

Robert Frazer's real name was Hans Heinrich Weber. He was by birth a German and by profession a spy. His 'nephew' was his British case officer, who controlled the messages Weber sent back in code by radio four nights a week to a receiving station in Hamburg. For even as a German spy, Robert Frazer was not what he appeared to be. To the German spymaster in Hamburg, who posed questions for which Frazer had to supply specific and sometimes complex answers, he was a loyal and trustworthy agent who risked his life every hour of every day and night in an enemy country. Frazer was in reality working for the British, under their close direction and total control. This uneasy situation was not of Mr. Frazer's choosing, but he accepted it because the alternative was even more unpalatable: death.

He had been offered this stark choice soon after his capture on arrival on the east coast of Scotland from a U-boat four years earlier. He accepted the offer to collaborate, was issued with a British identity card and a ration book in the name of Robert Frazer, and moved to the house in Finchley Park Road. This choice owed much to the fact that the house stood on relatively high ground, which helped wireless transmission and reception.

The officer who now posed as his nephew, explained to him that he fully realised how all agents, German and Allied alike, had a simple means of explaining to their controllers whether they were free or working under enemy coercion. Before they started on each assignment they agreed on a deliberate mistake to make in their messages in such circumstances. This might seem to Frazer a foolproof way of explaining his predicament, but if he used it, he would obviously receive no further signals from Hamburg. In these circumstances, Weber's value to the British war effort would also be at an end; so would his life.

Frazer was never allowed to tap the Morse key himself. His signals were all sent by a Royal Signals operator who had copied his style of sending – his 'wrist' as signallers called the way of tapping the key which, to the expert, can be as individual and identifiable as handwriting.

The fact that Weber/Frazer was captured within hours of his arrival was due to the activities of an electrical engineer who emigrated to Canada in the mid 1930s and then returned to Britain, working for a company dealing with Admiralty contracts. This engineer did considerable business with German companies and brought back items of technical information which he passed on to a friend in the British Admiralty. Early in 1936, he told this friend he would like to do something more active to help Britain against the increasing threat of war with Germany.

The friend informed the deputy Director of Naval Intelligence, who passed the engineer on to MI6. They investigated his background and gave him the code-name of Snow, and a few small routine jobs to test his accuracy and his loyalty. They also discovered that he was in contact with German Intelligence. No action was taken about this, because what he could pass to the Germans was thought to be of little value, and a double-agent might be of great value in time of war.

So it proved, and shortly before the war, MI6 told Snow that his association with the German Secret Service was known. Snow admitted he was about to receive a special radio transmitter from the German controller. It was explained to him where his future lay, and he agreed to work for the British, while pretending to remain a German agent. In case Snow had second thoughts, all messages to him from Germany were monitored. A five letter code was used. This proved to be the basis of other codes the Abwehr favoured, a discovery which helped many further German messages to be broken.

Under British direction, Snow visited the continent several times until April, 1940. When these visits became impractical after France fell, his German controller informed Snow where and when other agents would land in Britain. They were all duly intercepted, 'turned' or executed. Sometimes *The Times* carried a brief notice of these deaths. This reassured the British public that their security system was alert to foreign spies, and also made the Germans value all the more those agents in Britain who they wrongly believed were still free.

By May, 1944, German agents with strange British code-names like Tricycle, Father, Freak, Gelatine, Lipstick, Tate, Garbo, Worm and Teapot were ensconced in houses similar to the one in Finchley, sending out a stream of doctored information to their controllers in Germany. Each spy dealt with one specific area of information: political news, sabotage, public morale, troop movements, and so on. For the previous six months many had been sending answers to German queries about preparations for D-Day, the dispositions of certain divisions, and the most likely areas where the Allies would land in France.

So that their reports would appear genuine, they included true but harmless information which had to be passed by the authorities concerned in Britain before it could be released.

These agents and the reports came under the direction of a special organisation, The Twenty Committee. This title was usually written with the Roman numerals XX, meaning the Double Cross. Their work was immensely delicate and complex. For example, each agent had to appear to be maintaining a standard of life in England that German Intelligence would find credible. He might be a civilian clerk attached to an Army headquarters, or perhaps he said he shared a flat with a naval officer who worked in the Admiralty plans division, or with an officer in Combined Operations headquarters. He also had to have a 'life' that would bring him into contact with those who could help him with information – and he also needed money to pay for this information. This was sometimes delivered by Nazi sympathisers working in the London embassies of supposedly neutral countries.

Frazer told his German controller that he worked for the Ministry of Information. In this capacity, he had access to many newspaper stories before publication, and so could report on items that the censor subsequently removed. When his controller asked for substantiation of certain facts, he would give as his source a colleague whose office he shared, or an official from some other ministry with whom he played darts or chess.

Until May, his messages were generally limited to dealing with specific queries his German controller asked, but for the past two weeks he had been offering information about a man he called Nimrod, who he claimed was one of his most reliable contacts. Nimrod, he explained, was involved with French Resistance activities, and Special Operations Executive, and sought the opportunity to come to Northern France on an SOE mission. If he did so, he would naturally like to make direct but extremely discreet contact with German Intelligence. Nimrod could provide more information in one hour than Frazer felt could safely be sent by Morse in a month – for, of course, he could only send short messages for fear his transmitter was detected. As it was, he frequently complained how he had to carry his suitcase containing his set to all kinds of unlikely places – on high ground – Ken Wood, Hampstead Heath, the Dunstable Downs – to minimise the chance of the British putting a 'fix' on him.

German replies were at first evasive. Then they suddenly showed a sharp quickening of interest. Frazer, sitting in the back bedroom which had been turned into a transmitting station, with black-out blinds permanently drawn, watching the skilled hand of the Royal Signals operator on the Morse key, did not for one moment imagine that in other houses around England other German agents were sending messages that would corroborate his – just as his signals substantiated theirs. He imagined that he was the only German agent the British had caught. The others believed that they had that unfortunate and melancholy distinction. Frazer sat, morose and sallow-faced, under the naked electric light bulb, hating himself for what he was doing to his country, and yet rationalising in his mind that he really had been offered no option.

After each transmission, the housekeeper made Frazer a hot mug of Camp coffee, with extra sugar, and laced with rum. His case officer appreciated the extent of the melancholy which often seized Frazer after a broadcast, and would talk to him about music or photography, which they both enjoyed. Frazer would sometimes sit at the piano in the front parlour playing Strauss or Chopin, according to his mood. People he never met produced all the replies he sent to German questions; he simply had to be available in case of any unexpected come-back: a sudden suspicious question about his background, his family, the nickname of a relative no-one else could know.

On this particular evening, he sat, earphones on, watching the Royal Signals corporal take down an incoming message. The transmission ended. The corporal switched off and removed his headset. He handed the message to the coding officer, a tubby captain in his late thirties. Before the war he had been a lecturer in mathematics at a northern polytechnic; in his spare time he had devised cross-word puzzles for a chain of local newspapers.

Now he carried the sheet of paper, with its groups of letters neatly written in block capitals, into the next room. He filled and lit his pipe and began to decode the signal.

GIVE APPROXIMATE DATE TIME AREA NIMROD
ARRIVING STOP IS NIMROD ALONE QUERY

The captain took this in to show the case officer. He read it through twice, then picked up a telephone with a green mouthpiece, dialled a number and pressed the scrambler button.

'They're biting,' he announced cryptically. 'Want to know date, time and place of arrival. And is he alone?'

'We'll work on that,' replied the man at the other end of the line. 'May take a day or so. In the meantime, we'll send a D.R. tomorrow morning with some reply to keep the pot boiling. How's Frazer holding up?'

'Same as usual,' replied the captain. 'Touch of the glooms tonight. Perhaps he'd like to go back himself.'

'I'm sure he would. Be a certainty for an Iron Cross if he did. "For a handful of silver he left us, just for a riband to stick in his coat." '

'He's staying right here,' retorted the controlling captain. He was not a man for quotations, and anyway he had a lot on his mind. First, he had to remember the whole of Frazer's cover story, a huge and intricate tapestry of lies about his supposed existence; how and where he lived, and what he needed, what he spent, when he fell ill, and why. Then he had to store in his memory all manner of details about earlier messages, so that answers to questions asked weeks or months apart would never conflict. And always he had to stay alert for the slightest nuance of discovery. This might come in a curiously worded message from Hamburg, or from Frazer's facial reaction to some apparently innocent signal when they read it back to him.

Against one wall of his room stood three filing cabinets with double locks, containing nearly fifty thick files. These dealt with every aspect of Frazer's fictitious life in Britain; his health, his women friends, the games of chess and darts he was supposed to play; his promotion prospects in a non-existent job; his contacts and acquaintances.

The captain had been controlling Frazer since his arrival. So far, he had managed to answer every query from Hamburg, however oddly worded or obliquely phrased, without apparently arousing any suspicion about Frazer's loyalty to the Third Reich. But how long could he continue the extraordinary business of running not his own double life but someone else's? It needed only one slip, one slight instance of carelessness or forgetfulness, and Frazer's credibility would be shattered. With it could vanish German belief, not only in him, but in many more of their agents in Britain. The responsibility sometimes made him irritable; this was one of those times.

The Royal Signals operator disconnected the aerial, removed the key, pulled out the plug from the wall socket. Nothing could be left to chance.

Frazer's bedroom was an attic under the roof. The air felt stuffy on this warm night, for the skylight was boarded over in case he should become lax with blackout regulations, either deliberately or by accident. He glanced at the wireless programmes in *The Times* for that Wednesday, May 17. He had missed a play on the Home Service; 'The King of Lampedusa,' described as a 'Jewish fantastic comedy.' He felt he could live without listening to that. Now the BBC Midland Light Orchestra was playing. He did not feel in the mood for light music, and on the General Forces Programme there was even less to attract him. Jack Payne and his Orchestra, to be followed by John Blore and *his* Orchestra until the news headlines were broadcast at 10.59, and Close-down came one minute later.

He could tell a story that would never appear in any headlines, he thought bitterly. But no-one would believe him now if he told them the truth; he had lived for so long in a world of lies that he found it difficult to differentiate between what had really happened and what had been invented for him.

In the attic next to his, separated only by a lath-and-plastic wall, he could hear one of his Army guards settling down in his truckle bed; the others were on duty downstairs. He was a prisoner in a house from which he could not escape even if he wished to make the attempt. And if he did try, where could he go? Always, at this hour, he felt unutterably tired and lonely. And, as ever, the thought of the future haunted him. What would happen to him when the war was over and his usefulness at an end?

Had he by treachery really saved his life – or had he only postponed his execution?

# Chapter Eight

The bedroom exploded in a wild sunburst of light.

Rigby struggled up from his bed, blinded by the unexpected glare. Someone hit him in the face. Two other men seized his shoulders and pinned him against the wall. He fought to be free, to shield his eyes from the hammering brilliance of the blaze that beat into his brain. Gradually his eyes accustomed themselves. Four men in S.S. uniforms surrounded his bed. One held a Schmeisser three inches from his head.

'Who the hell are you?' asked Rigby, instinctively speaking German.

'Who the hell are *you*?' retorted the man with the gun.

Their questions rattled on. Why was he here? When had he arrived? Who had sent him? What had he done in England? Who forged his papers? What was his real name?

Suddenly, the lights died. The small reading lamp by his bed glowed like a friendly candle after their fierce intensity.

'Not bad for a first time,' said the man with the Schmeisser, now speaking English. He placed the gun on a chest of drawers, offered Rigby a cigarette.

'But you hesitated too much. We'll play this back to you in the morning. It's all been recorded, so you can hear your mistakes – and learn by them.'

'Thanks,' said Rigby. 'I didn't recognise you.'

'What we must hope is that no-one recognises you,' the man replied soberly. They filed out of the bedroom. Rigby lay back in bed, mouth dry, heart still pounding as though he had been running up a long hill.

He was in a house on the Beaulieu estate in Hampshire, used by

SOE for training agents. These four men were instructors. That afternoon, they had warned Rigby they would give him snap tests, but he had not expected this. He closed his eyes, but it was some time before he slept. Several houses like this, screened by high hedges or banks of rhododendrons, had been requisitioned for purposes unimagined by their pre-war occupants. In one house two Frenchmen due to parachute into Northern France to blow up an aqueduct were learning the intricacies of their assignment. In another, three Dutchmen were training to return to Holland for a railway sabotage mission. Elsewhere, Danes and Norwegians were rehearsing an assassination, and a kidnapping.

Each group lived and worked with their own particular instructors. They did not mix with others. Often they did not even know who lived next door, and they did not enquire; such knowledge could be dangerous. As in X-Troop, the less anyone knew about anyone else's activities, the safer it was for everyone. Also like the X-Troop, everyone here was learning to become someone else, to forget their true identities. Even the instructors did not always know the real names and nationalities of all the men and women they taught.

For Rigby, it was luxury to have his own bedroom and bathroom. Here he was due to stay for several days, the maximum time to spare in view of the urgency of his assignment.

'Obviously, we can't teach you a lot in this short time,' said Captain Angus, as they sat over a pint of bottled beer in the dining room before supper on the evening Rigby arrived. 'But we'll teach you as much as we can to help you come back safely.

'First, from now on, you will be Stéphane Dubillier.'

'Why that particular name?' asked Rigby.

'Because although the Resistance will be told you really are English, you must still appear to be French to everyone else. Also, you understand radio, and so will be familiar with the Dubillier condenser, which will help you remember your name. You'll keep your first name, so if anyone calls, you'll react quickly. You might not to another name.'

Rigby agreed, remembering the early roll-calls at Harlech and Aberdovey.

'We'll give you a suit made in France, and shirts, underwear, socks and shoes which have come out of France. You will learn to look left instead of right crossing the road – very important that, and surprisingly easy to forget. You will speak French here and learn to walk like a Frenchman, not like a soldier. The Resistance section will know you are English – but others must assume you're French. Remember that first of all you may have to convince the French you really *are* from SOE. If you fail, you will never leave the dropping zone. These people are risking their lives and their families' lives all the time. The slightest hint that you intend to make contact with the Germans will be the end so far as you're concerned.'

'And who am I supposed to be?'

'A wireless expert. You will land with a *bona fide* agent going back into the field. He will be told exactly what you will tell the French. The cover story is that radio reception from their transmitters is very bad – which it often is. You are there to try and boost their sets' performance. That should give you the excuse to move about a bit.

'You must contact the Germans within 24 hours of arrival. They will, in fact, probably seek you out before then, so don't worry on that score.'

'When will I be given the story I have to tell them?'

'When we leave here.'

Next morning, Rigby's briefing began. An officer who before the war had been a game-keeper on the Royal estate at Sandringham taught him how to snare a rabbit or a pheasant with a small length of wire. A theatrical make-up expert explained how cigarette ash rubbed into his hair would give it a grey tinge that would age him fifteen years, and how the same ash on his upper lip could produce a moustache passable in a badly lit room. A former burglar, also now holding the King's commission, taught him how to make an impression of a key with a piece of soap; how to copy a key by cutting the top of a tobacco tin with a pair of scissors; how to slide a sliver of tin or celluloid against the tongue of a lock to open a door.

Later that day, a car took Rigby to Empress Road, on the outskirts of Southampton. He was told to make his way to the Polygon Hotel, where Captain Angus would be awaiting him. Three instructors would shadow him. First, he had to discover them among the crowd of Saturday morning shoppers and then elude them. He learned that a 'tail' does not always walk behind his quarry, but sometimes level with him, on the other side of the street; that a shop window provides a convenient mirror in which to check discreetly whether anyone is watching him from across the road. Rigby spotted two of the men following him, but missed the third.

'On that showing,' Angus told him grimly, 'I wouldn't say you are a very good risk.'

'Do I have another chance?'

'No time. You'll need all your chances anyway when you're in France. Now we have to get you word-perfect in your story – and then seal it in.'

'How, exactly?'

'Hypnotism. Then your story should still stand up, even if they inject you with whatever truth drugs they are using now.'

The same car that had taken Rigby to Southampton now brought him, with Captain Angus, to a house on the outskirts of Portsmouth. An Army sign outside the large front garden announced that this was a branch of an army physical training establishment, which conveniently explained the arrival and departure at all hours of army trucks and cars, some containing large and muscular men in uniform or civilian clothes.

An orderly took them upstairs into a room overlooking the back garden which was screened from neighbours by poplar trees planted close together. The room was empty of furniture except for a long table. Fitted cupboards stretched along one wall. They had been part of the original built-in bedroom furniture and seemed incongruous in their matt white paint with gilt beading. A sergeant stood behind the table, a tape measure around his neck.

'Here's where we fit you out,' Angus explained.

'With clothes?'

'With everything.'

The sergeant ran the measure expertly over Rigby, and opened the nearest cupboard. It was filled with a variety of second-hand jackets and suits on wooden hangers.

'Try that coat, and these trousers,' he said as he threw them on the table. The jacket was a passable fit, but the trousers an inch too short.

'Try these then. What size shirt?'

'Fifteen and a half.'

'Right. Shoes?'

'Nine and a half.'

'Try these. A bit narrow? Here's a wider fit.'

Soon, Rigby stood dressed as a civilian, in a rather shabby suit with scuffed brown shoes.

'Now,' said the sergeant briskly. 'A few bits and pieces to help you on your way. The laces in those shoes, for instance. One contains a surgeon's trepanning saw, which is flexible as a piece of string. It has a loop at each end. Stick nails in these, or a bit of comb, or even your fingers. Then you have a saw that can cut through an iron bar.

'You'll note that your jacket has three buttons. Top and bottom ones contain a compass, like the buttons on RAF aircrew tunics. The top button has an ordinary right-hand thread. If the Jerries discover the compass, then they may start trying to unscrew the others. The middle one is simply an ordinary button, but the bottom button has a left hand thread. The more they attempt to unscrew it, the more they will tighten it up. Gives you a chance they won't discover that compass, which could be good news for you.

'The leather strips at the bottom of your trousers show you are trying to cover frayed turnups. Each one also conceals a tiny waterproof pack of benzedrine pills. No more than one every twelve hours, or you will forget what sleep is like. They are blue and round. There's also another pill, white and square, to enable you to recognise it in case you can't see it in the dark. That's your L-pill. L for lethal. You're out for ever in about two seconds flat if you swallow that. So watch it.'

'I intend to.'

'Here's a survival pack – a flat tin of Horlick's tablets, sealed with adhesive tape in case you get it wet, to keep you going. A handkerchief in your top pocket, but not to blow your nose with. Wash it in your own urine, and you'll get a map of the area where you land. Main towns, railway lines, roads and north compass point. As it dries, the map fades. But you can only piss on it twice. Third time, not even a horse could activate the dye.'

'But won't they find all these things if they search me, as they are bound to do?'

'Possibly,' agreed Angus. 'But then you are there as an SOE man, so it's only what the French – and the Germans – would expect to find. If they find 'em it simply backs up your story – so you're winning either way.'

'Maybe you could cut a bit off the sleeves?' Rigby asked the sergeant semi-seriously. 'They feel a bit baggy to me.'

'They're wearing 'em like that this year,' the sergeant retorted with a grin.

Rigby changed back into his uniform, then followed Angus upstairs to a room on the top floor. This contained a table and three chairs. On the table a dark green cloth covered what appeared to be a ball about two feet in diameter. Although it was early afternoon, Angus drew the black-out curtains and lit a small desk lamp. An orderly brought in two mugs of tea. Then a major, wearing medal ribbons from the Great War and campaigns on the North West Frontier of India, came into the room. He wore round glasses that magnified his eyes so that they seemed to swim behind the thick lenses. He did not introduce himself as he sat down behind the table, but nodded a vague greeting to them both. Then he addressed Rigby.

'I don't know how much anyone else has told you,' he began, 'so let's start from the basic principles.

'First, your task in Britain has been as an interpreter with No. 10 Commando. The Germans can check this unit fairly easily – and no doubt will do so, which is why I am starting with facts, leaving fiction to follow. Give someone one hard checkable fact, then two that *sound* true, and it's odds on they'll believe the fourth – whatever it is. A theory you might care to remember.

'In your job, you have had access to much information regarding Combined Operations and Special Operations Executive. You also know the location of various units preparing for the invasion, and the Germans have been fed wireless messages for months giving answers to specific questions as to the whereabouts of various divisions facing Calais. We will also furnish you with numbered copies of secret orders and other material obviously intended for very select distribution. These will be signed by officers whose names they can easily check and will involve British, American and Canadian units.'

The major paused and looked up at Rigby thoughtfully through his thick glasses.

'Now,' he asked. 'Are you *au fait* with political realities in Germany at this moment?'

'Only what I have read in the newspapers, sir.'

'Well, let me fill you in on the background, to show exactly how your visit could help to tip the scales. First, in the German Army there is the old professional officer caste, men with duelling scars and a long tradition of honourable service to their country.

'Then there are the thugs who have come up from the gutter, the Nazis who don't give a damn about tradition or chivalry. All they care about is their own advancement. As you can imagine, the old style officers, of whom the most representative and important at present is Field Marshal Rundstedt, cannot abide these carpet-baggers.

'He still refers to Hitler openly as the Bohemian Corporal, which is what Hindenburg used to call him. Rundstedt won't even speak to the Führer on the telephone if he can possibly avoid it. Hitler understandably resents this, but he needs Rundstedt for he is a professional, and Hitler is not. Hitler will make decisions on intuition, on what his astrologer tells him, or his mistress Eva Braun believes, what he may feel in his guts. In the early days of the war, when all the force was on Germany's side, some of these hunches paid off. They were bound to, because Hitler had little to beat. But things have changed since then. Now the Allies have the muscle. So a great rift yawns between the professionals and the politicians – but they still need each other to survive.

'Rundstedt and Rommel – who, mind you, are not on the closest terms of cordiality, partly because Hitler has deliberately not defined their areas of command – regard the site of our landings as a tactical matter. And rightly so. They put themselves in our shoes and decided that since we need ports to unload our troops and stores, the easiest way and shortest route across the Channel is from one very good port to another – Dover to Calais.

'They accept that we might also land at Le Havre or Cherbourg. Both are very good ports, but involve a longer voyage. They therefore want to place their troops so they can move this group or that to repulse a landing in any of those areas.

'Hitler, as I say, tends to judge events by what he feels, without necessarily employing any basis of fact or truth or even logical deduction to arrive at his conclusions. He is also a very cautious man, and he knows that feeling against him is growing in Germany – especially among the old school officers. They have seen their country ruined once in 1918. They don't want it to happen a second time. They *could* therefore get together and overthrow him, if the going suddenly gets as tough in the west as it is on the Russian Front. The key to this lies with the Panzer divisions. They owe allegiance to Hitler. He knows this well enough and keeps all their movements under his sole control.

'Right now most of the Panzer Divisions are within relatively easy distance of Calais, on the east of the Seine. That is where we wish them to stay until the invasion begins. Then the RAF and USAAF will blow the bridges – so they will find it difficult to cross the river.

'Now don't imagine you are going out there, just one man on his own, on a Mad Mike sort of exercise, The Man Who Won The War kind of thing. You are going on a mission which is only one part of a concerted team effort. The Germans will weigh the information you bring against what their agents over here have been telling them for months, what their own aerial photographs show.

'The Nazis will want to believe you, because you will confirm what the Führer believes and what his intuition or gut reaction tells him.

'The professionals may be more cautious, but even so they will find it difficult to argue convincingly against the information you will bring which is backed up by dozens, no, hundreds of other apparently independent reports. To borrow a Biblical analogy, you are not the heavy load the camel is carrying. You must regard yourself as the last straw that breaks the camel's back!

'Now I want to introduce you to someone who has been sending wireless messages to advise the Germans that you should soon be arriving. We started to hint at this for some weeks past, even before you volunteered. Incidentally, as Nimrod, you have been one of this man's chief contacts for some time.'

The major pressed a bell-push beneath his desk. The door opened and Robert Frazer came into the room. His case officer had driven him down with him from Finchley that morning. They lunched together and he had then enjoyed an unexpected cigar. Now as he stood framed by the doorway, in his shoddy wartime utility suit and cheap leather shoes, Frazer might have been a schoolmaster from a seedy private school, or a door-to-door salesman come to explain to his area manager why he had failed to reach his sales target. He looked with dull eyes at the major and then at Rigby. Suddenly, the muscles tightened around his mouth. Blood left his face. He removed his cigar.

'My God!' he said softly. 'You!'

'You!' repeated Rigby, equally amazed. For here was Mr. Werner, who years previously had given him piano lessons in Belvedere and then had taught him German; the man who had paid his university fees; who had asked him to find out the performance of British army wireless sets. What the devil was Werner doing here?

Rigby turned to the major.

'This man spied for the Nazis before the war. I went to the Embassy here when I wished to work in Germany. They put me on to him. He asked me to work for them.'

'And you refused?' the major asked Rigby.

'I did. But I must admit he arranged for the German embassy to pay my fees at the university.'

'Of course,' said the major urbanely. 'And for others too, no doubt. The Germans even put one or two cadets through Sandhurst and Cranwell and Dartmouth. Nothing unusual, Rigby, I assure you.'

'So you knew about this, then?'

'Not then, but afterwards. We also knew about your reaction. If it had been different, you would still be interned. And if you had shown a different reaction now, you would probably have gone back behind the wire, ek dum.'

'He was called Duncan then.'

'Now he's got another good Scottish name. Frazer. Know the motto of their clan, Rigby? "I am ready." Rather apt, I think. He's had several names – Werner, Duncan – and his real name is Weber. But, as the bard said, what's in a name?

'We have a number of former German agents working for us, so it seemed best to choose one with whom you had already some contact. You can then tell the Germans all about that, if you have to. They can check it up easily. Makes for confidence all round. Puts you in a stronger position.'

'My father was a Jew,' said Rigby. 'Do they know that?'

'Your mother is not Jewish,' replied Frazer.' I have made that point in several messages.'

'I don't think it matters either way,' said the major. 'After all, Heydrich was part Jewish. It simply made him all the more eager to prove his political reliability to the Nazis. Perhaps your wish to help stems from the same motive? They can check up on your real name, Rosenberg. Your army number shows you are in the Royal East Kents. Nothing to worry about there.'

'Where have Frazer and I met?' Rigby asked him.

'In the same public houses around London where you met before the war,' said Angus.

'None have been bombed, luckily,' the major added. 'We've checked.'

Rigby and Frazer sat talking, uneasily at first, and then gradually more freely. Both carefully avoided areas of controversy. At last, the major nodded to Frazer.

'You've quite a drive ahead of you,' he told him. 'And no doubt you are transmitting tonight?'

Frazer nodded. He stood up.

'It must seem strange to you in the circumstances that I should wish you luck,' he said to Rigby. 'But I wish you what I hope for myself. Good luck.'

'We will both need it,' Rigby replied.

'Me possibly just as much as you,' said Frazer softly. '*Wiedersehn.*'

The major left the upper room and a captain, wearing service dress, with the serpent and staff badges of the Royal Army Medical Corps, took his place.

Angus stood up.

'I'll wait for you downstairs,' he told Rigby.

The captain shook hands with Rigby, sat down behind the table and pulled the cloth from the globe.

This was a ball covered with segments of mirror glass, the type that Rigby had seen suspended from the ceiling at dances in North Wales, to reflect coloured lights. The ball was mounted on a square black base. The captain pressed a button, an electric motor inside the base began to hum, and the ball slowly revolved, scattering splinters of light across the walls and up on the ceiling.

'Now,' said the captain soothingly. 'I want you to lean back in your chair. Relax. Fold your hands in your lap. Don't look at me. Look at this revolving crystal. I will talk and you will listen. And then afterwards I will ask you various questions, and you will answer. I will tell you who you are about to become and what you will have to do. Then I will ask you to repeat these instructions to me. We will continue until you are perfect in the part, like a good actor. Then, if others ask you awkward questions, you will know exactly what to say. You understand me?'

He had a soft, persuasive voice. Rigby nodded. He kept his eyes on the small flickering mirrors, now ablaze, now dull as the ball turned. The contrast was not at all disagreeable; it had a soothing, almost soporific effect. Rigby began to wonder why.

The captain opened a file on the desk and started to read aloud in the light of the desk lamp. His voice was at first a whisper and then seemed to rise steadily until it boomed and echoed. Rigby was no longer in a small unfurnished upstairs room, but in a vast cavern which magnified each word the captain uttered. And soon the voice filled Rigby's mind. There was no other sound in the world, but the voice of the captain speaking to him, and to him alone.

Frazer sat with his case officer in the back seat of the little Hillman car that sped back over the empty roads towards Finchley. Next to the RASC driver sat another soldier; both wore revolvers. No-one spoke for several miles.

'That major mentioned the Frazer clan's motto,' said Frazer at last. 'Do you by any chance know whether the Duncans also have a motto?'

'Yes. I do. It's brief and applicable to all of us who wish to survive for as long as possible in this transitory life. "Learn to suffer." '

'Ach!' Frazer smiled bitterly. 'I am learning. These many years I have been learning. But what will happen to me when I graduate?'

The pilot of the Lysander was a thin and wiry flight-lieutenant who wore the ribbon of the D.F.C. Before the war he trained as an accountant and he had the lean pale face that not infrequently goes with members of that profession. Whenever he read a book or even a newspaper, his eyes showed incipient distrust, as though he expected to find at best a gross error, and at worst, a deliberate falsification or fraudulent entry.

He sat now in the briefing room of an airfield outside Chichester, smoking a cigarette and occasionally sipping a cup of black coffee as he checked his orders. He was to land two agents in Northern France and bring out one. Visibility with the moon should be fair, which his mathematical mind knew could equally well be a plus or a minus for success. From past experience, he personally preferred a moonless night, when he could see the improvised landing strip marked out in a field by parallel lines of plastic ping-pong balls coated with white luminous paint. When there was a moon, the Frenchmen on the ground were understandably less willing to advertise their position, and consequently the strip was sometimes more difficult to find.

He had memorised his route on the folding map with a scale of half a million to one, and pinpointed his target on the quarter million map. He had two copies of his gen card, which contained details of his flight plan, and he knew what landmarks he should look for, which way the rivers ran, which villages had churches with unusual steeples and which railway lines should be visible from the air. He anticipated no special problems, but he never liked these clandestine tasks. He hated that moment just before he landed in a dark unknown field, after spotting the pin-pricks of light from a signal torch, or the dim glow of the ping-pong balls.

He had not landed in an ambush so far, but several friends had, and there was always a first time. He wondered about the people he would carry out and who he would bring back, what they had done before the war, what they hoped to do afterwards. Theirs was a task for which he would never volunteer. It was bad enough having to land and be away within minutes. The risk of interception was largely confined to that time, but these men and women, of what nationality he had no idea, for they seemed to speak French, Spanish, Italian and German with equal facility, might be in France for weeks – if they were lucky. If they were not, by the time he was back and eating breakfast they could be facing torture or might already be dead. In accountancy terms, the risks they accepted were not notional, but deadly.

The door opened. Another RAF officer showed in two men, and closed the door behind them. Both wore civilian suits, rather shabby, with unpressed trousers and unpolished shoes. They were smoking Gauloise cigarettes. Agents outward bound frequently did this to mask any lingering scent of British cigarettes, and to impregnate their clothes and hair with the smell of French tobacco. When one was running the risks they faced, every detail that could be utilised to build up a believable picture of pretence became of great importance. They both looked very ordinary people, the sort who before the war had probably filled in their own income tax returns.

He shook hands with them.

'Coming with me?' he asked.

The first one nodded. He was about thirty-five years of age, sallow-faced, unshaven, with brown, unhappy eyes.

'I am Ricard,' he said. 'I've not flown with you before.'

His voice was flat, with an accent. He did not look English, but then he was not supposed to be English.

'Here is my colleague, Stéphane Dubillier. What time do we leave?'

'Twenty-three hundred,' said the pilot. 'Before we go, I suggest we check a few things. Carrying much gear?'

'Not a lot. Two small packs, plus cases.'

'If they are heavy, shove them under the seats. But watch they don't slip back into the tail. We'll never get them out if they do. Taking much money?'

'A bit.'

'In that case, put your bags on the shelf. Just in case you might leave them behind. Easy to do when you are getting out in a hurry. Now, have you any brandy or other booze with you?'

They shook their heads.

'I've a reason for asking,' the pilot explained. 'A number of you fellows carry brandy in metal flasks. Less chance of them breaking than bottles, I suppose. We had an instance where one of your chaps gave the pilot his flask to bring back. He stuffed it in his flying boot – and the metal threw the compass off, so he came out over the Channel Islands, instead of Cabourg! Now, shirts and pants clean?'

'So far,' said Ricard.

This was necessary because dirty underclothes could easily poison a wound.

'Anything I should know?' the pilot asked.

Ricard shook his head.

'Less you know the better. Except the target area.'

'I'm clued up on that. South of Bayeux. Where they have the tapestry.'

'Where they *had* the tapestry. They've moved it.'

'We won't be looking at it anyhow,' said the pilot. 'We'll leave that until after the war. Want a cup of tea, coffee, something to eat?'

They shook their heads.

'Flown in a Lysander before?'

'No,' said Rigby. 'Never.'

'It can be cold, but we're not making a very long journey. Now, when I come in to land, I'll switch on my lamp to "Morse" to give the recognition signal. When I pick up their reply, we go right in. If I am not absolutely satisfied that their signal's a hundred per cent right, or if it's coming from the wrong field, or I feel there is *anything* whatever fishy about it, we don't come down, but turn round and head back home. But if all's well, down we go – for as short a stop as possible.'

He turned to Ricard.

'You jump out first. You stay inside,' he told Rigby, 'And hand out the gear. Then out you get and in comes the fellow I'm bringing back.

Now, a rather awkward point. I must make it absolutely clear that if anything goes wrong when either or both of you are out on the deck, I take off even if I have to leave you there. Those are my orders. You've probably got yours. Sorry and all that, but those are mine. So let's hope it's a friendly reception committee. Any questions?'

Rigby shook his head. Since his final session with the hypnotist, which had taken place that morning, he felt curiously, almost absurdly relaxed. It was as though he wore invisible mental armour; he was immune to attack from all enemies. This state of semi-euphoria should last for several days, but thereafter it would grow progressively weaker.

Captain Angus had driven him to a house in Kent, and introduced him to Ricard. Neither had any real idea who the other was. Rigby knew that Ricard believed he was a wireless expert flying out with a case of equipment to boost the power of the sets the Resistance used. Rigby had been told that Ricard had undertaken several earlier missions in France and he was now returning; but what his duties were in France, Rigby had no idea. Neither man knew anything about the other's background; they were only names, and even these were false.

The three men walked in silence across the tarmac. The Lysander waited, surprisingly large and spidery in the dim moonlight. They climbed inside it.

'Parachutes under your seats,' said the pilot briefly.

Rigby nodded. His mind was already on their destination; the flight was incidental. The propeller began to turn and the engine fired. The pilot went through his pre-flight checks and raced the engine against the chocks. Then the aircraft began to taxi forward. Blue lights alongside the runway glowed to infinity. The engine roared. Rigby felt the floor tilt underneath his feet, his body pressed harder against the back of his seat. Then they were airborne, and circling the airfield. When its lights were no longer visible, the plane turned and headed south over the sleeping countryside towards the English Channel.

# Chapter Nine

The sea lay flat and empty beneath them; they might have been flying above a vast sheet of smoked glass. Inside, the aircraft felt chill and cheerless. The only light was a greenish-blue glimmer above the instruments. No-one spoke.

The drone of the engine and a faint vibration of the cabin's thin walls provided an uneasy background to Rigby's thoughts. It was difficult to accept that this was all actually happening, and to him. How often had he seen similar scenes on the screen in cinemas in Wales or Eastbourne! But now he was principal actor, and if his performance proved unconvincing, it would also be his last.

Time passed. The pilot moved the stick forward and they began to lose height. Soon they could see a row of dim blue pinpoints far beneath, which meant they were close to an electric railway. Five minutes later, a dull red glow moved across the darkness; the fire box of a locomotive going south. The plane banked to turn, and the railway lines gleamed. They flew over a darker area of forest. Then Rigby could make out faint outlines of houses and larger buildings – barns? factories? – to the left. The pilot straightened out, still losing height.

'Three minutes,' he said curtly over his shoulder. The pitch of noise changed as he feathered his propeller. He began to go through pre-landing drill; switched on the fuselage tank, moved the lever that turned the signalling lamp to Morse as opposed to direct beam; pushed down the seat arm-rests; adjusted the mixture control.

They seemed very low now, the engine hardly making any noise. Their speed was accentuated by the tops of trees in the dark forest that rushed away beneath them. Suddenly, the trees disappeared. Ahead, stretched fields, much larger than those left behind in England. In one, Rigby could see two parallel rows of small round dots, like faint glow worms in two straight ranks – the luminous ping-pong balls that marked the landing strip. Down on the ground, a tiny lamp flickered a Morse greeting.

'That's us,' said the pilot with relief and satisfaction. 'I'm replying.' His Morse lamp spelled out the recognition letters.

'Going in now. Elbows on your knees, heads down.'

Rigby and Ricard leaned forward as though in prayer, feet pressed flat against the floor, seat belts tight, heads down, elbows on their knees, in case the plane pitched on touching the rough earth in the field. For the first time, in he had forgotten how many years, Rigby murmured the words of the Jewish prayer his father had taught him during one of his visits to Vienna, a prayer to be used only at a time of extreme personal danger. *'Hear, O Israel, the Lord Thy God, the Lord is One . . .'*

Ricard made the sign of the cross. The note of the Lysander's engine changed abruptly, their wheels bounced once, twice and they were down. The whole plane trembled with resonance as the pilot slowed, turned his aircraft to be ready to take off into the wind, and taxied back to the edge of the trees. He cut his engine. After the buffeting from the wind and the vibration in the confined cabin, their ears rang with the sudden, unexpected silence. Rigby fought down an almost over-whelming wish to leap out and race for cover. They must present a sitting target, strapped to their seats in this fragile cage on wheels. How could they possibly have landed without the Germans hearing their engine and seeing the Morse light flash?

The pilot was already doing his cockpit drill for take-off; he was careful, unhurried, methodical. He would make a good accountant. He nodded to Ricard.

'Out,' he said briefly.

Ricard unclipped his seat belt, and opened the door at his side. Cool night air, heavy with the smell of honeysuckle and mint, filled the chilly cockpit. Ricard jumped down stiffly. Figures detached them-selves from the deeper darkness of the wood. Pass-words were whispered and replied to. Rigby handed out their gear and then jumped out on to the grass. Figures flitted silently into the safer dark-ness of the trees. One man ran towards the aircraft, climbed inside and shut the door. Someone slapped the side of the plane with the flat of his hand and called, 'O.K.' The propeller began to turn slowly against compression. A cloud of white smoke blew out from the exhaust. Wind from the propeller briefly flattened the grass, and then the Lysander was away, climbing steadily up into the night sky.

Three men were waiting in the trees. Ricard appeared to know them all. The leader was André, and the second in command, Jules. André's brother, Louis, was third in line. Ricard introduced Rigby as Stéphane. All shook hands formally. There was a strong smell of fear and sweat and garlic and Gitanes tobacco, although no-one was smoking.

'We have to move fast,' said André. 'You're late.'

'Not our fault,' replied Ricard. 'Maybe there was a head wind, or something.'

'Explanations later. We had better split up into two groups.'

He turned to Rigby.

'My brother Louis will guide you. Go with him.'

Louis pushed an old bicycle. Over the crossbar he had slung several hares and rabbits tied by their paws. Rigby balanced his case on the carrier.

'What if we are stopped?' he asked.

'Leave the talking to me,' Louis told him shortly. 'I'll try to buy them off with these hares.'

'What about my case?'

'We use cases like that for carrying Calvados. We have been taking some bottles to their officers' mess.'

'And if they want to look inside?'

Louis shrugged.

'Leave that to me, too, but whatever happens, let me do the talking. You say nothing.'

Soon they were through the wood, and climbed down a bank to a narrow, winding road. Hedges grew tall on either side, and branches of trees hung low just above their heads. An owl hooted. Unknown small animals rustled in the darkness which pressed on them like a weight. They came to a farmhouse. A dog barked in the yard and chickens clucked disapprovingly from a hidden perch.

Louis gripped Rigby's arm and nodded his head slowly towards the back of the house. They walked into the farmyard. Rigby could feel cow dung soft under his feet. Louis leaned his bicycle against a wall, picked up Rigby's case and went into a barn. He closed the door and lit an oil lamp. Rigby looked at him in surprise.

'Won't the light show?'

'No. We've seen to that,' said Louis. 'This your first trip?'

'Yes.'

They regarded each other warily. Louis had a narrow, thin face. His eyes were set close together, and he had not shaved recently. The corners of his mouth turned down, giving his face a discontented appearance. Rigby was not drawn to him; he sensed the feeling was mutual.

'Know anyone?'

Rigby shook his head.

'I've been over to England twice,' Louis told him proudly. Rigby nodded. The less he spoke the less he might have to retract or remember.

'How long do we stay here?' he asked.

'Until your work's done. We'll sleep in the loft.'

'Anyone see us come in?'

'No. My father owns the farm, anyway. Someone from the nearest German regiment comes most mornings to collect eggs. We get a good price. My old man even gives the soldier a glass of Calvados. They sit chatting for a bit. Then he goes off. We've not had the place searched so far.'

Touch wood, thought Rigby, and put one hand on the nearest wall.

'What's the regiment?' he asked.

'First battalion, Artillery Regiment, 352nd Division. Why?'

'No reason. Just asking.'

'I'll get some Calvados now. We could both do with it.'

Louis moved towards another door. Then he turned to face Rigby.

'Do you speak German?' Louis asked him suddenly in German.

'Yes,' replied Rigby, in the same language. 'A little.'

Louis came back to him and looked at him closely. Rigby could smell sweat and the sourness of the man's clothes.

'Who *are* you? You're not French. And you don't look wholly English?'

'I am English. I speak French and German fairly well.'

'No-one here has ever heard of you before.'

'Just as well,' replied Rigby. 'I hadn't heard of you either.'

He made his voice sound matter-of-fact, but he felt sweat gather on his back. Was he already suspected? Had he made some stupid mistake, without realising it? Had someone in England talked too much? Or had he simply been too eager to know the name of the nearest German unit?

Louis left the barn. Rigby waited for him to return, his heart beating strongly, sweat trickling down between his shoulder blades. If Louis already suspected him, to attempt to reach the Germans would be even more difficult than he had anticipated – and infinitely more dangerous.

He sat down on an upturned bucket and began to count slowly, forcing himself to relax.


The acting Intelligence Officer of the German Corps, a captain, who thought he should be a major, sat in the front room of a requisitioned château overlooking a drive of plane trees. He was plump, a law graduate from Heidelberg, bored with his job, and the length of a war that had brought him insufficient promotion. He had served in Poland, in France, in Italy, and now was back in France but still only as a captain, while others of his age and service, and in his opinion less well qualified for promotion, were majors and even colonels.

Captain Arngross sipped a cup of tepid acorn coffee and winced as he swallowed the bitter brown liquid. He suffered from stomach trouble, largely brought on by his personal discontent and frustration. For this reason he usually drank half a cup of water with a spoonful of bismuth twice a day.

He rustled papers he had been reading, the daily teletyped messages from 352 Division, 10 miles away. This division had only recently moved near the coast from Saint Lô. Some time before it did so, an order had been issued that teleprinters and telephones must always be used in preference to radio conversations, because it was now suspected that the Allies were monitoring wireless traffic. There was, of course, much evidence that members of the French Resistance were also tapping telephone lines and recording important conversations, and such calls were accordingly to be kept as brief and cryptic as possible.

Captain Arngross had recently attended a conference for Intelligence officers at Rommel's headquarters, when General Günther Blumentritt, Rundstedt's Chief of Staff, had spoken to them about the expected Allied invasion, and the paramount need for stricter security.

There was no need for the Allies to capture Army Headquarters in

106

order to learn their plans, the general declared, in an attempt at joviality. Allied agents simply listened in to radio links and telephone conversations! Secret and other important messages were therefore teletyped, or, if this was impossible, typed out and delivered by dispatch rider.

For the past ten days, Captain Arngross had received repeated enquiries by both these means, asking whether any enemy parachutist had landed in his area. Had any clandestine landings of small enemy aircraft been reported?

Of course, everyone knew that planes came in after dark to remote fields and flew out again, having delivered or collected an agent; sometimes several. But to know this and to catch the culprit was a very different matter. These small aircraft only needed a hundred metres or so on which to land and take off, and the fields in Normandy sometimes stretched for several kilometres in every direction.

Even if the locals were not particularly hostile to the Germans because they had not suffered at their hands, he also knew, as does every town-born stranger who chooses to live in the country, that villagers who may appear bucolic and simple invariably hedge their bets most shrewdly, and always aim to be on the winning side. During Arngross's last stay in France, this tendency had favoured the Germans; but not now.

Every night, each regiment in the area sent out special reconnaissance patrols to cover the most likely landing places. Some patrols went on foot, others by bicycle. They might have heard an engine coming down the sky, or seen a glimmer of light at the edge of a wood, but by the time the soldiers reached the area and forced their way through prickly hedges, there was no-one left for them to see, nothing to find. Each morning Arngross received the same reply: Nothing to Report.

Now, in front of him was an urgent message, that had originated from the senior Intelligence officer in the headquarters of the 7th Army, and which he believed could well have emanated from an even more senior source. He read it through for the umpteenth time, reaching automatically for the bismuth bottle in the drawer as he did so.

IMPERATIVE CAPTURE DISCREETLY AND UN-HARMED ENEMY AGENT NIMROD DUE ARRIVE AREA

CABOURG-BAYEUX STOP INFORM SENDER IM-
MEDIATELY WHEN APPREHENDED.

Arngross had risked a tapped line by telephoning the officer who
sent this message, speaking obliquely in case of unknown listeners.
These would not necessarily be French, for many army telephone lines
were also tapped by the German Secret Service, and for this reason,
senior officers who had to telephone controversial orders which might
afterwards be queried or even denied, would frequently invite trusted
colleagues to listen in on extensions, so that they could later verify
exactly what had been said.

'Just had your latest on the expected visitor,' said Arngross. 'We
have already given orders to all patrols to treat Nimrod kindly. But he
could still get hurt before they know who he is.'

'So could you, if anything happens to him,' came the uncom-
promising reply. 'I must repeat that if this man arrives he is not –
repeat not – to be harmed. I can't say any more, but for God's sake,
don't discuss such things on an open line.'

Captain Arngross pressed a bell for an orderly, who brought him a
glass of water. He shook some bismuth into it and stirred the milky
mixture with the end of a pencil. Then he personally telephoned the
Intelligence officer of each unit to ask the same guarded question: 'Has
anyone arrived?' The replies were still in the negative. One patrol had
reported hearing a low-flying aircraft early that morning, but no-one
had actually seen it, and did not know whether it had landed. Arngross
sat for a moment, sipping the drink and then sent for his clerk.

'Send a teletype to all Intelligence officers of infantry and Panzer
units,' he instructed him. 'Copies to commanding officers. On orders
from HQ 7th Army, they are immediately to increase investigative
patrol activity day and night to apprehend agent believed arrived in
area overnight. Agent answers to name Nimrod. He is to be brought
here immediately under guard for interrogation but must not be
injured or ill-treated. Headquarters 7th Army will hold the commanding officer in whose area Nimrod is apprehended personally
responsible for his safe arrival here.'

As Arngross waited for the clerk to type the message, he looked out
at the garden of the château. In peacetime it must have been magnificent, he thought, with its wide lawns and long flower beds bursting
with colour.

Even shabby and uncared for, it still spoke of wealth and a country contentment he envied. The sight somehow symbolised to Arngross his own predicament. He was the man in the middle, between orders and action, with all the prizes and the pleasures and the promotion going elsewhere.

He did not own this château, and he never would own anything like it. He simply occupied one room by force of arms; and soon even this short and increasingly uneasy tenancy could end. He massaged his stomach slowly, while he waited to sign the message.

In the room overlooking St. James's Park, the major with the thinning hair and the first war ribbons who had interviewed Rigby was looking at a report that his RAF liaison officer had sent to him.

The Lysander had landed safely at 01.03 hours that morning at the agreed place, disembarked two passengers and brought back one. Trip uneventful in both directions. No flak or searchlights.

The major glanced at his watch. It was now a quarter past nine in the morning. No doubt the sun was shining in France as strongly as it was here. He looked at the next report. Another bombing raid had been made on targets in the Pas de Calais area. German night fighters had intercepted the bombers, but no casualties were reported. Large fires had been started and left burning.

The major took out his pipe, filled it and pressed the tobacco down in the bowl with the ball of his thumb. His mind was miles away. He was imagining the edge of some wood or a loft or other hiding place in a village, which in happier days he might have driven through on his way south to his summer house in Grasse. There would no doubt be a local garage with its single pump by the roadside, an auberge, a shop, and old men sitting on benches in the sun or playing boules. Children might be running about in their school playground behind high iron railings. Flowers would wilt outside a roadside shrine – and some-where the young Jewish German who had pretended to be English was now in hiding, pretending to be French. He would be on his own now. No-one could help him; only God.

The major was not notably religious, but he knew how much depended on the success of this man's mission, and how slim were his chances of survival.

He thought of other young men in this war and the last. He remembered his own experiences at Ypres long ago. Then he lit his pipe, initialled the report, and to show he wasn't becoming soft and sentimental, rang his sergeant clerk to ask gruffly where the devil was the latest Sitrep (Situation Report) about FUSAG?

# Chapter Ten

Rigby and Elena were walking through the streets of Vienna. Sunshine gilded the old stone buildings he knew so well, and which she was now seeing for the first time. It was her first visit to the city, and he was experiencing happiness of an intensity he had never previously imagined.

Somewhere, out of sight, people were cheering. Gradually, the tone of this cheering changed. It became harsher, angry, menacing; the voice of the mob baying for blood. The sun retreated and the skies grew dark.

Streets now began to fill with people from side roads and alleys, as streams discharge into a main river. They were rough, with fierce scowling faces. Soon it became impossible to move without jostling strangers or being jostled by them. Shopkeepers were hurriedly putting steel and wooden shutters in place to protect their plate-glass windows. He saw his father wrestling with a heavy metal shutter outside his jewellery shop, an old frightened man in a world of the young.

Rigby forced a way through the crowd to help him. Together, they heaved at the sheets of steel and locked them in place. But his father's face showed no recognition of him. They might have been strangers.

Only seconds before, Elena had been by his side, but now the crowd had drawn her away, like a leaf on the racing waters of the Danube. He could not reach her, and as he struggled frantically the crowds dissolved and Elena vanished with them. Instead of their shouts, Rigby could hear individual voices, the rustling of straw, the clucking of hens.

For a moment, he could not comprehend where he was. And then his dream faded. He was awake, instantly alert in the way he had learned during training in Wales. He was lying on a large empty sack spread in a loft. Hay from a broken bale covered his case and shoes. Through an open trap door, he could see a ladder going down to the stone floor beneath him. The sun was shining, and the barn doors were open. Chickens pecked among bits of straw; inside a wood-wheeled cart, parked with its shafts up in the air, a cat dozed while four tabby kittens played around her.

The voices grew louder; they must have woken him. Louis was talking outside to another man about his own age, unshaven and wearing shabby, dirty clothes. As they both came into the barn, the sun threw long shadows across the floor. Louis began to climb the ladder. The other man waited, watching him. He held a pitchfork. Rigby saw that its two prongs were unusually sharp.

'Awake?' Louis asked him.

'Yes.'

The skin was tight across Louis's cheekbones; he looked pale and worried.

'What's the matter?' Rigby asked him.

'The Germans must have seen the plane last night.'

'How do you know?'

'They've captured Ricard.'

'Where?'

'A few kilometres away. With my brother André. They killed him.'

Rigby was already sitting up, putting on his shoes.

'They surrounded the house where Ricard was hiding. He had no chance at all. When they seized Ricard they kept asking if he was Nimrod. The patrol commander said he hadn't to be hurt or roughed up in any way. But that didn't go for the rest. André they shot. Jules got away – after a free for all.'

'What do we do?'

'We move you – now.'

'And my case?'

'I'll take that.'

Louis picked up Rigby's case and climbed down the ladder. Rigby followed him. Louis tied a length of binder twine around the handle of the case and crossed the yard to a well. He lifted up the round wooden lid and lowered the case carefully inside. He tied the other end of the twine to a metal ring two feet down from the mouth of the well, replaced the lid and scattered some wisps of straw over it so that it would not appear to have been removed. Then he motioned to Rigby to come into the house.

A woman with greying hair, wearing a black blouse and skirt, kept her eyes down as she stirred a pan of soup on the old-fashioned black leaded stove. She could have been Louis's mother; Rigby did not ask, and Louis did not introduce her. She ladled soup into a shallow bowl, opened a cupboard, brought out a slice of blackish bread. Louis poured one glass of cider.

'Aren't you eating?' asked Rigby.

Louis shook his head.

'I don't feel hungry. Not now.'

He sat down and lit a cigarette. Rigby ate thankfully; he had forgotten how hungry he was. As he finished, they all heard footsteps on the flagstones. Louis jumped up nervously. A little boy with shorts reaching below his knees, and wearing boots and a jacket too small for him, came running into the kitchen.

'They're up the road,' he announced breathlessly. 'Near the byre.'

'How many?'

'Ten. With bicycles.'

'Come on,' said Louis quickly to Rigby.

The woman picked up his half-empty bowl of soup, emptied it into the sink and threw the bread out to the chickens. Then she continued to stir the pan, as though nothing had disturbed her. Rigby and Louis ran out across the flagstones. The man with the pitchfork followed them. They went through an open five-bar gate, into a field of new wheat. Poppies blazed red like random splashes of blood. They ran half-doubled to keep their heads below the top of the hedge. The wind rustled the wheat, moving it like waves on some strange surrealistic sea. Soon the ground fell away, and they reached a copse near a stream about twelve feet across. Louis waded out into the centre. Rigby and the other man followed.

'In case of dogs,' Louis explained.

The water felt very cold, fresh and welcome at first, and then numbing to Rigby's ankles and feet. They walked through the stream for about 200 yards then came out on the other side, and sat down thankfully in a tangle of docks and thorn bushes.

'Patrols have been out for days,' Louis explained. 'They seem to be looking for someone special. Can't understand why. And who is Nimrod?'

113

He looked questioningly at Rigby as he spoke. Rigby said nothing. Louis unbuttoned an inner jacket pocket, took out a pistol, cocked it.

'Are you going to shoot it out?' Rigby asked him.

'No. They'd have reinforcements up within minutes.'

'Isn't it dangerous to have that on you, in case you're searched?'

'I won't be searched,' Louis told him confidently. 'And I may have to use it.'

The two men looked at Rigby with the suspicious eyes of peasants facing a situation they did not understand, a problem they could not solve.

'Are *you* Nimrod?' Louis asked him.

'I'm Stéphane Dubillier.'

'That's what your papers say, and what you say. But you are not French. And I somehow doubt you are English. *And* you speak German. We've never needed a wireless expert before. Always managed ourselves. And we were only expecting Ricard. Not you. And never before last night has anything gone wrong. The Germans have never given us much trouble, but – now!' He spread his hands in perplexity.

The other man spoke. He had a deep, gruff voice.

'We asked Ricard about you, but all he knew was that you drove to the airfield together. And soon as you land everything goes wrong.'

'Maybe you've been lucky up to now,' suggested Rigby.

'Maybe. But I am not happy about you. André's dead and Ricard and Jules are captured. You're the only one left.'

'And you two,' Rigby pointed out. 'I don't know what the hell you are going on about. I am very sorry about your brother, but this has nothing whatever to do with me.'

'Do you know Monsieur Cardan?' asked Louis.

'No.'

'Ever heard the name?'

'Can't say I have. In a car, the Cardan shaft drives the back axle. That's all.'

'What about Heloïse or Guillaume?'

Rigby shook his head.

'You're *sure*?'

'I am sure.'

'Just as well,' said Louis. 'Because I don't know them either.'

He smiled for the first time, but only with his mouth.

'Thought I'd test you. But I still don't understand why exactly you are here. That wireless business . . .'

He shrugged.

'When you're living on your nerves, like us, you develop a strong sense of survival. I've a feeling right here in my guts about all this. And I don't like it.'

'I'm sorry about that, but I'm not so happy about the way things are going, either. That case of bits and pieces has only to be found and the Germans will know there must be several transmitters hidden elsewhere. Now, where are we heading? What's the plan?'

'We will go to a friend's house across the fields, four or five kilometres away. He supplies the Germans with even more eggs and cider and Calvados than we do. They'll never suspect him. We will hide up for the rest of the day, or until the boy tells us the patrol's gone.'

'And then?'

'Then we will put you through a few real tests. Just to see how your story does stand up.'

In the distance, through the wheat, they heard a whinnying of horses. Louis and the other man stood up carefully. Rigby also stood up in case either of them jumped him. He felt curiously calm. He was younger and fitter than either of them; he was also trained to fight, to kill. They had adapted themselves to these necessities; he was a professional. His most dangerous time would come when they and their friends questioned him.

A number of birds had risen and were fluttering above the wheat with a great beating of wings. In the next field, four horses stood by a hedge, looking in the same direction. These signs of birds and beasts, revealing the presence of strangers, he had learned on so many patrols at Aberdovey. They marked exactly where the Germans were.

'Follow me,' said Louis. He put his pistol in his jacket pocket. The man with the pitchfork came behind, breathing heavily. Now and then he hawked and spat as he ran. They came out of the copse, crawled on their bellies across a flat unsown part of the field and reached a path. They stood up and walked slowly along it; to run might frighten the birds or the horses and draw attention to themselves.

In the distance, Rigby saw a grey stone farmhouse with a slate roof. Smoke spiralled up from its only chimney. The horses were moving along the hedge, still whinnying uneasily. Now and then one reared up nervously. The Germans must be on the other side.

They reached the outer extremity of the farm. Ahead lay a row of slate-roofed buildings. Milk churns stood on a cobbled yard. High up in the walls were little holes for doves. Some ducks and geese clucked around stagnant water in a pond; chickens pecked in the dust. It was going to be a hot day. Already the sky felt heavy with heat.

They could see the house clearly now. A middle-aged woman stood in the yard washing clothes in a huge wooden tub, her arms white with soapsuds up to her elbows. A rusty metal yard gate stood open with a high stone wall on either side. The scene was peaceful and rustic. For the first time since Rigby had landed in France, he felt safe.

They walked towards this gate, past nettles and docks. Louis began to whistle cheerfully. The woman turned and looked at them, shading her eyes against the sun. In her lined, brown face Rigby suddenly saw horror, fear, anguish. And then they were through the gate and the Germans who had been crouching on the far side of the wall dug the snouts of their Schmeissers into their stomachs.

'Hands high,' ordered a feldwebel cheerfully. This capture could mean promotion or leave, or both. A leutnant came towards them from the house, carrying a small black leather attache case.

'So who have we here?' he asked genially.

'I am from the farm down the road,' explained Louis. 'This is my cousin, Stéphane Dubillier, who is helping me, and my cowman, Paul.'

'Your papers.'

With right hands still raised, the three men put their left hands into inner pockets and took out identity papers. The leutnant looked closely at their photographs and then at them. They returned his gaze, all expression wiped from their eyes. The leutnant handed Louis's papers back to him, and did the same for Paul. Then it was Rigby's turn. But instead of examining the papers, he seized Rigby's right wrist, and twisted it sharply so that the palm of his hand was uppermost.

'A farm worker?' he asked sarcastically in French. 'Your hands aren't as rough as your friends', and your nails are not chipped.'

'True,' agreed Rigby in French. 'I've been ill.'

Instantly he regretted this, for the officer only smiled at him.

'In what hospital?' he asked.

'At home. It was only the *grippe*. But it lasted for a week.'

'Where is your home?'

116

'I am staying with Louis.'

Rigby answered each question automatically and quickly, without hesitation. The hypnotist had done his work well. He knew who he was, or at least who he was supposed to be, where he lived.

The officer put his case on top of the wall, opened it, took out a typed list of names and addresses. Over his shoulder Rigby could see that this contained details of everyone who lived in the area: their ages, how long they had lived there. The officer reached Louis' farmhouse. Rigby read that it contained a grandfather of seventy-two, a grandmother four years younger, a wife, an unmarried sister, a young brother and an infant son.

'I think you are mistaken,' said the officer quietly. 'No-one named Dubillier lives there.'

'I am lodging there,' insisted Rigby.

'Not last week. We checked these addresses then. Think again, Monsieur Dubillier.'

Rigby looked at Louis, at Paul, then at the German soldiers. They had lowered their Schmeissers in deference to the officer, pleasurably surprised that they had ambushed a man whose papers were so clearly false. The officer replaced the lists in his attache case, shut it.

'In fact, I would hazard a guess that your name is not Dubillier at all. Does Nimrod mean anything to you?'

For a second that seemed timeless, Rigby did not reply. Then he nodded.

'Yes. I have heard it.'

Louis drew a deep breath; so his instinct was right. He should have killed Dubillier in the copse. Emotion erupted within him. His brother was dead, his family compromised, and now he had been captured. And all because of this stranger who had suddenly arrived, unexpected and unknown – a traitor.

'You bastard!' he shouted. He ripped the pistol from his jacket and fired. The shot went wide. Two Schmeissers chattered a reply. Louis jumped like a marionette and dropped on the cobblestones. His pistol slid away, still smoking. A smell of cordite hung sharply in the air. Chickens ran clucking in terror. The woman at the washtub screamed and fled into the house. Paul stood, trembling with fear.

'Take him, but don't hurt him,' the officer ordered, nodding towards Rigby.

Two soldiers seized Rigby by his arms and ran with him across the

117

cobble-stones. Behind him he heard Paul cry out, but he could not look back. In front of the farmhouse stood a Kübelwagen with canvas hood and sidescreens erected. One soldier pushed Rigby into the back seat and then sat with his arm linked through his, Schmeisser across his knees, pointing at Rigby's stomach.

The second soldier climbed in behind the wheel. The officer sat beside him. As they drove away, Rigby looked back through the little celluloid window in the rear of the hood. The other soldiers were marching Paul to a truck. Rigby's mouth felt dry and sour with reaction. The leutnant turned, holding a packet of cigarettes. He offered it. Rigby shook his head. The officer lit one himself. The smell of Akita filled the little car, bringing back memories of Frankfurt and Vienna.

'Where are you taking me?' he asked.

'Headquarters. You speak German, I assume?'

'Yes.'

'Then let us continue our conversation in our mother tongue.'

'Do you know who I am?' Rigby asked him.

'Only that I think you are the man we have been looking for, Nimrod.'

'I wish to see your Intelligence officer.'

'You are on your way to meet him.'

The car turned off the road, down a drive of plane trees, and stopped outside a château. Lawns grew thick from a winter and spring of neglect. Stone figures holding stone torches peered from groups of trees; weeds clogged urns that had once overflowed with a blaze of geraniums. Rigby climbed out stiffly, with his guard behind him, the Schmeisser now only inches from his kidneys. They climbed the steps. An orderly looked surprised at the manner of their arrival.

'Captain Arngross,' the leutnant told him.

The orderly knocked on the door of a room, and motioned them through. The leutnant saluted.

'I have brought the man who I believe is Nimrod, sir,' he announced proudly.

Captain Arngross closed the drawer of his desk and stood up.

'You are Nimrod?' he asked.

'Yes,' admitted Rigby.

'Is he armed? Have you searched him?'

'Not yet, sir.'

'Well, hurry up about it.'

The guard went through Rigby's pockets, took out his French identity papers, his handerchief, a comb, a stub of pencil, his survival pack.

'He speaks German, sir,' said the leutnant.

'I'll conduct the interview,' said Arngross sharply. His gut had begun to pain him. 'Wait outside, please.'

When they were alone, Arngross walked around Rigby, looking at his shabby suit, his soaked trouser legs and sodden shoes, his whole unshaven scruffy appearance.

'I wish to see the senior Intelligence Officer in Army Group "B" Rigby told him.

'Why? You have been arrested as a member of the French Resistance. You gave a French name and address.'

'I had to. But I have been working in England for the Abwehr. I understand that my arrival here is expected.'

'It is,' agreed Arngross. 'We've been waiting for you for days.'

'Which makes it all the more imperative I see him as soon as possible. It is a matter of the highest priority.'

Their eyes met.

'I'll take you over myself right away. In the meantime, while I inform him of your arrival, let me offer you a coffee. It is only acorn, but at least it's wet and warm.'

Arngross handed Rigby's belongings back to him, and sat down behind his desk.

119

# Chapter Eleven

Ahead of the Kübelwagen, the road stretched grey and uninviting in the afternoon rain, empty as a dead man's eyes.

To the left towered giant white cliffs roofed with grass thick as green thatch. Here and there, huge holes gaped blackly in the cliffside; the mouths of tunnels bored deep into the heart of the hill centuries ago. Some had vertical planks of wood across them; from the road these resembled huge teeth in open mouths. Several houses perched uneasily on small promontories, shutters drawn discreetly across their windows, as a man afraid of heights will close his eyes. The walls of these houses were yellowish and their shutters brown or grey, sad colours that added to the sense of chill and emptiness. Owners had gouged garages out of the base of the cliff at the roadside, but with no petrol available, the little Citroëns and Renaults stood inside on flat tyres, gathering dust.

To the right lay water meadows, and then the wide broad sweep of the Seine curved like a shining scimitar. The river seemed placid and still; three barges going upstream, one behind the other, produced a herringbone washboard effect of ripples that stretched from bank to bank. Beyond the river stood quarries, some filled with water, and a few houses, with power-line pylons marching into the distance to forests shrouded by rain.

The Kübelwagen turned the final bend of the road. Ahead lay La Roche Guyon: a crossroads with an inn, Aux Vieux Donjon, and on the left the castle that dominated the whole village. It soared up against the vertical face of white cliff like something from a fairy tale, so tall that its grey roof tiles, glistening with rain, reached up almost as high as the cliff. And above it, on top of the cliff, loomed the ruins of a

120

donjon tower, originally part of a Norman stronghold that for nearly a thousand years had stood sentinel above the whole area.

This castle had been the home of the Dukes de la Rochefoucauld for the past 400 years. The present Duke and Duchess and their family still lived in the upper storeys, but all other floors and rooms were taken over by the German Army. The castle was now both home and headquarters for Field Marshal Rommel, commanding Army Group 'B', responsible for defending the coast of France.

German engineers had transformed deep caves and tunnels in the cliffside into bomb-proof briefing rooms, a communications centre, and rest rooms for officers. The rear wall of the castle stood so close to the cliff that the back rooms were almost always damp and dark.

The front overlooked a long sunken lawn. To the left of this was a formal riding school, with prancing stallions carved in stone above the doors. On the right was the main entrance to the castle, with a gravel courtyard at the end of a short drive, part cobble-stones, part tarmac, up from the main road.

One side of this drive was bordered by rows of lime trees, pollarded so that their thick branches formed a deep roof of leaves. At the end of the drive, black gates tipped with gold opened on to the courtyard. Opposite this was the 15th century church, where each morning at six the church bell would toll the angelus. In peacetime, this was the signal for the pious in the village to bow in prayer, to cross themselves and seek God's guidance for the day. Now the bell marked the end of the previous night's curfew, for after dark and until dawn, no-one, apart from the military, was allowed on the streets.

German sentries were posted outside the castle gates, and at strategic street corners. They stood, capes shining with rain, as the car turned up the drive. It passed the village war memorial, still with a wreath of flowers, on to the Rue d'Audience, where, in earlier years, villagers would wait to petition the Duke, and stopped in the castle yard. Two soldiers closed and bolted the gates behind it.

'We get out here,' said Arngross, opening his door.

Rigby stretched himself thankfully after a journey squeezed between the captain and the leutnant, who had brought him in. They had spoken little on the way. The road had been almost empty of other vehicles, for it was unwise to be out on any main road during daylight, unless on most urgent business. The risk of British or American aircraft shooting up a convoy or an individual car was very great. They had passed a few local lorries with wood-burning generators, and towing trailers piled with logs to fuel them, and some heavy horses and oxen pulling carts. These were used for delivering perishable food that could not survive long delays on the railways caused by bombing and increased sabotage by the French Resistance.

The air smelt fresh and newly washed. The Seine shone silver through the rain. No birds were in the trees, and no-one was in the streets. Rigby's first impression was of total tranquillity.

The two officers took him up the steps, through French doors that towered thirty feet high, into a corridor panelled with oak. As they walked along its tesselated floor, Rigby heard the clatter of type-writers from offices on both sides.

Arngross knocked discreetly on a heavy door. They entered a high-ceilinged room that looked out across the lawn to the road and the river. Arngross saluted very smartly.

'Reporting with Nimrod, sir,' he said.

A colonel with staff tabs on his uniform stood up behind his desk. Another man wearing a civilian suit, a smaller older man, with oily black hair brushed down on his skull, remained seated. He wore horn-rimmed glasses, and his eyes did not leave Rigby's face. The intensity of his gaze and his rather seedy appearance, like a middle-aged actor down on his luck, seemed incongruous, almost grotesque against the architectural elegance of the room. Thick Persian carpets covered the floor; de Rochefoucauld ancestors peered down at them haughtily from oil paintings on the walls. The room appeared infinitely more luxurious than the room in which the major had interviewed him over-looking St. James's Park, but the atmosphere was somehow the same; both rooms housed men with unusually alert minds.

The colonel gave the Nazi salute almost as a routine gesture expected of him, and motioned Rigby to a chair.

'I am Colonel Ritter,' he said. 'This is Herr Mannheim, my civilian opposite number. So you are Nimrod, who we have been expecting for the past few days? I am told by Herr Mannheim that you have fully lived up to the standards of your eponym and have hunted out all manner of information – particularly for agent Weber.'

'I have done my best, sir,' replied Rigby.

It was easy to lapse into German again, and also surprisingly comfortable, like putting on carpet slippers after a long day wearing shoes one size too tight.

122

'But you are *not* German?' asked Mannheim.

He had an aggressive way of speaking.

'I am, sir,' Rigby corrected him. 'I was born in Frankfurt. But I have spent most of my life in England.'

He explained how this had come about. A uniformed clerk sat at a table in one corner making shorthand notes as they spoke.

'How have you arrived in France? This is your first visit?'

'The first time since 1939 that the opportunity of making the journey presented itself, sir.'

'We understand you have been working in Combined Operations, and with the Special Operations Executive Office in Baker Street, in London?'

'Off and on, sir,' admitted Rigby. 'Not permanently, though.'

'So where do you have lunch when you are in, say, SOE head-quarters, off and on, as you put it?'

'Usually at The Wallace Head public house.'

'Where is that?' Colonel Ritter asked. It was clear to Rigby that he did not agree with Mannheim's abrasive, suspicious tone.

'I was in our London Embassy before the war. In the Military Attaché's office. I did not know that public house.'

'It would be a bit out of your way from the embassy, sir. It is in Blandford Street.'

'Is there any name-plate outside the SOE office in Baker Street? How would I recognise the place, were I to make a call?'

'There is a plaque, with the words, "Inter-Services Liaison Department" on it.'

Mannheim and Ritter exchanged glances. Rigby stood at attention, with the two officers a pace behind him on either side. The clerk waited, pencil in hand. Outside, in the road, an army convoy was moving over the crossroads towards Mantes. Rigby found something soporific, almost hypnotic in watching the trucks follow each other, a set distance between them. He felt strangely calm, as though he was not personally taking part in this question-and-answer charade. He might be one of an audience watching it happen in a play, for he had no idea what would come next; and yet he was confident he would survive. Was this confidence justified – or was it simply a nervous conse-quence of what had already happened? Was this the way a tired body and a worried mind reacted on each other after days of danger?

Here he stood, Rigby, formerly Rosenberg, now Nimrod, in the headquarters of the most famous Field Marshal in all the German Army. Somewhere in this castle or perhaps in a house elsewhere in La Roche Guyon, would be experts who might be called upon to extract the truth from him by any means they saw fit, so long as it produced a quick answer.

He knew and accepted this. Had he not signed a paper that began rather pompously: 'I understand the risks . . .?' But how would he stand up to torture, whether physical or psychological? He had no idea, and yet the prospect did not seem to concern him; he felt beyond discovery, above any of its consequences.

Herr Mannheim took out a packet of Akita cigarettes, offered it to the colonel and then to Rigby. The leutnant obsequiously struck a match. Rigby inhaled the pungent smoke.

'You are not superstitious, then? Three cigarettes from one match.'

Colonel Ritter was doing his best to keep the conversation on a friendly level.

'No, sir,' said Rigby.

'Who did you deal with in London?' asked Mannheim. His tone was also more conciliatory now, less hectoring.

'A man I first met before the war. He taught me the piano. He was called Werner then and later, Duncan. I know him now as Weber.'

'How do you report?'

'By telephone.'

'To his house?'

'No. To a telephone box. He sends me a note with a list of several numbers. Not the exchanges, only the numbers. The exchange is the name of the town that he puts as his address. This name changes week to week. If the call box is occupied, I come back every five minutes until I reach him.'

'How long do you wait?'

'No more than 15 minutes – three attempts.'

'And then?'

'And then I try the next number. Sometimes we meet.'

'Where?'

'The saloon bar of a public house.'

'You give him information. What has he given you?'

'Pound notes – when he has them. But I am not doing this for money.'

'I never suggested you were. But every labourer is worthy of his

124

hire, Nimrod, and you have been labouring a long time over there. Tell me – why haven't you been caught?'

'Why hasn't Weber?' retorted Rigby quickly.

Mannheim nodded; he took the point.

'Some of our people *have* been captured,' he went on. 'One of our very best, who Herr Himmler personally selected four years ago to kill Churchill.'

'Who was that?'

'He had a Dutch name. Jan Willem Ter Braak.'

'I heard nothing about him,' said Rigby.

'I wouldn't expect you to. He was found shot in an air raid shelter in Christ's Pieces in Cambridge. On April the first, 1941, the day the English call All Fool's Day.'

'I have never heard of Christ's Pieces,' said Rigby slowly. Was there such a place – or was this an attempt to trap him?

'I am sure Ter Braak wished he hadn't heard of it either,' replied Mannheim easily. 'It is an open space. No-one knows exactly how he died. Maybe the British found out who he was. Some of our people think he ran out of money and panicked and took his own life. Maybe his nerve deserted him. You need steady nerves in our business, eh?'

Rigby said nothing.

'What military unit are you with?'

'I enlisted in the Royal East Kent Regiment, The Buffs, Army Number, 6300414.'

'And your latest unit?'

'No. 10 Commando.'

'Where did you join them?'

'In Harlech. North Wales.'

'Where are they now?'

'Split up, all over the place,' said Rigby. 'My particular Troop is in Sussex.'

'And you were interned, I believe?'

'Yes, sir. First in London and then in Canada. Not an experience calculated to endear the British to me. I was allowed out on the understanding I joined the Pioneer Corps in England.'

'Weber has given us quite a bit of information about you,' said the civilian. 'So have other people whose advice we value. By the way, how was Weber when you last saw him?'

'In pretty good shape, sir.'

'What was he wearing?'

'A brown suit.'

'Where did you meet him?'

'The King of Bohemia, Hampstead.'

'He met you there several times, I believe?'

'Yes. Hampstead is on a hill. That helped his wireless signals.'

Mannheim nodded and turned to the colonel.

'Anything you want to ask him?'

'Yes.'

Colonel Ritter glanced at a sheet of paper on the desk in front of him.

'Who is the commanding officer of No. 10 Commando?'

'Colonel Dudley Lister.'

'What does he look like?'

'A big man. He won the Military Cross in the First War. And he boxed for the Army. Heavyweight.'

'I would like to ask you one specific question, more about the matter that brings you here, than about yourself. Where is the 58th British Infantry Division?'

'It is part of the First United States Army Group, sir. FUSAG. Under the direct command of the 2nd British Corps.'

'Do you know where they are stationed?'

'Not the exact location, sir. But I believe near Grantham, in Lincolnshire.'

'Our reconnaissance photographs clearly show several army camps there,' the colonel admitted. 'They do not appear to be very well camouflaged. Indeed, some are barely concealed at all. The question has been raised as to whether they are just fake camps. We do the same sort of thing over here, of course, to draw the bombers. Dummy gun emplacements. Fires of boiling oil, and so on. What do you say to that theory, Nimrod?'

'I categorically deny it, sir. The camps are real. I can vouch for that. You must remember England is a small island, with only a limited number of open places around the East Coast where troops *can* congregate in large numbers. In that particular area, there are few woods. Camouflage is therefore much more difficult. And so many troops are in the area it is impossible to conceal them all.

'We – they – have what is called a restricted zone, all round the coast for 10 miles inland. Virtually no-one is allowed any nearer the coast unless they live there. So the only way the camps can be spotted is from the air. And they have to chance that.'

'Are any exceptions allowed, for anyone to approach the coast if they do not live there?'

'Only four. If you have business, or a wedding, or a funeral to attend, sir. And if you wish to visit someone over seventy who is dangerously ill – the inference being that if you don't see them soon, you won't see them at all.'

Again there was silence in the room. The convoy had gone and the road lay empty in the rain. A small tug pulled a string of barges down the Seine, moving slowly against the current. The colonel gave a brief nod to Herr Mannheim. Then he turned to Rigby.

'You have answered our questions frankly,' he said. 'You must bear with Herr Mannheim and with me if some seemed tedious. But we must be certain you are who you say you are.'

'I appreciate that, sir.'

'Now, have you brought any papers with you?'

'Copies, sir, sewn into my right cuff.'

Rigby removed his jacket. The colonel turned the sleeve inside out, picked up a pair of desk scissors and began to snip away at the lining. A small oilskin pouch fell out on to the desk. He opened it, shook out half a dozen negatives, the size of postage stamps. He pressed a bell for an orderly who brought in a projector and drew the curtains over the high windows. Mannheim fed the first negative into the machine. On the white wall, was a black and white enlargement of a movement order for the 4th Canadian Armoured Division. The order was stamped 'Top Secret'; it was number 41 of 59 duplicated copies.

The second slide dealt with instructions from the Royal Electrical and Mechanical Engineers for waterproofing tanks; what modifications needed to be made to exhaust systems; vulnerable joints to seal; how the ignition could best be protected from spray or total immersion in salt water. The page was also stamped '4th Canadian Armoured Division, Aldershot.'

The third slide was a photograph of a memorandum from the Chief Medical Officer to the U.S. 3rd Army in East Anglia about the issue of anti-sea-sickness tablets, and possible side effects on soldiers allergic to certain drugs. One paragraph noted the full effects were only required for a maximum of six hours, so care must be taken not to issue tablets too long before embarkation.

The operator clicked his switch; photograph succeeded photograph on the far wall; tanks in Suffolk; petrol bowsers in East Kent; landing craft in Essex creeks and river mouths; maps of the Pas de Calais printed on silk squares like scarves; lists of steep gradients, narrow bridges, the tonnage they could bear, sharp corners that could prove difficult for an armoured column to navigate; known German defensive positions around Calais and the units involved. At last, all had been examined. The orderly switched off the projector and opened the curtains.

'Where did you find these?' Colonel Ritter asked Rigby.

'Some in the briefcase of a General Staff Officer, Grade II, a major, visiting Baker Street. He had locked it in a cupboard for safe keeping. I had another key. Others in different desks in various offices I visited.'

'How did you photograph them?'

'With a camera Weber provided. He developed and reduced the negatives.'

'He was always good at that, even in the old days. Cameras and music were his hobbies.'

The colonel stood up, obviously impressed.

'That will be all for now, Nimrod,' he said.

'I have a great deal more information to give you, sir,' Rigby pointed out. Now that he had begun, he wanted to continue, to pour out all the figures and dispositions of regiments that he had learned with the hypnotist in the upper room of the house outside Portsmouth. He found a relief in telling what he knew, as someone making confession to a priest feels uplifted by releasing the burden of his secrets.

'I appreciate that, but I wish to show these photographs to others without delay for they are of great interest. Meanwhile, I have arranged quarters for you here. An orderly will look after you.'

He nodded dismissal to Rigby and his two companions. Captain Arngross clicked his heels and saluted. Rigby walked out of the room with them, up a long flight of stairs to the bedroom he was to occupy at the rear of the castle. Its one window was only a few feet from the side of the cliff. The stone walls of the castle were a metre thick, and felt cold to the touch; even the air was damp. No sun could reach this room and Rigby was immediately aware that no-one could escape from it. The drop outside was sheer and probably forty feet.

A truckle bed was made up in one corner and near it, a narrow doorway opened on to an old-fashioned bathroom with brass taps.

'Don't be alarmed by the questions they ask you,' said Arngross.

128

'They have to be sure.'

'Of course,' said Rigby. 'I would be the same in their position. Who exactly is Herr Mannheim?'

'One of Admiral Canaris's lot. Quite a high official. But not someone I can take to particularly.'

'Nor me. He looks a hard man.'

'His trade makes for hardness,' said Arngross. 'You should know that. Now get some rest and later we can dine together. I've been posted here to show you the ropes.'

'But aren't you the Corps IO?'

'Only acting. The real IO's back from leave. Which is why I'm here. Makes a job for me.'

Just for a moment, resentment darkened Arngross's face. Then he closed the bedroom door behind him. Rigby waited until he heard his footsteps going down the stairs and then cautiously turned the ornate door knob. This turned easily, but the door stayed locked. As he had half-expected, he was a prisoner.

He stood for a moment, looking out at the dull limestone of the cliff. The window sill was stained with bird droppings, and the window was far too narrow to allow him to squeeze through – even if he could survive the drop. But why was he even considering escape? He had not finished what he had come here to do. Worse, he had barely begun. Could he convince whoever he had yet to convince he was who he claimed to be – and the information he brought was true?

On his own, without the stimulus of an audience, without the spur of danger, Rigby's confidence sagged. He felt physically cold. He considered taking a benzedrine pill. The thought was tempting, but he fought it. To give himself something to do, to occupy his mind and divert his thoughts from his predicament, he began to search the bedroom systematically. He found what he was looking for high up behind one of the curtains; a microphone on a rubber base.

That is the one I am meant to find, he thought. There will be another somewhere else, one they think I'll never look for. That is what the instructor had told him in the house at Beaulieu. He decided to put theory to the test and crawled over the floor on his hands and knees, seeking a loose board, feeling the skirting for a piece of canvas painted to resemble wood that could conceal a microphone.

He finally found it, neatly inserted into a base of a lamp on a chair by his bedside. The clue had been a slightly thicker flex than a genuine reading lamp required. He did not disconnect either microphone; this would instantly have aroused suspicion. But he must remember not to talk in his sleep, and to be discreet in his discussions with Arngross. He tried to recall what he had said about Mannheim, but the effort of remembering made him feel even more tired. He had a bath, and came back into the room with a towel round him. The door had been opened and closed in his absence and he had not heard anyone enter, but a clean pair of underpants and socks, with shirt and clean army trousers and tunic lay neatly on his bed. Apparently they had been put out by an orderly. On the dressing table was a tray with a bottle of lager beer, a round metal cover over a plate of bread and liver sausage. Rigby changed into the new clothes, ate and then lay down on the bed.

He thought of Elena, wondering what she was doing, whether she was at that moment thinking of him. He had been foolish to rush off as he had done, simply because he had discovered she had lied to him about her husband. He had also lied to her. He should have heard her side of things, and tried to understand. Instead, he had acted precipitately, like an idiot. What did it matter if Jack *was* alive? Surely they could sort out something between the three of them? They must do, as soon as they both returned.

Rigby closed his eyes. Presently, he slept.


In his room overlooking St. James's Park, London, the middle-aged major broke the red wax seal on the brown envelope and shook its contents out on to his desk.

A dispatch rider had brought the letter from the secret code-breaking centre at Bletchley Park where German radio messages – from unit to unit, army to army, ships to shore, aircraft to ground – were deciphered, then typed out on sheets of flimsy paper and sent within hours of receipt to those most closely concerned with the information they contained.

The major sifted through the pages, searching for any mention of Rigby's movements after his arrival in France, but there was nothing. No hint, no rumour. Nothing.

He lit his pipe, looked out at the Park, wondering whether absence of news was good or bad, whether indeed it signified anything at all. By now, Rigby had been on French soil for nearly eighteen hours. Surely he must have made contact with the Germans? But if he had done so,

130

why had none of the people involved – the unit to whom he should have reported, maybe some higher echelon – not mentioned this over the air? Were they deliberately keeping silent? Were they using the telephone instead – or had Rigby simply gone to ground?

Captain Angus opened the door.

'Seen the latest traffic from SOE?' he asked.

The major shook his head.

'Not yet. I have been looking through these signals from Bletchley. Nothing about Rigby here. Not a dicky bird. Anything with you?'

'Yes. The Germans have him. They killed André, who was head of section. Ricard's captured. So is André's brother, Louis, and two others. And our man.

'The general feeling is that Rigby was a bad 'un. Admitted he knew Nimrod, the fellow the Jerries were after. They've warned us to check his movements and contacts here. They think he's a stool pigeon. Apparently, Louis didn't trust him from the start. Meant to put him through a few tests to prove his loyalty. Lucky the Germans got him first.'

'For whom? Rigby or us?'

Angus shrugged.

'I hope both,' he said.

He crossed the room and stood, hands in his trouser pockets, looking through the window.

'I hope both,' he repeated. 'But I'm not that hopeful. Rigby didn't have enough training for the job. But there wasn't any more time. He had to go as he was, or stay. Must say, I don't like the sound of things.'

'I never did, right from the start,' agreed the major. 'But beggars can't be choosers. And it was worth a shot, sending him. Now, if the poor bastard ever does escape from the Germans, he'll have the French Resistance looking for him, too, to kill him. And he won't even know it.'

'You a betting man?' Angus asked him.

'Used to be. Don't have much time now. Why?'

'If I were a bookie I'd offer a hundred to one on Rigby getting back safely.'

'For?' asked the major in surprise.

'Against,' replied Angus.

# Chapter Twelve

Field Marshal Rommel raised his rifle, took careful aim and then first pressure. Gently, he squeezed the trigger.

The crack of the shot echoed around the small forest clearing, loud as a cannon in the confined space. A flutter of birds scattered in the sky. The hare at which he had aimed leaped in the air as though it would join them, hung for a second and dropped. Rommel reloaded.

He and several staff officers from his headquarters at La Roche Guyon were making what they called 'an armed promenade'. He was an enthusiastic hunter, an interest that had begun some years before the war when he commanded the Goslar Jaegers. On arrival at the regiment's headquarters he was surprised to discover that, despite the name of their regiment – the Goslar Hunters – none of the officers really knew how to hunt game. They were like officers of a cavalry regiment that had long since been mechanised; of the old tradition, only the name remained.

With typical enthusiasm, and the single mindedness that characterised his whole career, Rommel immediately arranged that the officers should all be taught to hunt, and at the same time he decided to learn himself. The first time out he shot the wrong buck. As a punishment to himself, Rommel decided that the next buck he shot must be one with deformed antlers, and the third with antlers like corkscrews. Only then would he allow himself a shot at a six-pointer. He could be as strict with himself as with others.

Now at La Roche Guyon he used what little free time he had to follow this pastime. Sometimes he did not shoot, but simply observed the wild life. Frequently, Admiral Friedrich Ruge, his naval adviser, accompanied him on these outings. Ruge favoured a machine pistol which had been adjusted to fire single shots; Rommel used a hunting rifle. On some days, they might walk for hours and not see or shoot anything. This had been one of those days – until they had spotted the hare.

As they began to walk on, they heard a strange rustling in the bushes and paused. A stag, antlers high, walked slowly into the clearing and stood only a few yards away facing them. Then slowly he moved back into the forest and was gone.

'He's quite safe, sir,' said one of the party regretfully. 'He must know it is the close season for deer.'

'But not for us,' replied Rommel with a wry smile. 'No close season in war, gentlemen.'

The others nodded agreement. Within days, weeks at the most, the dangerous lull they had known for months must end. The Allies would invade. All knew and accepted the fact that the Allies had air superiority and also outnumbered them in tanks and guns and other equipment of war. But they also knew that in order to exercise this supremacy, the Allies had first to achieve a safe landing and hold a bridgehead long enough to allow their men and material ashore.

If the German defenders could hold and break this invasion on the beaches, the American and British armies would be forced to return to their bases in England. The invasion would then take months to remount – and this might not be achieved successfully that summer because of deteriorating weather conditions.

The blow to the Allies' Service and political morale could be all but mortal. One result might be that Americans would decide to concentrate on the Pacific theatre of war in preference to Europe. Among other advantages to the Germans, this could erode the faith of the people in Nazi-occupied countries in Allied ability to keep their promises of deliverance. If the right political atmosphere could be arranged in Germany, perhaps with Hitler's removal, a negotiated peace in the West might even be possible before the dreaded Russian armies swept in from the East. The political consequences of such a setback to the invasion could be virtually incalculable. Everything from the German point of view therefore depended on a quick victory along the coast – but along which part of the coast?

Rommel personally believed the invasion was still several weeks away, and when the Allies did come they would land between the Somme and the Bay of St. Malo, with possibly other subsidiary or feint landings elsewhere. The High Command in Berchtesgaden believed that the main landing would be around Calais and Cap Gris Nez, because this would involve a shorter sea voyage and, once ashore, the enemy troops would still be close to their supply bases in England.

That morning, Rommel had read the weekly report compiled by his Intelligence officers, from all available sources; German spies in Britain, intercepted radio messages, aerial reconnaissance photographs.

Some increase in radio traffic from members of the French Resistance was reported, and the BBC were broadcasting an increasingly large number of apparently meaningless sentences which obviously had some significance, such as 'Uncle Jean has lost his legs again,' or 'Maria does not like cold water,' and 'The beetroots are ripe.' While the Allies were known to be in what the compilers of this report described as 'a high degree of readiness' it was not believed that invasion was imminent.

Rommel privately thought that the most likely time would be in early July when tides and summer weather would be more propitious than in May or June. He had initialled the report, and it was already on its way by dispatch rider to Field Marshal Rundstedt in his headquarters at St. Germain-en-Laye, 13 miles west of Paris. Here, Rundstedt's Intelligence officers would add any other material that might be relevant, and no doubt suitably rephrase or elaborate parts of the report that could redound to their credit. The document would then be flown to the OKW in Berchtesgaden for them to show to the Führer, either as it stood, or else after further editing had removed or emasculated any items that might offend him and bring on one of the moods of gloom or frenzy that had grown increasingly frequent and violent over the previous few months.

As the shooting party moved on through the wood, chatting among themselves, Rommel walked a little to one side, occupied with his thoughts. It was useless to telephone OKW, or even to telephone Hitler to give his views on the most likely locality for the invasion, and how best to combat it. He had done this on several occasions already, without any result. The surest way was to go to Berchtesgaden himself and see Hitler personally about the whole concept of defending the coast and to explain how important he regarded the correct positioning of the Panzer divisions. It was privately said that the last man to speak to Hitler persuaded him; he must be the last man.

Rommel remembered one of the maxims of the 17th century Duke de la Rochefoucauld, whose portrait now hung inside the castle: 'We have all enough strength to bear the misfortunes of others.' But did he possess sufficient strength to bear the mistakes of others, principally Hitler? Rommel knew without any self-aggrandisement that he was the one man in Germany who could defeat the Allied landings. As Churchill had remarked of Admiral Jellicoe at the Battle of Jutland in the First World War, he was the only man who could lose the war in an afternoon.

His mind made up, Rommel began to take an interest in the conversation of his colleagues. One of the great advantages of working in Army Group 'B' was that the officers could speak their minds freely, which was too dangerous to do elsewhere, and when among strangers.

Some weeks earlier, Admiral Ruge had found a tortoise which he brought back to the castle. The staff's pet dog had been afraid of this new arrival and the noise of his barking brought other officers out from their offices to look at these unlikely companions. Now, dog and tortoise had come to terms.

An Intelligence colonel had then remarked, partly in jest, that their relationship was much the same as those between the army and the political wing of the Nazis. He meant, an uneasy compromise, with distrust on both sides. Rommel's headquarters was unusual because it did not have a Nazi political officer attached to it. The staff trusted each other; they said what they thought to a greater degree than in other headquarters, and they personally liked each other. Rommel possessed the rare gift of being able to mould people of different outlooks, backgrounds, political and religious persuasions into a team, which thought as a corporate body, not as a group of individuals.

'Any visitors due to join us for dinner tonight?' he asked an aide.

'No, sir.'

'Good. An early night, then.'

Frequently, Rommel had to entertain some visiting minister from Germany, which meant a formal meal that could last for hours. He ate sparingly himself, and when he visited units under his command he preferred to sample a meal from the troops' field kitchen rather than the more elaborate fare some commanders enjoyed.

When Rommel entertained a visitor from Germany who might help him to gain weapons or supplies that would otherwise be impossible to acquire, his chef would produce a superb meal. But generally Rommel would be in bed by 10 o'clock. He always breakfasted at six each morning.

The shooting party reached the main road, and his colleagues automatically fell into step with the Field Marshal. Sentries presented arms smartly as they came up towards the Hotel Au Vieux Donjon at the crossroads, next to a pantile-covered market where old women sold flowers and homemade produce and bric-à-brac.

They walked up past the war memorial into the castle yard. The windows of Rommel's office on the ground floor overlooked a terrace of rose trees. Its walls were hung with Gobelin tapestries. His desk dated from the Renaissance, and sitting at it 259 years earlier, Louis XIV's war minister, the Marquis de Louvois, who organised France's first standing army, had signed the revocation of the Edict of Nantes. This Edict had given to members of religious minorities the right of worship and the right to hold political office. Its revocation drove hundreds of thousands of loyal French families into exile in England and Germany.

Now Rommel sat down at this desk to read a message from his adjutant. The colonel of Intelligence wished to see him urgently. Rommel picked up his telephone.

'Send him in,' he ordered.

The colonel who had interviewed Rigby came into the room, clicked his heels and stood to attention. He carried a buff coloured folder. Rommel invited him to sit down.

'Something I think you should know, sir,' the colonel began. 'One of our prime sources of information in Britain, who has supplied agents there with material for a long time has just arrived here.'

'Here?' repeated Rommel in surprise. 'Why here?'

'Agents in England reported that he was hoping to arrive in France, ostensibly to visit the French Resistance, and he wished to make contact when he was here. He could obviously bring more news in a personal visit than in any amount of wireless messages. We knew roughly where and when he was expected, so we put out patrols to locate him. An Intelligence officer brought him here this afternoon, sir.'

'But why *here*? We don't have any direct dealings with agents in Britain from our Army Group. That's an Abwehr matter, surely?'

'I agree, sir, but he had been supplying our agents there with details of enemy troop dispositions for the invasion, so he thought it might be

136

useful to cut across formalities and bring him here so that we could interview him.'

'These Abwehr people get very touchy if they think anyone is poaching in their preserves. We must take care not to let them think we have anything like that in mind.'

'For that reason I asked Mannheim of their Paris office to come and check him first. Mannheim gave him a pretty vigorous questioning in my presence. In a fairly friendly way, of course. The man stands up well. I rather took to him.'

'Have you spoken to him yourself about invasion dispositions?'

'Not in any depth, sir. He has brought several copies of orders with him which I have had copied myself. Here they are.'

He placed the folder on the desk. Rommel examined the photographs carefully, poring over some with a magnifying glass. He lingered longest over the pictures of tanks.

'I thought you might like to meet him, sir,' suggested the colonel.

'I would,' said Rommel. 'With you present.'

'And Herr Mannheim, sir?'

Rommel paused imperceptibly.

'Not immediately. He has already interviewed him, so you tell me. I would rather keep this a military thing, at this stage, at least. Since this is a bit unorthodox, treat the matter as prudently as you can. There need be no mention of this in the War Diary, for instance.'

'Very good, sir.'

The War Diary was the day-to-day record of every official happening at headquarters: who arrived and who left, and with what purpose; who telephoned to another unit and which units were in contact with Army Group 'B'. But some matters of political or military delicacy went unrecorded.

'Now, how does this man appear to you – as a man? What's his name, by the way?'

'He's known as Nimrod to our people over there. That's not his real name, of course. I should tell you he is Jewish, sir. Father's name was Rosenberg. His mother is Catholic.'

'Anything much known about his background?'

'Mannheim put a call through to Paris for an urgent check on that, sir. His father owned one and probably two jeweller's shops in Frankfurt, and then moved to Vienna. He left for Switzerland in 1938 just after the Anschluss, and died there, apparently. We're awaiting full details. Mother went to England, then to Canada. Other traces are cold.'

Rommel smoothed the top of his desk thoughtfully with the palms of his hands.

'One thing in his favour, sir,' the colonel continued. 'The agent Nimrod has worked most closely with in England was there under another name before the war, and made contact with him then. Taught him the piano when he was a boy. Government funds actually helped put Nimrod through university.'

'So you think he is genuinely who and what he seems? There is no chance that he has been simply sent over here to help some of us believe what the enemy might want us to believe?'

'A difficult question, sir. Most people like him are devious, of course. They have to be to stay alive. But he is a Commando soldier and looks you in the eye, and, more important, what he says is backed up by our agents in England and aerial reconnaissance.

'If he had just arrived out of the blue, as it were, then I'd have no doubt whatever he was here to deceive us. But his background seems impeccable. And he has risked his life, coming here. Not only with the French, but with us. I think that says a lot for him, sir.'

'It says he has courage, certainly. Let us then hear what he says for himself.'


An orderly shook Rigby awake.

'Colonel Ritter is here, sir.'

The colonel entered his room.

'Get up and dressed,' he told Rigby. 'Field-Marshal Rommel will see you.'

Rigby swung himself out of bed, dashed cold water on his face at the basin, combed his hair, opened the cupboard and took out his suit. It had been pressed while he slept.

'Wear the clothes we have given you,' suggested the colonel. 'They're smarter – and cleaner.'

'I know, sir. But I'd rather stick to my own things.'

'As you wish.'

Rigby smoothed down his lapels. The slight springiness in his left lapel had gone; so they had discovered and removed the trepanning saw. But they had left his survival kit. Probably they had opened that as well and found it only contained Horlicks tablets. As he put on his

138

shoes, which had been brushed, he felt the pliable metal in the left lace. They had not found that saw. Or if they had, they had let it remain. He would have to wait until later to know whether they had discovered the secret of the buttons, and the pills beneath the leather strips on the bottoms of his trouser legs.

'Ready, sir.'

They left the room together and walked along the corridor, down the main marble staircase. A sergeant stood on sentry duty outside the Field Marshal's door. He opened it and announced the colonel. Rigby followed him into the room.

Rommel stood, back against the window, framed in the dying afternoon light, a stocky figure, jaw and stomach thrust out, hands clasped behind him.

'Nimrod, sir,' said the colonel, introducing Rigby.

'That is not your real name, I understand,' said Rommel.

'No, sir,' said Rigby. 'My code name. My real name is Rosenberg.'

'Your father is dead. And your mother is in Canada?'

'Yes, sir. Montreal.'

'And you have been working for us in England, while apparently serving in the Commandos? That must have been a strange division of loyalties?'

'Not really, sir. I have only one loyalty. To my country. To Germany.'

'Quite so. And how did you combine your Commando training with the gathering of information about the projected landing?'

'My duties involved translating newspapers and training documents, sir. This gave me the excuse to visit various headquarters, such as Combined Operations and Special Operations Executive.'

'Your father, I believe, was Jewish? The National Socialist political record for the last few years has not been, shall we say, very friendly towards Jews.'

'My mother is Catholic, sir.'

'And you follow her faith?'

'No, sir. But I think there is much to be said for all religions.'

'Have you studied all religions?'

'Only in the sense of general reading.'

Rommel walked around his desk, hands still behind his back, looking at Rigby all the time. His blue eyes were sharp, alert; neither friendly nor hostile, simply aware.

139

'So two days ago you were in England in the Commandos?'

'Yes, sir.'

'Less than a week ago, I interviewed two British Commando officers here. In this room.'

Rigby stared at the Field Marshal in astonishment. Had there been some duplication of his task? Had two others arrived on the same mission?

'You are surprised?' asked Rommel, watching him closely. 'They were captured on the French coast while examining our defences in the Somme estuary. It was fortunate for them that my Chief of Staff, General Speidel, heard about them, because standing orders are that such intruders are turned over at once to the SS. He thought I might care to meet two British Commando officers, and indeed I was most interested to do so.

'They had been blindfolded, of course, so they would not know where the car was taking them, but one of them kept asking me where he was. He explained that he wished to come back here after the war with his children and show them the exact place where we met and talked. I appreciated the compliment, Nimrod, but I did not gratify his curiosity – which might not, after all, have been as altruistic as he would lead me to suppose.

'Incidentally, he also had some theories as to Allied intentions. He was certain they planned to land in the Somme area.'

'Who was he, sir?' asked Rigby, anxious to keep the conversation on this level until he could regain full control of his own emotions.

'His name was Lane. Lieutenant George Lane. Educated at Oxford. A charming man, and a brave one. Why, is there anything wrong?'

'No, sir. Nothing.'

'Do you know this officer?'

'Lane? It is a fairly common name,' said Rigby, desperately playing for time, a chance to compose himself.

'What did he look like, sir?'

'Well built, fit. In his twenties. A very good presence.'

'Then I don't think he is the officer I knew, sir. There was a Captain Lane in a pay office I knew by sight. But he was thin. With glasses. Where's Mr. Lane now?'

Rommel looked at Colonel Ritter enquiringly.

'He was taken for preliminary interrogation to the Hotel Continental in Paris and then for further questioning to Fresnes. Even-

140

tually, he will be sent, in the normal course of events, to a P.O.W. camp.'

'What do you mean by "the normal course of events?" ' Rigby asked the question without really intending to do so. He bit the inside of his lower lip to prevent any further spontaneous questions.

'Well, our people will check on him, make sure he is who he says he is – and so on.'

'Of course.'

Rigby could feel sweat ooze down his back. What the devil had George Lane been doing here? Or was this all a German trap to catch him out?

He glanced at the colonel, but his eyes were on the Field Marshal. The three men stood in silence for a moment. Then Rommel turned to Rigby.

'I understand you have brought some details of the disposition of Allied forces in England?'

'Yes, sir.'

'Come with me.'

He crossed to a smaller room where a large map of the south and east coasts of England and the opposite coast of France covered one wall, lit by a spotlight. Two other officers were already waiting in the room. Rigby saw that they had placed enlarged copies of the photographs he had brought with translations of the text, on a side table. Little red and blue-headed pins were stuck in the map from Lowestoft to the Thames Estuary, and on to Dover and Folkestone, with corresponding green and yellow pins in France.

Rommel handed the folder to Rigby who crossed to the map, consulted the papers for a moment, and then began to speak. Working south from Yarmouth, he pointed out locations of tank and truck parks; camps for infantry and artillery regiments; the positions of auxiliary troops, field hospitals, REME workshops and light aid detachments. He gave the locations of groups of tank and infantry landing craft, disguised airfields and fuel storage depots.

He spoke in a calm unhurried voice, explaining the various brigades and divisions involved, naming their commanders, and the heraldic sign for each unit. Sometimes one of the officers consulted a file, perhaps checking on the name of a formation or its leader. In a corner of the room a uniformed stenographer took a shorthand note of all that he said. Rigby knew he was speaking more confidently than he had

141

done to Colonel Ritter in his office. That had been a tricky dress rehearsal; now he felt relaxed before the audience for whom the play was intended.

At last he finished, placed the pointer on the table, and bowed towards Rommel. The field-marshal nodded.

'We will not ask questions now. When we have studied the papers you have brought, and a transcript of our discussion here, we can then formulate any points which we would like elaborated or elucidated. Right, gentlemen?'

The other officers nodded appreciatively, clicked their heels, bowed, and left the room.

'We had another unexpected visitor here the other day,' Rommel told Rigby conversationally. 'General Hans Cramer, formerly commander of the Afrika Korps. He was captured in Tunisia last May and taken to England as a prisoner of war. He had been repatriated to Germany on health grounds, largely through the good offices of the Swedish Red Cross.

'It is noteworthy that he gave us much the same information as you have given us now. The Allies treated him with most unusual courtesy. On his way through London, he actually had dinner in London with the American General Patton, who was introduced to him as the Commander-in-Chief of the First US Army Group. He then met various divisional commanders. There was no question of him being treated as their prisoner; he was treated as a guest, an equal. It was an occasion almost unique in my experience between officers of this rank who are at war. I suppose they did not realise that Cramer understood English, because at dinner some were openly discussing the projected landing in and around Calais.

'Cramer had been held in a POW camp and when the time came for him to embark from Harwich he was taken to the port by car, so the English could not very well hide the extent of their build-up of troops in East Anglia. It was just as you have described. In Berlin, General Cramer had a medical check-up, then he went to Berchtesgaden to give his report personally to the Führer.'

'Everything that General Cramer – and Nimrod here – said is fully borne out by our Intelligence reports,' said the colonel.

'I am sure it is,' replied Rommel.

Rigby eyed him cautiously. Was the Field Marshal being sarcastic?

Rommel nodded a dismissal. Rigby sprang to attention, bowed and left the room. Arngross was waiting outside to conduct him back to his bedroom.

Rommel waited until the sound of their footsteps faded and then walked to his own office with Colonel Ritter. He sat down behind his desk, leaned back in the chair and glanced quizzically at the colonel.

'What do you make of all that?' he asked him.

'He corroborates much that we already know from our own agents in England, sir, and what our aerial photographs show.'

'So you have already told me. But then that is what I would expect him to do.'

'You have doubts about his integrity, sir?'

'No. Not about his honesty, or his courage. I think he believes what he has obviously taken great risks to discover, and came here in person to tell us. It is his conclusion that gives me cause to doubt. I wonder whether you recall the words of an English advocate who once spoke on behalf of the notoriously unfaithful Queen Caroline, the daughter of our Duke of Brunswick and wife of the English King George IV?

'She had been conducting a number of flagrant affairs throughout Europe, which he dismissed successfully as "odd instances of strange coincidence". I submit that here we have three instances of coincidence so strange that they simply cannot be accepted as chance.

'First, General Cramer is sent back from England on the grounds of ill-health. But when he is examined by Army specialists in Berlin, his health is declared sound, apart from some asthma. On his way home, the British and Americans introduce him to his rival commanders. He sees – and the important point is that he is *allowed* to see – concentrations of troops whose destination can only be across the Channel at its narrowest point – in other words, Calais.

'Next, the British officer Lieutenant George Lane is captured on the coast, and brought here. He leads me to believe that the Allied invasion is also planned for this area.

'Third, this envoy Nimrod arrives fortuitously with documentary evidence that the main landing will take place in the Pas de Calais.

'Three visitors, two German and one English, all bearing the same message. Coincidence? More likely all part of a plan to deceive us as to Allied intentions – even though these men may not know it.'

'So should we have Nimrod interrogated thoroughly, sir?'

'Possibly. But not just yet. Field Marshal Runstedt may wish to arrange a more thorough examination of what he tells us, or the

Abwehr, or even the OKW. As I say, I am sure he is genuine and believes the information he has brought us. But that does not mean that we should follow him blindly in his belief. When I was in Italy, I frequently heard people quote an Italian proverb that I think I could quote here myself. *Chi pia sa, memo crede. Who knows much believes less.* Let us work on that basis for the time being, keeping our minds and our options open. And our thoughts to ourselves.'

# Chapter Thirteen

Because of Allied bombing, the Abwehr had been forced to move their headquarters from 72-76, Tirpitz-Ufer in Berlin to a concrete bunker in the centre of a pine wood at Zossen, outside the capital. They shared this area, known as Camp Zeppelin, with the Army General Staff. The camouflaged bunker stood in a small clearing surrounded by pine trees. Its concrete walls were several feet thick and sweated continuously. The offices inside always felt damp; breath hung in the air like fog.

Mannheim was sitting now at a desk in the main office with the papers Rigby had brought from England spread out on the table in front of him. A powerful reading light illuminated them and accentuated the sparse furnishings and general bleakness of the room. Beyond the glare of this electric bulb sat another officer, older and fatter than Mannheim, with a pale soft face and a sandy coloured moustache. He wore the uniform of an SS colonel and tapped the papers from time to time with his steel-rimmed spectacles.

Mannheim had come here from La Roche Guyon as quickly as he could, not only because it was vitally important to have a headquarters' assessment of Rigby and his information, but also because he realised that his own career, perhaps even his own survival, could depend on drawing the correct conclusions.

Petrol was strictly rationed, but a staff officer had given him a lift in his car to Paris, and then he had flown in a service aircraft taking a general to Berlin. Here, he had begged another lift out to this bunker in security zone Maybach II.

As they drove around the outskirts of the capital, and Mannheim saw the increasing devastation caused by Allied bombing, he recalled visits he had paid to the previous head of the Abwehr, Admiral

145

Wilhelm Canaris, in his familiar third floor office in the Tirpitz-Ufer.

He remembered with warmth, almost affection, the small white-haired admiral in his unpretentious room, with its camp bed, shabby leather armchairs, books piled on the floor, and, in one corner, the folded Army blankets where his two pet dachshunds, Seppel and Sabine, slept throughout each working day.

Now, not only had the Abwehr changed its location and its style; not only had the organisation lost independence in a drastic political reshuffle, but, worst of all, the admiral who had built it up and controlled it for the previous nine years had also gone.

Throughout the war, Himmler, the SS Reichsführer, had sought to wrest control of the Abwehr to add to his own private Intelligence empire. Canaris had thwarted these attempts, largely because Hitler highly regarded his abilities as a spy master. After all, Canaris had introduced such revolutionary ideas as microdot photographs for agents' messages, ultra-photography, which enabled a picture to be taken of a defence installation, even through thick fog or beneath camouflage netting, and the 'Afus' radios for agents, which could fit into a small suitcase. In addition, he had built up a wide network of Abwehr informants in the USA and Britain, and in France, Rumania and Czechoslovakia. But Canaris was never a rabid Nazi, and owed his allegiance to his country rather than to the Party.

Over the past two years his star had steadily declined. As head of the Abwehr, he took responsibility for several grave failures from which his political opponents extracted full advantage. The Abwehr had landed eight specially trained spies on the east coast of the United States – and lost them all. Canaris had attempted to create uprisings in South Africa, in Western India against British rule, even in the Caucasus against the Communists. All had failed dismally. The final crucial fiasco, resulting in his dismissal and the end of the Abwehr as an independent Intelligence organisation, had taken place five months earlier in January.

Canaris visited Field Marshal Kesselring at his headquarters in Italy, and personally assured him that no further Allied landing would take place in Italy in the near future. Yet, he had barely left Kesselring's office when 300 Allied landing craft discharged their troops on to the beaches at Anzio.

Hitler, who only weeks previously had awarded to Admiral Canaris the German Cross in Silver for 'exceptional contributions to the

146

military conduct of the war,' now removed him from command of the Abwehr. The little admiral was being held prisoner in a 13th century castle, Burg Lauenstein, overlooking the Loquitz Valley.

This castle was also the Abwehr's workshop where scientists produced invisible ink, microdot equipment and the false passports and passes that agents required. It was very heavily guarded, and the only news Canaris received from the outer world was grave: he was to be formally removed from the Navy's active list on June 30.

Now Himmler had gathered the Abwehr into his fiefdom, along with other previously autonomous Intelligence agencies. The man responsible for its day-to-day control was his deputy, SS General Ernst Kaltenbrunner, one of the few men whom Himmler feared.

Kaltenbrunner, as Mannheim knew, was everything that Canaris was not: rough, tough and uncultured, a heavy drinker, with a vicious temper. Whereas Canaris had assisted Jews to escape certain death in concentration camps by claiming that he could use them as potential overseas agents, Kaltenbrunner consistently refused to release any prisoner, however prominent, or to relax the strict Nazi rule in occupied countries. He had been responsible for thousands of deaths.

Canaris was often affectionately known as 'the little admiral,' or sometimes 'the wily Levantine,' because of his shrewdness and the fact that his ancestors originally came from Northern Italy. Kaltenbrunner was simply called 'the old gorilla'. He currently enjoyed exceptional favour with the Führer, however, and as such his word could mean instant promotion or equally swift disgrace.

Mannheim, sitting in the damp, airless room, removed from reality by layers of concrete, by the pine forest, and its electrified fences and guard patrols, accepted with resignation that he had served the wrong master. It was imperative that he prove his indispensibility to this new regime. One mistake about Nimrod, and he could also be removed.

He sensed that the colonel across the table was in a similar predicament. He had been newly promoted and could not afford to make any mistake at this stage of his career or at this stage of the war. Tempers were taut and rivalries that had hitherto been discreetly concealed for years were now out in the open. No-one wished to express any opinion too strongly in case it disagreed with the view of a superior. This was not simply a matter of tact or prudence, but of sheer survival.

'What is *your* opinion of Nimrod?' the colonel now asked Mannheim, trying to keep all hint of doubt from his voice.

Mannheim stroked his chin before replying. He had decided that it would be easier (and safer) to be the devil's advocate, and let someone else defend Nimrod. His aim now was surely to defend himself.

'You will see from the transcript, sir,' he replied, 'that he has satisfactorily answered every question we put to him. However, I feel I should say that one thing gives me some cause to doubt.'

He paused for the obvious question.

'What is that?'

'Simply that everything in his account ties up just too perfectly. There are no loose ends, no questions without answers.'

'But surely that is only what we would expect? We have more than 100 skilled agents still in Britain. Of course, you will not be familiar with all their reports, but I can assure you that they back up what this man says. They cannot *all* be wrong, surely?'

Mannheim glanced around the room, which still contained the books of Admiral Canaris. Suddenly, he saw a copy of Somerset Maugham's *Ashenden* on a shelf and took it down.

'Listen to this, sir,' he said, and began to read:

' "Fact is a poor story-teller. It starts at haphazard, generally long before the beginning; then rambles on inconsequently and tails off, leaving loose ends hanging about without a conclusion." '

'I know all that,' the colonel replied irritably. 'I have, of course, instructed Control in Hamburg to find everything they can about Nimrod. So far, all our people over there speak most highly of him. Weber, who has known him for years, greatly misses him as a source of highly secret information. But he admitted that when this opportunity to fly to France came up unexpectedly, Nimrod had to take it. What does Field Marshal Rommel think about all this?'

'He is unconvinced, sir. He does not doubt the bravery of the man, but feels that his story should be treated with caution.'

'Very wise. Nimrod is, of course, a Jew.'

'His mother is Catholic, sir.'

'So I understand.'

'If the British wanted to send someone here with false information they might be forced to send a German Jew – simply because they would have no other German available.'

'I take your point, Mannheim. But this information on the desk before us – First US Army Group, dispositions of fuel and ammunition dumps, even the power of landing craft engines which enable our experts to calculate that they are unlikely to risk a long and rough Channel crossing – is far from false. It corroborates what others have already told us. You cannot deny that, can you?'

'No, sir. Perhaps you would care to interview Nimrod yourself?'

'I would indeed.'

The SS colonel consulted his diary.

'I have to be with General Kaltenbrunner on *Heinrich* tomorrow, but any time thereafter would suit me.'

*Heinrich* was the name of the special train which Kaltenbrunner, Himmler, and others of high rank in the integrated Intelligence organisation, used as a mobile headquarters.

'I will contact Army Group "B" immediately, sir.'

'Do that. I see I have to go to Paris later in the week. That is always a pleasant trip. I could see him there. Also, it is not so far to bring him. I feel from your attitude that you rather doubt what this man says?'

'It is in my profession to be a doubter, sir.'

'And mine. Don't forget tha⁺,' replied the SS colonel sharply. 'You must remember that we also have the interrogation report on the SOE agent Ricard, who landed with him. He insists that Nimrod is a genuine radio expert.'

'Which is what we would expect, sir.'

'What makes you so dubious, then?'

'When I was working under Admiral Canaris before the Allied landing in Sicily, there was that business of the body of a British major washed up in Spain. A brief-case of papers that hinted at a landing in Sardinia and Greece was chained to his wrist. The Admiral doubted their authenticity, for their arrival at that precise moment seemed altogether too fortuitous. The Führer overruled him.'

'Are you hinting that the Führer acted wrongly?'

'No, sir,' replied Mannheim vehemently. 'I would never do that. I think that the Führer acted as he did because the Admiral did not make out his case strongly enough to him. No doubt he was at fault. But here I feel we have a similar situation. Then, the Allies used a dead man. Now, they send a living messenger.'

The colonel smiled at him across the desk, and placed the tips of his fingers together. The light reflected from the lenses of his spectacles.

'That must be a bonus, Mannheim. Surely you will admit that? It gives us the opportunity of extracting the full truth of this matter from Nimrod when I see him in Paris.'

# Chapter Fourteen

The nun led her crocodile of little girls through the huge iron gates into the vast park that stretched in a green summery haze of lawns and trees.

On the right, as the girls walked, trying to keep in step, stood the palace that dominated the Paris suburb of St. Germain-en-Laye. Louis XIV had given this palace as a magnificent *pied à terre* to King James II during his exile in France; Napoleon III converted it into a museum. Now the German Army used the building as a barracks.

The palace extended, grey and impressive, for possibly two hundred yards. Then, across a garden, stood a smaller building of cream-washed stone with neat green shutters. Ivy climbed its walls, and under the morning sun, the slate roof shone like polished pewter. A fan-shaped glass canopy sheltered the front door, and above a royal crest on the end wall was a relief in black and gold of a baby's cot with the legend: *Ici Naquit Louis XIV*. This house was known as the Pavillon of Henry IV, and beyond it the park dropped away precipitately. A popular treat for the schoolgirls on their morning walks was to stand against the railings here and enjoy the incredible panorama, hundreds of feet beneath them. Paris lay at their feet; spread out with its bridges spanning the Seine, its famous and familiar buildings, a living life-size map of the city of light.

Sometimes, an elderly man with a set, lined face and wearing a beautifully pressed grey uniform, would come through the iron gate into the park from the house where Louis XIV had been born. He invariably carried a bag of sweets which he would distribute among the girls. Frequently, he was accompanied by one or two younger officers who would wait impatiently while he talked to them, or to the nun who

150

led them. The younger girls did not know his name, but the seniors and the nuns knew that this was the German Supreme Commander in Western Europe, Field Marshal Gerd von Rundstedt.

When Rundstedt left the Pavillon by car, he used another entrance that opened on to the Rue Thiers. This was a cul-de-sac with large houses on either side; grey walls, grey slates on the roofs, grey shutters. These houses were large by most standards, and only appeared small when related to the size of the palace. Iron railings and a hedge concealed thick green metal plates that protected the Pavillon's courtyard from curious eyes or attack. A guard room was partly concealed by ivy; horizontal slits cut in the metal plates and the wall itself allowed machine guns to cover the whole street.

At sixty-eight, Rundstedt was as set in his ways as any man of that age. Habit and tradition ran strong in him. He rose late every morning, usually between ten and ten-thirty, and then took a walk down the immensely long and wide path by the edge of the park. To the right, as he walked, lay Paris. To his left stood a huge square of horse chestnuts. A statue marked the end of his promenade. When Rundstedt reached this it was time to turn back.

Sometimes, on the way, he talked to one of the old gardeners working in a flower bed. He was a keen gardener himself, and had been annoyed when, during a brief leave, Hitler had taken advantage of his absence to order that an underground air raid shelter should be constructed beneath the Pavillon's lawn. In doing this, the foreign workers employed had unfortunately caused a privet hedge to die.

Rundstedt was frequently accompanied on his walks by his son, a lieutenant in his forties. Before the war he had made a name as an historian and archivist. He was strictly a wartime soldier, and having worked his way up through the ranks, was now on his father's staff.

Rundstedt was an austere man, but possessed a sense of humour. When the Germans first occupied Paris four years earlier, two large maps of the city were pinned on a wall in his orderly officer's room. One contained blue dots and the other red; blue marked the location of restaurants worth a visit, while red dots indicated entertainment of a more intimate nature. Entering the room one morning and seeing young officers keenly studying these locations, he remarked drily: 'Why, your red map isn't *nearly* full.'

As a child, Rundstedt had been brought up by an English nursemaid. He spoke English well, and enjoyed the English custom of taking tea on sunny days at half past four in the garden as much as he enjoyed his morning walks. On this particular day, however, as the little girls looked expectantly at him when he came through the gate into the park, he hardly saw them. His mind was on more important matters. He had just studied the latest Intelligence report, headed 'Confidential: Estimate of Allied Intentions,' which by evening would be on Hitler's desk in Berchtesgaden.

There was still no firm news of the expected Allied invasion, but plenty of theories as to its time and place. In the opinion of the compilers of this report, the most probable area now seemed the sector from the Scheldt to Normandy, which involved a distance of approximately 450 kilometres. It was 'not impossible' that Brittany might also be attacked. Concentrated air strikes on coastal defences between Dunkirk and Dieppe could mean that the Allies might land there, too. The whole report was ridiculously vague, virtually no more than a list of various possibilities along nearly 3,000 miles of coast and frontier.

The general concensus of opinion, however, was that invasion was still not imminent. Even so, Rundstedt knew that it could not be long delayed; he planned to leave on an inspection of Normandy defences on Monday, June 5. The Commander-in-Chief 7th Army, stationed in Normandy and Brittany, was carrying out an exercise at Rennes. Some units would be 'enemy' and others the defenders.

Hitler had earlier suggested that a landing might take place in Normandy. Although Allied bombing was heaviest around Calais, the two peninsulas of Normandy and Brittany were being gradually cut off from the rest of Western Command by the systematic bombing of bridges and railways. Sabotage on railways to the coast was increasing and road convoys were coming under stronger aerial attack. Rundstedt personally feared there might be Allied airborne landings around Paris, and indications from German agents in Britain, plus the fact that General Montgomery had been seen in Algiers and Gibraltar, caused the OKW to move more forces south against attack from the Mediterranean.

Rundstedt ruled out a major attack through Spain because of difficulties in crossing the Pyrenees. Even so, he had to be prepared for too many eventualities. It was impossible to be strong everywhere, for his armies were being drained of men to reinforce the Eastern Front. He recalled the words of Frederick the Great: 'Little minds want to defend everything; sensible men concentrate on the essential.' But Hitler did

152

not know which were the essential areas; perhaps no-one did.

Then there was this curiously fortuitous arrival of the German from England, bringing papers that gave added credence to the view that the Pas de Calais was the most logical area to expect attack. But, like Rommel, Rundstedt had his doubts. An Intelligence officer suggested that he should personally interview this man, but he had declined. However, Rundstedt had discussed the matter with his son, and they continued this conversation as they walked.

'Do you think he is genuine?' his son asked him bluntly.

Rundstedt shrugged.

'Very probably, he is. But on the basis of what I have heard so far, I doubt the accuracy of all his information. I know we receive constant Intelligence reports about how strong Allied forces are in south east England. General Cramer saw these concentrations himself, so there is no doubt that they exist. But what is happening elsewhere along the English coast, from Dover to Land's End? No-one can tell me.

'Our reconnaissance planes seem able to photograph the Thames Estuary easily enough, but they cannot approach the Isle of Wight, Portsmouth, Southampton or Plymouth without being shot down. They are obviously being kept out of those areas for a reason. My guess is that this is because that is where the Allies have their strongest troop concentrations. And if my theory is correct, then they will land much farther to the west.'

'So you think our planes are simply being allowed to photograph what the enemy wish us to see?'

'In the main, yes,' replied Rundstedt grimly. 'We must therefore keep the Panzers ready to move wherever they are needed. It is imperative we preserve the initiative of movement to deal with the enemy wherever they land.'

That morning, in the underground bunker beneath his lawn, Rundstedt had studied a large scale map of Northern France with his staff.

'Count the bridges over the Seine, gentlemen,' he had advised them soberly. 'Twelve carry railway lines, and fourteen carry roads. If we have our Panzers, or worse, the whole 15th Army, concentrated in the east – as at present – and the Allies bomb those bridges, how do you propose we can move them west – should we need to do so urgently?'

'We could build pontoons within hours, sir,' an engineer officer suggested hopefully.

'In ideal conditions, we could. But not in the conditions under which we would find ourselves then. We would be facing heavy and constant aerial bombing. Roads would be choked with refugees. There would be sabotage on every side by the Resistance, and panic by the rest. In these conditions we could not be certain that our pontoons would even reach the river in time. And time is vital.'

Now, walking in step on the crisp gravel, with sunshine bright on the chestnut trees and the sound of children's voices faint in the distance, both men remembered his words.

Rundstedt's son broke the silence.

'And the Führer still refuses to see this?'

Rundstedt nodded.

'Our Bohemian corporal always believes the man who spoke to him last – and loudest. And he hates to alter any view he has once expressed. He thinks that this shows weakness, whereas, of course, it shows just the opposite.

'Rommel wants the Panzers up near the coast. He believes he can best defeat the invasion on the beaches. He might be right – if they land on the beaches. But what if they land inland by air 200 or 300 kilometres from the sea? Anyway, Hitler would not listen to Rommel. The Führer keeps as tight control over the Panzers as a nagging wife keeps her hands on her husband's income.

'General Guderian went to see him on the subject. What was he told? "Go back and discuss the matter with Rommel and Rundstedt."

'So we are exactly whre we started. The Panzers stay under Hitler's direct control. We cannot move them without his approval. And by the time he gives it – *if* he gives it – there may be no way of moving them, and indeed by then no reason to move them. And yet I find it impossible too to converse with him.

'We both speak German, the Bohemian corporal and I. The trouble is we do not speak the same language.'


The fir forest stood on its side as the Storch light aircraft came in to land at the military airstrip outside Berchtesgaden.

This town had originally become prosperous in the days of the old Bavarian kings because one of them had built a hunting lodge there, and then a castle. The nearness of Berchtesgaden to the Austrian border helped local people grow rich through smuggling; a brisk and more legitimate trade in carved crucifixes was also done with tourists during the summer.

When Hitler was a boy in Linz, he bought a lottery ticket, and weaved dreams about building a huge house in the hills should his number come up. In the 1920s, when he had been released from prison, he stayed in the Purtscheller Haus in Berchtesgaden to finish work on *Mein Kampf*. He liked the area; he could see Austria from the hills, and the poet Dietrich Eckart, who first gave him the name 'Führer,' encouraged him to visit Berchtesgaden regularly with other founders of the Nazi Party.

Albert Speer, later to be Hitler's architect and finally his Armaments Minister, and second only to the Führer in terms of power on the home front, built a house for himself there, and this decided Hitler to do the same.

The financial success of *Mein Kampf* gave him his chance. He bought Haus Wachenfeld, which had been built by a businessman during the First World War. Then he bought the hotel next door, called Türkenhof because a veteran of the Turkish wars had once lived in a house on the site. Finally, in 1936, Hitler decided to build the house of his boyhood dreams, a palace worthy of Europe's leading head of state, the Berghof.

A barbed-wire barricade ringed in the whole area. An elite squadron of SS troops, with 'Adolf Hitler' embroidered on their left sleeves, guarded all its doors, operated the telephone exchange, and, under the command of Hitler's chauffeur, a special squad were on constant duty in the car parks in case of an 'emergency'. This was a euphemism for any attempt to kill or overthrow the Führer. This was most likely to come from an Allied parachute landing, but there was also the growing possibility of an internal coup. To conceal the outline of the house from the air, camouflage nets had been flung across parts of its roof and surrounding outbuildings. High in the hills, in specially made clearings, groups of German soldiers were on duty with smoke generators. In the event of an air-raid warning they could blot out the whole area within minutes.

As Martin Bormann told them all: 'A minister's uniform is no justi-fication for him being here.' Every visitor therefore had to produce a special pass before being allowed to approach the house. Some months earlier, a routine search had revealed a hand grenade in a soldier's pack during manoeuvres at which Hitler was present. The man had admitted he had intended to assassinate the Führer. Bormann was determined that such a situation should never arise again, and this general air of suspicion and unease communicated itself to everyone associated with the Berghof. Even Eva Braun, Hitler's mistress for many years, felt uneasy in its strange and unreal atmosphere.

Seven miles away, on the other side of the hills, lay the village of Obersalzberg, literally High Salt Mountain. Here, relays of prisoners from Dachau dug out the salt for commercial purposes. Between these two extremities of the Reich – the Führer's guarded palace and the equally heavily guarded slaves in the salt mines – stood the Reichskanzlerei, the headquarters of the German High Command. Here, Colonel-General Alfred Jodl, Chief of Operations, controlled Germany's armed forces, always subject, of course, to Hitler's overriding authority and wishes.

Jodl, shrewd and ambitious, owed his promotion largely to his considerable skill in anticipating Hitler's wishes. He could always think one move ahead of his master and would never disagree with his views, however wrong or even absurd these might appear. Sometimes he skilfully manipulated people and information so that both would appear to reflect the Führer's superior wisdom. Jodl was the perpetual man in the middle. On one side of his office lay absolute power; on the other, absolute misery in the salt mines.

Hitler always rose late, and guests in the Berghof were therefore advised not to run baths in the morning, because the house was largely built of concrete, and the noise of running water could disturb the Führer's sleep.

Jodl prudently rose early so that he could acquaint himself with the military situation on all fronts and be able to answer any question Hitler might put to him. He usually breakfasted just after six on a soft-boiled egg with a single cup of coffee and a slice of brown toast. Then he would read overnight battlefront reports in his small and sound-proof office. Because of this soundproofing, he did not hear the Storch arrive bringing Rigby from Paris.

Arngross had kept up a lively conversation for most of the journey, alternating in German and English. The noise of the engine, and the constant need to keep his face as expressionless as possible, Rigby had found very tiring. And this trip was only the prelude to who knew how many more interviews with loaded questions from dubious questioners? The prospect depressed him. The effects of hypnosis were beginning to weaken, and his confidence was correspondingly diminished.

As the pilot switched off his engine, Rigby unbuckled his canvas safety belt and leaned back thankfully in his seat for a moment, eyes closed, his head throbbing with weariness. Then he climbed down stiffly on to the tarmac and stood breathing deeply in an attempt to overcome the staleness he felt.

The mountain air was cold and clear, and the sun bright, casting sharp shadows. They walked briskly to a car that waited to take them down to the headquarters building. After a wash and a cup of acorn coffee he felt more cheerful. Then Arngross took him into an office and Rigby's spirits sank; behind a long table sat two colonels. To one side of them was Herr Mannheim.

The older colonel shook hands with Rigby. He had duelling scars on his face, and cold blue eyes.

'You have had a pleasant flight?' he asked.

'Yes, sir.'

'Good. Quarters have been arranged for you here. Now, we have examined the material you brought from England and also transcripts of your conversation with Herr Mannheim here, and our colleagues in Army Group "B". What you have to say appears to agree with what other sources of ours have also been advising us. But just as you have taken a great risk in coming to France personally, we take an even greater risk when we commit a concentration of our forces to any one area. You risked your life. We risk more than our lives. We risk our country, even our whole future. We would like you, therefore, to answer some more questions.'

'I will answer anything I can, sir,' said Rigby. He looked from one face to another. These were worried men. In their eyes he could read doubt and fear. He remembered the words of the major with the thick-lensed spectacles in the house outside Portsmouth: 'The Nazis will want to believe you because you will confirm what the Führer believes . . . The professionals may be more cautious . . .'

'Now,' said the colonel briskly. 'You have already explained how you came to be in possession of these papers. But how, as a German, could you join the British Army, apart from in some non-combatant capacity?'

'I was brought up largely by an English family. I adopted their

157

name. Before the war, I met, as you know, Duncan, who is now Weber. I tried to work in Germany then. You can check all that for yourselves, sir.'

'We have already,' said Herr Mannheim softly. 'But that is not the colonel's question. Please answer his question.'

'I worked for a wireless factory, and was interned, first in London and then in Canada, when war broke out. The British authorities gave some of us the chance to return to England if we volunteered to join the Pioneer Corps. They wanted cheap labour, I suppose. Anyway, I volunteered.'

'Why?'

'Because I thought that I might eventually be able to serve my own country in some way. Certainly, I would never have the opportunity in an internment camp on the other side of the Atlantic. After some time in the Pioneers, I was allowed to transfer to a more active unit. Several of us did so. I joined the Royal East Kent Regiment, The Buffs – as a private soldier.'

'Why that regiment particularly?'

Rigby smiled.

'I had no choice, sir. I was simply drafted into it.'

'Where were you then?'

'In Canterbury, in Kent.'

'Where in Canterbury?'

'Chaucer Barracks.'

'And then you joined the Commandos?'

'Volunteers were called for. I joined No. 10 Commando. It came out that I could speak German, and from time to time requests came in to our unit, and I suppose to others, for people who could speak any foreign language. I was detailed to make myself available to any department, should they want me.'

'And did they?'

'I visited SOE headquarters in Baker Street and translated papers for them, sir. I examined captured documents and training manuals and so on at Combined Operations HQ. Elsewhere, in a propaganda office, I translated leaflets – advice for civilians – to be printed in German and French. Leaflets to be dropped from the air. That sort of thing.'

'Had they no-one else to do that?'

'Many people, sir. But as a soldier with a German background I was

158

asked for my opinion as to the value and phrasing of certain items.'

'Where did you stay in London?'

'At the London District Transit Camp, Marylebone Road. The former Great Central Hotel.'

'A railway hotel near Baker Street,' said Mannheim. 'I myself have stayed there.'

'Have you personally visited any of the assembly points for American and British troops training for the invasion?'

'I have, sir.'

'Which ones?'

'Areas in Suffolk. Near Bury St. Edmunds. And, of course, near Canterbury and Folkestone.'

'On what pretext? We understood you to say that travel is forbidden within 10 miles of the south coast?'

'Not for all soldiers, sir. I had a 72-hour leave pass, and as I had joined up in The Buffs, I said I wanted to go back to see my friends.'

'Where did you stay in Canterbury?'

'Bed and breakfast in a house in York Road.'

'Show me on this map where the troop concentrations were.'

The other colonel pushed a large scale map of the Kent coast across the table towards him.

'Here, I counted 118 tanks, parked out of sight of the road on the edge of a wood 10 miles out of Canterbury.'

'How did you find them if they were out of sight?' asked Mannheim sharply.

'I hired a bicycle in Canterbury. I thought I might be coming over here, so I decided to see all I could. I saw a number of Austin pick-up trucks and Jeeps in Canterbury. I asked one of the drivers where they were stationed and he told me, up the road. I said I had a cousin in the Royal Armoured Corps and wanted to see him. I would still have missed the tanks, if I hadn't looked out for the marks of their tracks across ploughed fields.'

'We have examined aerial photographs of that area,' said the older colonel. 'Why were the tanks in the open?'

'The woods were too thick to drive them in between the trees. The ground was marshy elsewhere, and I heard that farmers had objected to their land being ploughed up.'

'We have the same sort of trouble,' agreed the colonel. 'What make of tanks were they?'

159

'Mostly Shermans, sir. And some General Grants. All were water-proofed, with long exhaust pipe extensions and so on. Jeeps and trucks were all waterproofed so that they could go through water up to their bonnets.'

'How did you get to Suffolk?'

'Train to Bury St. Edmunds. I got through to the coast easily because I was in uniform. I knew one unit up there. A detachment of the 15th Worcesters.'

'What were they doing?'

'They were older men posted to guard the landing craft. I counted 200 landing craft, all self-propelled.'

'What sort of engines did they have?'

'Chrysler Marine six-cylinder engines, sir.'

'Were they in a state of readiness?'

'The motors were run every day.'

'Who gave you the impression that these vessels and tanks were destined for France? They could land anywhere, I take it?'

'Yes, sir. But a long voyage would be unlikely from the River Deben. They would have to go south, cross the mouth of the Thames, then along the south coast of England. They would be slow and vulnerable all the time. If the sea were only slightly rough, everyone aboard would be very sea-sick.'

'Would they not be sea-sick crossing the Channel to Calais?'

'Possibly, sir. But that voyage would be so much shorter.'

Rigby picked up a map-measuring instrument from the desk and rolled the wheel around the south east coast of England until he came to Eastbourne.

'You see, sir, that is at least 400 kilometers. At the best pace those vessels can travel it could still take days, even if there is no tide. Then they would face refuelling and revictualling problems. Calais was the only possible target. Also, the men were being issued with silk squares, street maps with Calais printed on them, and larger scale maps of Calais and the towns and roads and bridges within a twenty mile radius. They wouldn't do that now if they planned to land, say, in Bordeaux, would they?'

The colonel turned to Mannheim.

'Anything you want to ask especially?'

Mannheim had a number of questions about civilian and service morale. How popular was Mr. Churchill? What did people think of the

160

Royal Family? There had been reports of poor distribution of vegetables and milk in towns. Was this so? He asked about the railways, whether they were being used more than convoys of trucks on the roads. Were there any instances of looting? How strong was the black market, and in what commodities? Then, almost as though he had forgotten to raise the subject sooner, he asked about Weber.

'Where exactly does he live?'

'Somewhere north of London. I have never actually been to his house, and he has not told me much about it except it was cold last winter. There was a severe coal shortage.'

'What work does he do?'

'In one of the Ministries, I believe.'

'When did you last meet?'

'A few days before I came over here.'

'How many days?'

'It is difficult to say,' said Rigby slowly, trying to think back. Days and nights seemed like a concertina of time.

'I really can't remember. I know it was within a week.'

'Where did you meet?'

'In a public house. In Hampstead.'

'The King of Bohemia?'

'I think it was. Yes.'

'At La Roche Guyon you said it was.'

'That's right,' agreed Rigby. But why the insistence on it? he wondered wearily. The officers he felt some sympathy with; but not with Mannheim. It was a basic chemical reaction. They distrusted each other, and because of the urgency of the hour, this distrust could very easily become dislike. That might be dangerous for him; he must keep all irritation out of his eyes and his voice.

'A fix has been taken on his transmissions', said Mannheim. 'Sometimes they come from near Dunstable, and sometimes from North London, the Highgate or Hampstead area. The signals always appear strong, so he probably lives on a hill. Did he seem all right? Was he short of money?'

'He didn't mention that to me.'

'When did you start to deal with him?'

'I have already told you,' said Rigby irritably. 'We met before the war.'

'But that is five years ago,' said Mannheim reproachfully.

161

Rigby could feel sweat trickle down his shoulders again. A pulse began to beat heavily in his forehead. The room was very quiet, almost airless. He closed his eyes wearily. It was becoming more difficult to remember what he had been told so many times in the upper room outside Portsmouth. Another two days and the effects of the hypnotism would have vanished. That was when his real danger would begin, when he could convict himself by forgetting what he had said earlier. Then he remembered what he had to say. Relief poured through his body.

'He was the only person I knew who had any contact with Germany. I had a telephone number to ring in North London from those days. I rang, but he had moved. I found him eventually.'

'Were you surprised to know what he was doing?'

'We have both tried to help our country in our different ways.'

'And your way,' said the first colonel heartily, 'is one of the bravest. As with Weber, it calls for calculated courage where no-one can see it and no-one even hears of it. You could so easily play the coward.'

He turned to his colleagues.

'I think we are tiring him. Any further questions, Mannheim?'

'Not at this moment, colonel.'

Both colonels stood up.

'I suggest we adjourn, gentlemen.'

Captain Arngross clicked his heels, bowed smartly. Rigby followed him out into the bright sunshine. Clouds pressed down on the tops of the hills; bells on cow harnesses tinkled from the distance. He stood for a moment, enjoying the cold air, absorbing the peace of the view.

After a meal he was taken to a ground-floor room which contained a bed and a wash basin. He took off his shoes and jacket, lay down on the bed and tried to sleep.

He must have done so because it was early afternoon when Arngross returned in a mood of great excitement.

He was to prepare himself immediately for the most important interview of his life. There was the strong possibility that he would be personally presented to the Führer.

# Chapter Fifteen

For nearly an hour, Colonel-General Alfred Jodl, Hitler's Chief of Operations, had waited patiently outside the Berghof. The morning's conference seemed likely to be tedious and fraught with tension, for the Führer's behaviour had been growing more and more irrational, his temper less predictable, with each day that passed.

Next to Jodl waited Field Marshal Wilhelm Keitel, Chief of High Command of all German Armed Forces. Like Jodl, he had never been heard to disagree with the Führer on any decision. Indeed, his acquiescence was even more obsequious than Jodl's. Other generals referred contemptuously to him as 'Hitler's head clerk' for he expressly forbade any officer to express any criticism of Hitler's plans in the Führer's presence, even if the officer's expert opinion was explicitly requested. Keitel's favourite words were: 'Jawohl, Mein Führer' – 'Certainly, sir.'

Across from them stood General Kurt Zeitzler, the Army Chief of Staff, a man renowned for his loud voice and crude insensitive manner. Hitler had selected him for this post after a quarrel with his predecessor, General Franz Halder, an officer of culture and independent mind, who viewed Hitler's projects and plans with the appraising eye of a professional soldier, not a pander.

Zeitzler and Keitel were not on good terms; each recognised a rival for the Führer's favour. When the Russian army had cut off the German VIth Army outside Stalingrad two years earlier, Zeitzler explained the gravity of the situation to Keitel and sought his support for his own request to Hitler that the Army should make a tactical retreat before it was too late to do so.

Keitel agreed, but knowing how Hitler hated the prospect of retreat

163

anywhere, realised he might turn this to his own personal advantage.

Zeitzler made his request, which, if granted, could have saved the entire VIth army. But Keitel interrupted him with an anguished cry to Hitler: 'Do not leave the Balkans!' Hitler immediately refused to sanction the withdrawal. As a result, the entire Army was captured, but Keitel felt he had scored a point against Zeitzler. That to him was the important thing.

Near these three men of power stood other staff officers holding brief cases and folders of documents. All waited stoically for Hitler's morning conference. Like their superiors, they accepted that it would be a waste of time, a pointless exercise in sycophancy, while the real action was elsewhere. Some stood, hands behind their backs, legs apart, admiring the view and making the most of the warm May sunshine. Others smoked nervously, inhaling with almost exaggerated intensity, for in Hitler's presence no smoking was allowed.

They all appreciated the fresh air because, although the conference room possessed a huge picture window that could be raised and lowered electrically, this was invariably kept closed. Hitler had altered Albert Speer's plans for the house, and the garage was now underneath this part of the building. In certain windy conditions there could be a strong smell of petrol in the room. A ventilation system had been installed to counter this, but Hitler insisted that the ducted air caused him headaches and attacks of giddiness, so it was rarely used.

Because the enormous window with its magnificent view acted as a lens that increased the heat within the room, the heavy curtains were usually drawn, and spotlights lit maps and other documents that might have to be studied. Sometimes it was difficult to know what time of day or night it was in the stuffy darkened room where they could be closeted for three or four hours. This sense of timelessness heightened the feeling of unreality at these daily meetings.

The double doors at the top of the stone steps opened and an adjutant, speaking like a butler, said: '*If* you please, gentlemen.' Starting in order of seniority, the officers began to file up the stairs. The house was furnished in what Speer privately called 'ocean liner style.' Some rooms had beer steins placed on the wooden windowsills as ornaments. Books that no-one had been seen to read packed the shelves, with atlases and numerous Morocco-bound copies of *Mein Kampf*. Giant candles, never lit, stood in wrought-iron holders.

The officers' jack-boots rang hard on steps carved from marble

164

brought from the Dolomites. They filed deferentially into the conference room that overlooked the mountains. Because of its size, this was known as the Great Hall. Tapestries covered the walls and muted the sound of conversation. The officers stood in order of rank around a long table of reddish marble. On this lay three maps, each about five feet wide by eight feet long, pasted together. They showed the northern coast of France in great detail.

There was only one chair in the room, which Hitler would occupy. Next to this was a stool upholstered in leather, which had been brought for Goering's use; he was so fat that he found standing for several hours extremely tedious.

When the officers were all inside the room, Hitler arrived. Most of the photographs which Goebbels had printed by the thousand for distribution to Party members and their families, showed Hitler as he had been before the war; hair dark, moustache closely trimmed, face alert. The man who now entered the room had greatly aged. His hair was grey. His hands trembled slightly, a failing he attempted to minimise by clasping them behind his back or in front of his uniform.

Hitler did not care to admit to worsening eyesight, and Eva Braun had therefore ordered that several sets of steel-rimmed glasses were to be discreetly placed around the house. Reports submitted to Hitler were always retyped by his private team of secretaries using special typewriters fitted with extra large type so that he could refer to them in public without using his spectacles. He had a tic in one eye which caused him to blink rapidly. His face was pallid and waxy, partly from the strange hours he kept; he was seldom in bed before four o'clock in the morning and always rose late, and partly because he rarely took any outdoor exercise. His personal physician, Dr. Theodor Morell, administered daily injections of drugs to counteract the sleeping draughts he took every night.

The Führer's alsatian, Blondi, which accompanied him everywhere, and like him, ate vegetarian food, came in at his heels and flopped down on one of the carpets. The officers all sprang to attention. Hitler bowed. They stood at ease uneasily.

'Well, gentlemen,' he began in his slightly hoarse voice. 'What is the latest news from Italy?'

This was a bad start: Rome was about to fall; the Germans were already in retreat. The Eastern front also offered nothing for their comfort, beyond the fact that the Soviet Armies had not yet started their expected summer offensive. But this was simply danger delayed, not averted.

'And France – what is the situation regarding the proposed invasion about which the enemy talks so much?'

Before the meeting, the officers and their staffs had written resumés of every available prognosis about Allied intentions. This time could have been spent more profitably dealing with other urgent matters, because these reports were simply regurgitations of second-hand theories, but so far as Hitler was concerned, this noon conference was the highlight of strategic thinking. All else must be subordinate to it. But as everyone in the room realised (although none would openly admit) decisions made in deference to Hitler's opinions frequently bore no relation whatever to hard realities beyond the sunlit hills around Berchtesgaden.

Now each officer read his report in turn like a schoolboy reading an essay in front of the class, and then waited, head bowed respectfully for the Führer's comments.

Several weeks earlier, Hitler had believed that a landing would take place in Normandy. One of the Abwehr's agents in Britain had actually provided the date, the time, the site and even the hour. But this had to be balanced by reports from other German agents in Britain concerning Allied landings planned for the Bay of Biscay, the Mediterranean coast, anywhere along the north Atlantic coast from the Scheldt in Holland to the Cherbourg Peninsula, in addition to the Pas de Calais.

Hitler listened to each officer, nodding in approval when he heard something with which he agreed, shaking his head irritably when he did not. When they finished, he began to talk. He reiterated what they told him, throwing in gratuitous recollections from his service in the First World War or items of unrelated information without relevance to the discussion. Did they know that during the 1914-18 war, the British gunners would stop their artillery barrage at four o'clock every afternoon in order to brew tea? Or that eels tasted best when fattened on dead cats? As a vegetarian, he rarely missed an opportunity to remark on the disgust he felt for those who ate fish or meat.

Then Hitler returned to the theme of the Anglo-American landings. The whole operation must not be allowed to last for more than a few hours. The example to follow was the landing in Dieppe two years earlier when the British and Canadians had stayed for barely a morning, suffered heavy casualties and made no progress inland whatever.

A speedy defeat for the Allies would have four major consequences. First, the enemy would never risk another invasion attempt. Next, the fearful blow to American national pride and morale would end President Roosevelt's chances of re-election as President. Third, in Britain there was a growing weariness of the war, which had already lasted for nearly five years. This feeling would reach its peak if the landings failed, and Mr. Churchill's influence would not be able to rally the nation for a second attempt. And, most important of all, Germany would then be able to transfer their divisions from Europe to the east with catastrophic effects on the Russian armies.

All this, of course, the staff officers had already heard many times; minutes passed in slow procession. One o'clock came and went. Two o'clock. Three.

The officers shifted their weight uneasily from one foot to another, wondering when they could be free to begin the real business of their day. Sometimes these conferences lasted until four o'clock, and then lunch would be served, so it might be evening before they could return to their offices. But today Hitler did not seem anxious to delay the conference much beyond three hours.

'We have heard the accounts of Allied intentions from our various Intelligence services, gentlemen,' he said. 'To be frank, I do not believe them. The British and the Americans are not fools when it comes to disseminating false information. Perhaps they have learned from us. I am personally convinced that these reports do not all emanate from our agents – as some of you keep assuring me – but from the Allies.

'I thought for a time, as you know, that Normandy would be the focus of their attentions. But the navy do not consider the terrain there suitable for landing troops on a large scale, and the coast lacks a suitable port. Since 1942 I have believed that Calais would be the prime target. Very likely there will be diversionary landings in Normandy and the Mediterranean, but it is around Calais that we have built our heaviest defences, where we have sited our largest and most powerful guns – and for several reasons.

'It is the nearest point across the Channel from England – and remember, a soldier is a land animal. He does not like the sea. Therefore, it is obvious that the enemy will wish to keep their soldiers at sea

167

for as short a voyage as possible.

'Next, we have, as you know, no less than fifty-five stations around Calais, with ramps, quarters and all ancillary equipment and services to launch our flying bombs against London.

'It is likely that the enemy knows that some new and deadly weapons are being prepared, because they have seen the launching ramps from the air. And these all point to London, fingers of retribution. Mr. Churchill knows it is essential for London's survival, and for any continuance of government in Britain, that the Allies neutralise these sites as quickly as possible.

'And there is a third reason, gentlemen. Should they succeed in landing in Calais, they will be infinitely closer to German soil than if they land to the west and have to fight their way through France to reach our frontier.'

Hitler paused, looking from one face to another, searching for their reaction.

'With your permission, Mein Führer,' one officer began carefully. 'I agree with you that the likelihood is for an attack to be made in the Pas de Calais. But Field Marshal Rundstedt and Field Marshal Rommel are firmly of the opinion that this may not be the main attack.'

'Opinions!' retorted Hitler. 'We have heard too many opinions. I prefer facts.'

'Would not our very heavy defences around Calais maybe influence them to land elsewhere, sir?' another officer asked cautiously. 'The Allies must have a good idea of the strength of our defences from their reconnissance flights.'

'On the other hand,' said Keitel, expertly gauging the delicacy of the situation, 'our aerial photographs show heavy troop concentrations in South East England. This bears out what our agents report to us. Their only possible destination from this particular part of England must be Calais.'

Hitler nodded approval.

'Other facts, Mein Führer, bear out your belief about Calais. First, our patrols have recently found a flashlight and shovels and other equipment hastily abandoned on a beach near there. Our experts believe that this landing party were removing samples of sand to take back to analyse, to discover whether it would bear the weight of tracked vehicles.'

'In addition, sir,' added Jodl, 'we have the testimony of General

Cramer about the Allied build-up in South East England, and the two British Commando officers who came ashore in the Somme estuary in a rubber dinghy from a British naval vessel, were also obviously examining the beaches with a landing in mind. And now we have further corroboration. An emissary, one of our trusted sources in England, is actually at this moment in OKW Headquarters. He has had access to secret material in various headquarters in London. Somehow, he managed to come to France on the pretext of advising the French Resistance near Bayeux.'

'He is here now?' said Hitler in surprise.

'It is true, Mein Führer,' replied an Intelligence colonel, gathering courage from Keitel's bravery in speaking. 'Agents with whom we have implicit trust in different parts of England confirmed in advance that he was expected to arrive. Army patrols from our units around Bayeux located him.'

'Then have this man brought here at once. Why waste time with opinions when he has arrived, armed with facts?'


Arngross burst into Rigby's room.

'The Führer wants to see you,' he announced excitedly. 'That is wonderful news! He is so sharp that no detail escapes him, however small. Think of the honour for me – and for you! I have never been to Berchtesgaden before, and now, on my first visit, I will meet Herr Hitler personally!'

'I share your pride,' Rigby told him. 'You can imagine what this means to me.'

A car was waiting outside with an escorting officer. Within minutes they were through the barbed wire barricade, and walking up the wide steps of the Berghof. As they approached the conference room, two guards opened the vast doors. Rigby waited outside while Arngross went in to report their arrival.

Rigby could feel his heart beating heavily; his mind was a kaleidoscope of conflicting emotions. The hoarse voice with a shrill edge to it that he could hear plainly through the doors must belong to the most hated and feared man in Europe, possibly in the world. How many thousands of those who had suffered at Hitler's hands, as a result of his orders; who had lost relations, friends, freedom itself, would give their lives to be standing here – gladly ready to kill him with their bare hands? Rigby swallowed and held his breath to steady his heart and compose himself.

The doors opened. He walked into the room. The doors closed behind him. Hitler motioned him to come closer to the table. He stood next to Arngross and looked at the other officers, recognising some faces from newspaper photographs and cartoons, awed by the concentration of power in the huge, dimly lit room. The spotlights gave their features a curiously ethereal appearance; they might almost be ghosts in grey uniforms, heavy with medals.

They regarded Rigby with equal interest and some surprise. They had not expected such an important emissary to arrive wearing a shabby suit. His shirt was clean, but his shoes were badly worn. He looked more like a well-built, athletic labourer than a man who brought immensely significant news from the headquarters of their enemies.

'Captain Arngross, Mein Führer,' said Arngross smartly, raising his arm in salute. 'This is the messenger from England.'

Hitler nodded. He walked towards Rigby, who saluted and stood at attention as though on parade in Eastbourne or Aberdovey, thumbs in line with the seams of his trousers.

'You have come from here with special information about Allied invasion plans?'

'Yes, sir.'

'And how did they allow you to leave England with this news?'

'I have a degree in wireless engineering, sir. A chance came to visit French Resistance units who had been experiencing trouble with their sets. I took that chance, Mein Führer.'

'A very grave risk to run. What is your name?'

'My code name is Nimrod, sir. My real name is Rosenberg.'

'Any relation of Alfred Rosenberg?'

'No, sir.'

Alfred Rosenberg, the Reich Minister for the Occupied Eastern Territories in the USSR, had been educated in Russia. Subsequently, he worked in Berlin and Munich among groups of Russian immigrants and the German Workers' Party, which eventually became the Nazi Party. Over the years, he held several positions in line with his standing as the party 'philosopher.' One was Führer's Deputy for Supervision of the Entire Spiritual and Ideological Training of the Nazi Party.

'What have you come to tell us that we do not already know?'

170

For a moment Rigby stood, before replying. His mouth was dry; he wet his lips with his tongue. Here, only feet away, stood the man whose whim for years had directly or indirectly influenced the fate of millions. He felt his body tremble with hatred, as he remembered his father and friends who had disappeared in Vienna and Frankfurt, faces he would never see again. The oppressively stale atmosphere of the room made him feel dizzy. He closed his eyes and put out a hand to steady himself.

'Come, now,' someone said sharply. 'The Führer is waiting.'

Rigby nodded and began to speak. His voice, at first thin and nervous, gradually gathered strength.

'The object of my journey, sir, is to inform your officers that, from all the evidence I can gather, the main Allied attack will take place amphibiously from the south and east coasts of England aimed towards Calais.'

'You see, gentlemen?' said Hitler, looking triumphantly around at the others. 'Some of my colleagues consider that the Pas de Calais is too heavily fortified to warrant attack. What do you say about that?'

'Mein Führer, the Allied High Command accepts that you have had four years in which to fortify it very heavily. But they plan an overwhelming aerial bombardment and a barrage from the sea before the invasion to soften up these defences.'

'That would not necessarily destroy our fortifications,' a general pointed out. 'Some have walls thirty feet thick.'

'It could shatter the minds and nerves of the men who have to fire the guns, sir,' replied Rigby. 'It could blind them, disorientate them. The Allies would then attempt to put those defences behind them – as the German army bypassed Maginot Line obstacles in 1940. There are also other considerations. Dover to Calais is the shortest route across the Channel – and the easiest to supply. Main roads and railways in England run to Brighton, Dover and other sea ports in the South East for embarking vehicles and other stores. And Calais is the nearest big French port to the German frontier.'

'What about Cherbourg? Or Normandy? Biscay? The Mediterranean?'

'I cannot answer for the last two, sir, but I understand there may be subsidiary landings – diversions if you like – in Cherbourg, and possibly elsewhere along that coast.'

'Which will come first?' asked Keitel.

171

'My information is that one or more of these subsidiary landings will occur first in an attempt to draw your reserves. Then they will strike at the main target – Calais.'

'*Facts*, gentlemen,' remarked Hitler approvingly. 'We are dealing here with facts and not opinions. Has anyone any questions he wishes to ask this brave man?'

The officers looked at each other; some uneasily, others carefully concealing their eagerness to be away. A spy's informant did not rate more highly in their estimation than the information he had brought. As professionals, they had already made their own assessment of Allied intentions. No-one spoke.

Hitler turned to Rigby.

'I thank you on behalf of the German staff for your courage and your endeavours.'

Rigby clicked his heels smartly. Arngross saluted. They bowed and left the room. Orderlies closed the double doors behind them. Outside, Rigby leaned on the marble balustrade, trembling with reaction and nausea. Arngross understood how he felt, and took his arm. Slowly, they went down the stairs, through the great hall and into the fresh mountain air. For different reasons, their hearts felt full; neither spoke a word.

Upstairs, in the conference room, Hitler looked questioningly at his staff.

'Well, gentlemen, what is your opinion?'

'He seemed a convincing witness, sir,' said one officer.

'We have proof from other sources of a great deal that he says, sir,' agreed a second. Other voices murmured approval. If Hitler had found the man trustworthy, they would not wish to voice private doubts or contrary opinions.

Hitler looked at them all for a moment with a half smile on his face. Then he brought his right fist down on the marble table with a crash that made the lights tremble. Even his alsatian Blondi looked up reproachfully from where she slept on the Persian carpet.

'I know all those things, gentlemen. But what about the *value* of the information he brings? Do you *agree* with what he says?'

'It certainly does tie up with other indications we have received about Allied intentions,' said Jodl diplomatically.

Other officers nodded sagely; this was exactly how they viewed the matter.

172

'So you are of the opinion, gentlemen, that this is a brave agent, a loyal servant of our country, who has come here at the risk of his life, to tell us that the Allies are going to land on the Pas de Calais? Is that how you view the matter?'

Again the officers nodded, but more warily now, for Hitler's voice was moving slowly up the scale.

'My hair is no longer so dark as it was,' said Hitler slowly. 'And do you know why? It is going grey because of the conduct of my generals. Do you seriously subscribe to the view that the British and Americans would allow some obscure person of no rank whatever, a private soldier, of German-Jewish origin, to fly out to France on a nebulous mission to the French Resistance in the hope and expectation that we would capture him so that he can tell us this story?

'Such a naive supposition is monstrous and beyond belief. This man may well be one of our most trusted sources of information in Britain. I leave that to officers concerned with Intelligence to determine. Let them judge that. But *I* will judge the truth or falsity of the message he brings.

'He may, as I say, believe what he tells us. I hope for his sake that he does, for I wish him to be questioned most closely on this matter. It is always instructive to see inside the enemy mind. My own instinctive feeling is that he is simply a creature of the Allies. They are deliberately using him, while he believes he is rendering us a most valuable service. His arrival is too convenient, too trite, too stage-managed.'

He paused.

'So you think, Mein Führer, that what he tells us is totally false – and that the opposite is true? There will be no important invasion on the Pas de Calais, but the main landings will be elsewhere?' asked Keitel. He was eager to know exactly what Hitler believed, so that he could follow his line of thought, and if necessary amplify it.

'Of course I don't think that. And why not? Because that is precisely what the Allies most desperately wish us to think. That is why my hair is grey, gentlemen, because you generals cannot think even one move ahead. You accept events at their face value.

'A man flies here from England on what may be the eve of the world's most decisive battle. He brings us news that corroborates information we already have from other sources. But his arrival here at this precise moment is altogether too fortuitous to be genuine. I think we are agreed on that. So what do you then suggest – that we ignore his

173

message and do exactly the opposite of what he suggests? Cannot you appreciate that this is *precisely* what the enemy is hoping we will do? They are using this man Nimrod in the expectation that we will do just this and move our forces – and especially our Panzers on which the whole defence of Europe can depend – away from Calais.

'We would then be everywhere, but nowhere in sufficient strength to throw them back into the sea. This is not what the Americans call a double cross, gentlemen. This is something more. This is a treble cross.

'Nimrod arrives to tell us that the enemy will land in Calais. We immediately react by moving our troops away to defend other likely areas. But in point of fact, the enemy *will* land in Calais, *because they calculate we will not now be expecting them to do so.*

'Nimrod is totally expendable, a messenger written off by the enemy the moment he left England. But his message remains. We will therefore reinforce our defences in the Calais area to the limit of our powers. For that is where the main Allied force will land – as I have for long steadfastly believed it would.'

# Chapter Sixteen

For several nights now, lights had burned late behind the heavy black-out curtains in the house in Finchley Park Road. They also burned long into the early hours in similar houses across the south and east of England where other collaborating German agents lived and worked. This was their busiest time since capture. The moment of invasion was almost at hand. On the success of their final efforts now, much of the success of the Allied landing in France could depend. And many believed that on their individual help and dedication could also depend how they personally fared after the war. Would they be given British citizenship, perhaps a chance to begin a new life in another country with a new identity and a gift of local currency? Or would they be abandoned as creatures who had served their purpose, and now must pick up the shattered pieces of their lives as best they could?

In addition to Weber's case officer, the Royal Signals corporal who transmitted and received the messages, his housekeeper and his guards, two middle-aged civilians were now living in the house, sleeping on camp beds in the front bedroom. They had arrived to help to analyse the queries pouring in from Weber's Control in Hamburg.

A clerk made three copies of every message on his Army Oliver typewriter. The two visitors and the case officer studied the latest ones intently.

SUPPLY FULLEST PERSONAL FAMILY PHYSICAL PROFESSIONAL DETAILS NIMROD URGENTEST STOP URGENT CROSS CHECKS REQUIRED NIMROD PARENTAGE, BOYHOOD SCHOOL COLLEGE AC-

TIVITIES PLUS LIST CURRENT INFORMATION
SOURCES STOP GIVE GRADINGS THEIR RECENT
MATERIAL STOP SEND ADDRESSES ANY NIMRODS
CONTINENTAL BLOOD RELATIONS FRIENDS STOP
SUPPLY DETAILS NIMRODS RACE RELIGION
POLITICS MOTIVATION STOP

Weber sat in his attic waiting for his cup of Camp coffee to cool. He
turned the wireless set to the Forces Programme, then over to the
Home Service and back again, while in the room beneath the three
men discussed the messages.

'We can send some replies tomorrow night,' said one of the new
arrivals. 'No problem. But they will take time to answer in detail.'

'When does Weber usually transmit?' asked his colleague.

'Between 23.00 and midnight,' replied the captain.

'Put him on the air late tomorrow morning then.'

'That barely gives us twelve hours.'

'Agreed. But it shows how we value Nimrod – or rather how highly
Weber values him. And it should give us time to dress up some sort of
answers to all these questions. After all, God made the world in six
days and rested on the seventh.'

'But He had all the material at His disposal.'

'So will we,' said the captain. 'If we work round the clock. After all,
it's the least we can do to help that poor bastard Nimrod.'


The teletype was also busy in the locked, most secret room in the
castle of La Roche Guyon. The captain in charge (for no-one below
this rank was allowed access to this particular machine, connected
directly to the OKW office at Berchtesgaden) tore off the thin strips of
paper each time the machine paused, and clipped them together. When
the message ended, he read it through before he took it to the colonel of
Intelligence.


MOST SECRET STOP FROM OKW TO ARMY GROUP B
STOP SENIOR INTELLIGENCE OFFICERS EYES
ONLY STOP FOLLOWING REFERS VISITOR NIMROD
STOP VISITOR TO BE KEPT UNDER DISCREET BUT
TOTAL    REPEAT    TOTAL    SURVEILLANCE

PREPARATORY FULLEST INTERROGATION PARIS
STOP DETAILS FOLLOWING STOP IF VISITOR
QUERIES SURVEILLANCE EXPLAIN TACTFULLY IT
IS FOR HIS OWN SECURITY MESSAGE ENDS STOP

The Storch aircraft that took Rigby to Berchtesgaden brought him
back to Paris. There, Rigby and Arngross found seats in a BMW staff
car bringing an artillery colonel to La Roche Guyon. The road had
been machine-gunned outside Orgeval by USAAF aircraft that afternoon, and other raids were possible, so they waited until dark and then
drove with dimmed headlamps. It was late when they reached La
Roche Guyon.

Rigby's room smelled damp as a newly dug grave when he entered
it. He shivered, and on the impulse took off his jacket and did twenty
press-ups on the floor. Not only would this warm him; the exercise
would help to keep him fit for what he realised would now be the most
difficult part of his assignment – escape. He had just finished, when
Arngross came upstairs to escort him to the small mess used by
visitors.

'Bit of good news,' he announced cheerfully. 'Just heard I'm staying
here with you.'

'Good. Any idea how long we'll both be here?'

'The longer the better, so far as I'm concerned,' replied Arngross
vaguely. 'Matter of fact, I think they want to ask you a few more
questions.'

'I see.'

Rigby did not wish to stay in La Roche Guyon for an hour longer
than was absolutely necessary, but he remembered the two microphones in the room and did his best to appear calm and indifferent to a
further interview, although he felt deeply concerned at this prospect.
How long after the invasion would the OKW take to realise that Calais
was not the main target – that the information he had brought was
false? Unease began to spread through his body, like indigestion after a
bad meal. He went to bed early that night, but it was a long time before
he slept.

By six o'clock on the following morning, Sunday, June 4, Field
Marshal Rommel was already finishing his breakfast. As he ate a thin
slice of toast, he read the latest Intelligence report. All remained quiet
along the north-west coast of France. Heavy enemy bombing was

reported overnight in the Pas de Calais region, but this was nothing new; the previous week had seen 246 air raids on areas north of the Seine, but only 33 south of the river. Clearly, the Allies intended to neutralise as many of the German defences there as possible, presumably as an essential preliminary to landing. But wherever the invasion might come, the writers of this report did not expect it within the next few days; the weather was so bad that German aircraft were grounded and German navy vessels were keeping in harbour.

Rommel had not been on leave for several months. Despite his professional optimism when he visited defence positions around the coast, he was greatly depressed by Hitler's vacillating policies and absurd contradictions based on what he called his intuition. For several months now, officers whom Rommel trusted, and civilians he admired, had secretly and at enormous risk to their own lives, urged that he should lead a faction to overthrow Hitler and attempt to negotiate peace terms with the Allies - while there was still time to do so.

On the Eastern front, German armies awaited the next Soviet offensive, expected within weeks. Italy had negotiated a separate peace and the German forces were withdrawing from Rome. Japan was now on the defensive in the South Pacific and Burma. Time and again Rommel would quote to his Chief of Staff Lieutenant General Speidel, as they walked after dinner in the gardens, Hitler's own words from *Mein Kampf*: "When the Government of a nation is leading it to its doom, rebellion is not only the right but the duty of every man. Human laws supersede the laws of the State . . ."

To believe this was one thing; but to act directly on this belief and directly against the Führer - this was treason and against the solemn oath of loyalty he had taken exactly 10 years earlier. Such an act might be morally justified - but could it be achieved successfully? So Rommel delayed, hopeful of some outward and unmistakeable sign that could be his guide; but already, although he did not know it, he had delayed too long and too dangerously.

Now, military rather than political considerations occupied his mind. When General Speidel had visited Berchtesgaden in April before joining Rommel as his Chief of Staff, he had asked the Führer specifically for a definite operational directive. Hitler replied that this was quite superfluous. They had to defend the coast. There was no room to manoeuvre or deviate from these instructions. That was the only operational directive.

But in order to carry out this vague order, Rommel needed to control all his means of defence; and in particular this meant the Panzer divisions. In a last attempt to solve this problem, Rommel had confirmed an appointment with Hitler's adjutant for a personal interview with the Führer. At this meeting he intended to insist on his right to conduct the defence of France as he felt best, for Hitler would never visit the front to see problems for himself. He appeared fearful for his own safety.

After the heavy air-raids on Cologne, the mayor of that city had personally invited the Führer to visit the bombed areas – as the King and Queen and Mr. Churchill had visited bombed cities in Britain. Hitler refused. The mayor then asked that he at least receive representatives of the rescue workers at his headquarters; a gesture that would give them heart and encouragement. Hitler would not do so. Now, when he travelled across Germany in his special train from Berchtesgaden to Berlin, he would pull down the window blinds, so that he need not see the devastation that Allied bombs had brought to his country.

Rommel had asked Rundstedt to join with him in appealing to Hitler for a workable defence policy. But Rundstedt, old, tired and cynical, replied cautiously: 'You are young. The people know and love you. *You* do it.' This Rommel was determined to do, but he had deliberately not told Rundstedt – or anyone else – of his intentions. He also had a personal reason for wishing to go on leave: to celebrate his wife's fiftieth birthday.

At seven o'clock he walked down the steps to his black Horch car. His adjutant, and a colonel to whom he was giving a lift, climbed in the back. Rommel sat as usual in front beside the driver. The big car set off on the road to Paris.

From an upper window, Rigby watched Rommel leave. The orderly escorted him down to a room on the ground floor where Arngross had unexpectedly told him they would eat in future, away from the visitors' mess. Rigby did not altogether like this new arrangement. It had a slightly ominous ring; it smacked of a prisoner eating with his escort. He would have felt even more uneasy had he known of the Intelligence colonel's orders to Arngross late the previous evening. He had called him into his office to tell him that he must not let Nimrod out of his sight.

'It is not that we don't trust him,' he added, 'but there may be attempts from the Resistance on his life. You must be armed at all times. If you require any colleagues to share these duties, then see me. But if anything happens to Nimrod – *anything* – I will hold you personally responsible. You understand that?'

'I do, sir,' replied Arngross.

After breakfast, he walked with Rigby past the church and the war memorial, along the Rue d'Audience. The houses were very old, many with roofs fallen in, and the road itself was too narrow for a car. An air of shuttered, almost sinister quietness hung over the Rue d'Audience. Some houses had been empty for so long that ivy fronds grew across their shutters and doors.

They turned into the main street, with its Bar Tabac and the Maison de la Presse, and then strolled back towards the castle. The whole promenade had lasted barely ten minutes; it was far too soon to return. On the impulse, they walked along the Rue du Docteur Duval, past Le Saint-Georges Inn. Some houses stood on either side, nondescript and empty. Soon the road petered out. A raised stone platform with four lamp posts marked its end, overlooking the Seine. They stood, elbows on the low wall that surrounded this platform, watching the fast-flowing river. Here and there a fish leapt at a fly with a flash of silver scales. Out in mid-stream three barges, long and thin, chugged towards Cherbourg. Rigby glanced at his watch; a quarter to ten in the morning.

'They are the safest means of supply now,' Arngross explained. 'It's much harder to bomb a barge in the middle of the river than to blow up a bridge or a level crossing.'

'What do they carry?' Rigby asked him.

'Cement for fortifications. Food, petrol, ammunition, mines for the beaches. All kinds of things. And they bring back vegetables and cider from Normandy.'

'Day and night?'

'All the time,' replied a voice behind them. Both men turned; they had not heard anyone approach. Herr Mannheim was standing on the top step of the platform, smiling at their surprise. Rigby glanced down at his shoes. They had soft rubber soles.

'So you had the rare privilege of meeting the Führer,' Mannheim began. 'I envy you. I have never been so fortunate. But then you rightly deserve the honour, Nimrod.'

'Thank you,' replied Rigby. Was Mannheim being sarcastic? He experienced the same feeling of hostility he had known during his questioning in the castle and the OKW office. This man disliked him, probably suspected him. Why? What mistake had he made?

'I am only one of a team,' Rigby continued deprecatingly.

'And, as I believe the English, with their love of sport, like to say, the team resembles a chain. Only as strong as its weakest link. Now, if you please, gentlemen.'

Mannheim produced a small camera from his pocket and quickly took two photographs of them.

'What's that for?' asked Arngross.

'My album. It is my hobby.'

Mannheim put the camera back in his pocket, gave them a farewell wave, and set off back towards the castle. His shoes made no sound as he walked. Rigby and Arngross looked at each other.

'These Abwehr people . . .' began Arngross uneasily, and then stopped in embarrassment, remembering his companion was also an Abwehr man. 'Come on, let's get moving.'

They walked along the edge of the river, past a long line of trees with their tops joined in topiary, like those outside the castle. To their right, a grass bank sloped down to a cobbled promenade and then the water. Several small rowing boats were moored to stakes; old men squatted on collapsible canvas stools, fishing. Beyond the river, silvery and slow, the far bank appeared thick with bushes and trees, empty as an eighteenth century landscape.

They turned to the left, along an unmade track. Large houses stood on either side. Like the others, they were mostly empty, hedges uncut and gardens thick with weeds. At the top of the track was a no entry sign – 'Sauf aux Riverains' – where it joined the main road.

As they walked once more past the Bar Tabac, Rigby saw Mannheim sitting in the window, apparently absorbed in a newspaper. From that viewpoint, Rigby realised, Mannheim could see both roads that led to the river, but he could not be seen himself unless – as now – someone peered in through the bar window. This made him feel even more uneasy about Mannheim. Was he deliberately watching his movements? He did not wish his likeness to be preserved in Gestapo photographic records, but there was nothing he could do about that now. As he entered the castle courtyard, he wondered how long it would take for Mannheim's dislike of him to turn to active distrust – if it had not already done so.

On Monday morning, after breakfast and their usual walk, Arngross was again called into the office of the Intelligence colonel. Immediately afterwards, he came to see Rigby.

'News for you,' he said brightly. 'We are moving.'

'Where to?'

'Paris. The Abwehr people want to question you on life in England and so on.'

'When do we go?'

'Wednesday. Six-thirty. If there are no air-raids, that is. They are actually sending a car. Shows how highly they think of you.'

Or else, thought Rigby grimly, it is because they want to be sure I arrive. He had either made a grave error somewhere, or something about him or his story had struck a false and jarring note. He remembered the microphones in his room. Had he talked in his sleep?

He sat on his bed, head in his hands, after Arngross left him, trying to puzzle out what had gone wrong. He felt a feeling of foreboding about going to Paris, farther inland, away from the coast, where he should shortly be heading. Why was he going? Could this only be due to a basic animal animosity on the part of Mannheim? Or was the reason more sinister? Either way, his dilemma was desperate.

He must not do anything that would arouse suspicion about himself before the landings began. But for how long could he hold out if he were not just to be questioned, but tortured?


General Speidel had high admiration for Rommel, but this did not extend to sharing the Field Marshal's liking for frugality and early nights. Speidel was more intellectual and more convivial, and on that Monday evening, the first after Rommel's departure from La Roche-Guyon, he invited some private guests to dinner at headquarters. One was a German consul-general who had been interned in Algiers two years earlier and only recently released; the German writer, Ernst Jünger, who was serving on the staff of the German Military Governor of France; a war correspondent; Speidel's brother-in-law, and a naval liaison officer from the 15th Army.

In Rommel's absence, they had no need to observe early hours, and the party broke up around midnight. At half past one, a teletype message came in from headquarters of the 7th Army on the east coast of the Contentin peninsula: enemy paratroops were being dropped.

Shortly afterwards, 15th Army headquarters in the north reported enemy paratroops landing between Caen and Deauville.

Admiral Friedrich Ruge did not go to bed, but sat up awaiting any further reports.

Shortly before Christmas, the Admiral had begun to make his own notes on events and impressions, for he realised that he was living through a decisive time of history. Now, in the small hours, while most officers in Headquarters were still asleep, he wrote sadly of 'the endless tug-of-war about the 12th SS Panzer division command, which was OKW reserve and placed too far back.'

It was 'very disadvantageous that the Panzer Divisions were not positioned as the Commander-in-Chief had requested over and over again . . .'

At daybreak, more teletypes were received from different vantage points along the Normandy coast. All confirmed that an armada of Allied ships was approaching. In some places, landings from them had already begun.

But was this the real invasion at last, or was it only an impressive diversionary attack to draw fire? No-one could be sure at this early stage, but it was sufficiently important for Speidel to order a signal of the highest priority to be teletyped to Rundstedt's headquarters at St. Germain-en-Laye, outside Paris:

MOST IMMEDIATE. FIFTEENTH ARMY REQUESTS ARRIVAL OF TWELFTH SS PANZER DIVISION. ARMY GROUP B REQUESTS MOVEMENT OF PANZER GROUP WEST TO POSITIONS EAST AND WEST OF LISEUX.

In the Pavillon Henry IV, on the edge of the park at St. Germain-en-Laye, Rundstedt lay asleep. An adjutant awoke him with the news of landings by sea and from the air. The old man read the teletype reports and the message from General Speidel. Far beneath him, on that early Tuesday morning, Paris stirred.

Rundstedt's first reaction was that this could not be the main invasion. There was no major port in Normandy, and a port was essential for disembarking supplies on a large scale. But it seemed serious, despite that.

'Two Panzer divisions, Panzer Lehr and the 12th SS Panzers are to proceed to the coast immediately,' Rundstedt told his adjutant. Then he paused, considering the order he had just given and its possible political implication. He had no authority to move these Panzer divisions, although this was clearly the correct thing to do. They came under the exclusive direction of the OKW, which meant, in effect, that they could only be moved on Hitler's express directions.

But the Führer, as Rundstedt knew, was an even later riser than he was himself, and rarely dressed until noon. It was unlikely that anyone on his staff would wish to awake him with bad news of enemy landings. Rundstedt felt certain that Hitler would – must – agree to move the Panzers as soon as he heard of the landings. But by then precious – possibly vital – hours would have been lost. The tanks had a long way to go to reach the coast, and if this was a serious invasion attempt and not simply a large Commando raid, it would be covered by heavy air support, which might prevent the Panzers moving at all. The sooner they were on their way, the greater their chance of reaching the objective before travel by road became impossible.

This was obvious to Rundstedt's trained military mind, but he realised that this did not guarantee the Führer would agree. So the Field Marshal sat at his desk, stroking his still unshaven chin pondering the situation – and his own position – if Hitler objected to his order. He was too old a soldier to be caught out on a technical point; he must cover himself completely in what he had done. Rundstedt turned back to his adjutant.

'Now send this message to the OKW,' he said briskly. 'If this is actually a large scale enemy operation, it can only be met successfully if immediate action is taken. This involves the commitment on this day of all available strategic reserves, including 12th SS and Panzer Lehr Divisions.

'If they assemble quickly and start early they can enter the battle on the coast during the day. Under the circumstances, Commander-in-Chief West therefore requests OKW to release these reserves.'

This was simply a formality, a statement for the war diary, so that no-one could accuse him of discourtesy. It was also his personal insurance policy. Satisfied, Rundstedt went into his bathroom to shave.

Within minutes, while teletype machines still clattered in St. Germain-en-Laye and Berchtesgaden, alarm sirens were sounding in Panzer divisional headquarters. The Panzers were on the move.


Early morning mist draped the mountain peaks around Berchtesgaden like a wedding veil. The SS guards were standing-to, machine carbines at the ready, as was their custom for half an hour before every dawn and dusk.

In Colonel-General Jodl's office, the duty officer read the message from Rundstedt's headquarters and glanced at his watch. Like Rundstedt, although forty years younger, he was wise in the ways of the army. He did not care to take responsibility for disturbing the general with news of an enemy landing at such an early hour. There had been several incorrect reports of landings during the past few weeks; he had no reason to believe that this was anything more than another false alert or, at worst, a small scale raid.

He sent a formal acknowledgement of the signal back to Rundstedt's headquarters, simply to record its arrival. Then, to cover himself from any subsequent unpleasantness about his action – or inaction – he prudently telephoned his opposite number on Hitler's staff. This officer awoke Admiral Karl Jesko von Puttkamer, Hitler's naval adviser, to tell him there had been reports of what he called 'some kind of landing' in Northern France.

He chose Puttkamer on the basis that since enemy ships were involved, a naval officer should know best what action to take. Puttkamer also took the course of prudence and decided against informing Hitler at such an early hour. The Führer had gone to bed at his usual time of four o'clock that morning, taking a sleeping draught. He would be fuddled and heavy with drugged slumber.

Jodl, however, like Rommel, was an early riser and by six o'clock was reading reports of the landings. He considered them less important than the grave news that had poured in overnight from Italy. Rome had fallen; German troops under Field Marshal Kesselring were in retreat to the north.

In Russia, the German army, stretched thinly across a 2,000 miles front, waited with resignation for the summer Soviet offensive. Like the Allied invasion, this had been expected for weeks. Would either ever come? Or had one arrived this morning?

As Jodl read the reports, already wondering how to translate them into less bleak terms for Hitler's eyes and ears, his desk telephone rang. General Walter Warlimont, his deputy, about to leave for Italy to discover at first-hand whether the military situation there was as desperate as it appeared, was on the line.

He explained that he had just seen a message from Rundstedt's Chief-of-Staff about the Panzer reserves. They wished to move them at once into the invasion areas – and indeed orders to this effect had already been given. The teletype message requesting this had been acknowledged by the OKW duty officer.

This information rang instant alarm bells in the careful mind of Jodl, the trimmer, the man who never deviated from Hitler's wishes, whether spoken or assumed. He knew how jealously the Führer regarded his command of the Panzers. It was not for Jodl, or for anyone else, to give permission for which he had no authority.

'What makes you so sure this *is* the invasion?' he asked soothingly. 'I genuinely believe it is only a diversionary attack, part of an Allied deception plan to draw off air forces from the Calais area.

'Rundstedt should deal with this with the forces he already has. This is not the time to release the Panzer Reserves. We must wait for further clarification of the situation before we consider that.'

What he meant, of course, was that he must wait for Hitler's approval. Back went the teletype order to Rundstedt's headquarters: PANZERS MUST NOT REPEAT NOT MOVE WITHOUT OKW'S CONSENT.

Rundstedt, accustomed to beginning his working day well after ten o'clock, was already in a bad temper at having been awakened so early. As he read the transcript of this message, his face reddened with anger. The thin calipers around his mouth deepened sharply. He called for his Chief of Operations, Lt-General Bodo Zimmermann.

'What do you make of this?' he asked, showing him the message.

'Can't understand it, sir,' replied Zimmermann. 'I advised Colonel-General Jodl's duty officer we had ordered the Panzer Divisions to move. He raised no objections at all. And neither should he. It was the obvious move to make.'

'They appear to disagree,' replied Rundstedt grimly. 'Get on to OKW again and remind them of the urgency of the situation.'

The Field Marshal felt too angry to speak to anyone in OKW, so Zimmermann spoke to the OKW's Army Operations Chief, Major General von Buttlar-Brandenfels. He attempted to explain the position informally, as between officers of approximately equal rank and seniority.

The release of the Panzers must not be countermanded, he said. Indeed, they were already on the road, and to order them back now would mean loss of morale, a considerable waste of fuel, and worst of all, a very serious loss of time. They had a long way to travel, and movement under Allied air attack might be difficult or even impossible later in the day. Delay now could deny them to the defenders when their presence was essential.

All this seemed really too obvious to require even this explanation, and Zimmermann listened expectantly, certain that some subordinate had somehow misread the earlier messages, and that his colleague would instantly appreciate the true facts of the situation. But Von Buttlar-Brandenfels had not served in OKW in his capacity without realising the imperative need for delicacy in every matter concerning the Führer. He had no intention of now being odd man out.

'Have I to explain to you yet again that these Divisions are under the direct control of the OKW?' he asked coldly.

'You had no authority or right whatever to alert them without our prior permission. You are to halt all the Panzers immediately. Let me repeat, not *one* tank is to be moved until the Führer has made his decision.'

'With respect, sir,' replied Zimmermann, also angry now. 'I feel that the Führer will agree we have done the right thing, in fact, the *only* thing in the circumstances. We *must* move the Panzers.'

'Do as you are told!' shouted the OKW general in reply and slammed down the receiver to end the conversation.

Zimmermann told Rundstedt what had happened. The old man stood for a moment, looking out of the window across his lawn towards the bridges of Paris. As Field Marshal he had the right of direct access to the Führer. He could have picked up the telephone and spoken to him as easily as he could telephone his adjutant in his office next door. But he did not do so. Pride, resentment, dislike and contempt would not let him. He was unable to bring himself to pick up the telephone and say the words that might have changed history. Zimmermann waited for a moment, and then went silently from the room to order the Panzer divisions to stop their advance.


In La Roche Guyon, further messages poured in, reporting Allied landings by sea and air. German troops had rushed to intercept what they believed was an airborne attack in one area only to find that paratroops were actually dropping miles away. The Germans had been deceived by dummies wearing paratroop uniforms. In their packs were concealed recording devices that broadcast the sound of guns firing and men shouting.

Sabotage by the Resistance on roads and railways, on truck convoys and rolling stock, suddenly increased dramatically. Whatever Rundstedt or the OKW might care to believe, this was certainly a major landing. In General Speidel's opinion, as he read these messages, this was the main invasion. He felt so concerned that he telephoned Rommel at his home in Herrlingen. Rommel at once contacted his adjutant, on leave in Stuttgart; they must return immediately to La Roche Guyon. Their expected time of arrival would be early evening, depending on the condition of the roads and whether any bridges had been bombed.

Shortly after half past nine that Tuesday morning, the BBC broadcast news that 'Under the command of General Eisenhower, Allied naval forces, supported by air forces, began landing Allied armies this morning on the Northern coast of France...'

German time was one hour behind British time. At nine o'clock German time, about half an hour after the rest of the world knew of the invasion, Hitler's staff decided that they could no longer delay informing the Führer, although no one was particularly anxious to bring these grave tidings to him.

Finally, after some discussion, his adjutant, Major-General Rudolf Schmundt, knocked lightly on the door of the Führer's bedroom. Hitler and Eva Braun were still asleep. The Führer jumped out of bed in his nightshirt.

'At last we are going to meet our real enemies face to face!' he cried excitedly, when Schmundt informed him of the Allied landing. Hitler was about to leave the bedroom to consult his maps, when Eva Braun pointed out that a white cotton nightshirt was not the most suitable garment in which to greet his generals.

Hitler hurriedly put on a dressing gown, and requested the immediate presence of Keitel and Jodl. They brought little more news of the progress of the landings.

'*Is* it or *isn't* it the invasion?' Hitler kept repeating. 'Is it or isn't it?'

In the tenseness of this meeting, in the unreality of their surroundings in an overfurnished drawing room outside Hitler's bedroom, approached by a velvet-covered staircase and usually out of bounds to all, no-one remembered to mention Rundstedt's requests about the Panzer Divisions.

# Chapter Seventeen

Rigby leaned over the wall on the raised platform at the end of the Rue du Docteur Duval, looking down at the Seine. Early morning rain had ceased; sun glittered on the wide sweep of river.

Arngross stood a few feet away, breaking off small pieces of twig to throw into the water and watch them float away. In mid-stream, three barges struggled against the same current. Rigby surreptitiously glanced at his watch; a quarter to twelve precisely. On Sunday morning, the barges had passed at a quarter to ten. Probably they did so at fifteen minutes to each hour throughout the day and night. Arngross might know, but Rigby did not dare to ask him; the question might make him suspicious.

The scene was so peaceful, so remote from war, that he found it difficult to believe that roughly 100 miles away, British, Canadian and American soldiers were fighting ferociously for a foothold in Normandy, while German armies were equally desperately trying to force them back into the sea. He might only be 100 miles from freedom himself, but he could equally well have been a thousand, for how could he hope to escape when Arngross was so obviously determined not to allow him out of his sight? The fact they were due to leave for Paris in the morning worried him even more now that the Allied landings had begun. He should be travelling west and not east, for it could not take the OKW long to realise that the landings in Normandy were not simply diversions, but must be the main attack. From that moment on, he would be a doomed man. Also, it would be infinitely more difficult to escape from Paris, with roadblocks and plain clothes Gestapo men at every railway station.

'Penny for them,' said Arngross.

'Sorry we're leaving tomorrow,' replied Rigby truthfully.

'So am I. It has been a very pleasant diversion here. I'm going with you to Paris. And then, who knows?'

Who indeed, thought Rigby. The effect of his hypnosis had now all but worn away. He felt more alert but also more nervous, more aware of the risks and odds against him. Before, his sense of danger had been cushioned by a euphoric feeling of superiority; somehow, he would overcome. Now, he felt less confident. If Mannheim really suspected him, he might never even reach Paris. The more Rigby considered his situation, the more depressed he became. He forced himself to break out of this downward spiral of acceptance. For no reason at all, he remembered a visit with Duncan to the Hind's Head Hotel in Bray. In the hall, over the mantelpiece were the words: *Fear knocked at the door. Faith opened it. No-one was there.* He must open the door to his own future, not cower behind it. He felt strengthened, more confident.

The barges bound for Cherbourg had already reached the nearest bend of the river.

'What's the next town in that direction?' Rigby asked Arngross.

'Bonnières, seven kilometres down river. Has the Singer sewing machine factory and a railway station, but that's about all. We should be lucky. Paris in the spring, eh?'

Rigby looked sharply at Arngross whose eyes were glowing at the thought of restaurants, theatres – and what else? An idea began to take shape in Rigby's mind, a thought that could conceivably help him to escape.

'When we reach Paris, we may have to split up,' he said slowly. 'So what about a night out here before we leave? I've some French money.'

'Not much doing here,' replied Arngross doubtfully. 'We could get a meal of sorts, I suppose. But – wait a minute. Officer I'm sharing a room with says there is a house he goes to sometimes. Only two or three girls, but all quite clean, of course. Inspected regularly. We *could* go there this evening. Can't get anything in the way of food, apparently. But we won't be out for the eats, will we?'

He giggled. Rigby found Arngross's anticipation of lust disagreeable, and glanced down at the river more intently in case these feelings showed on his face.

'Can you fix it up then?' he asked.

'Delighted. But I must take you back to the castle first. Can't let you wander about alone.'

190

'Why not?'

Arngross shrugged; he had said too much.

'Well,' he explained as casually as possible, 'the French might get a bit rough. They've never been terribly involved up here with the Resistance until the last few weeks. But now the enemy has landed at last, things may change. And if any of them recognised you – even from a description – you could be in trouble.'

They walked back to the castle. Then Arngross went off on his own. Rigby read German newspapers in his room; the door was locked from the outside, as it had been when he first arrived. Arngross came to collect him and they lunched together, looking out at the damp dirty whiteness of the cliff.

'We'll eat about nine,' said Arngross.

'What time does the curfew start?'

'Doesn't affect us. So long as we are back by midnight. That should give us enough time, eh?' He sniggered, meaning one thing.

'I very much hope so,' said Rigby, meaning another.


Six hundred miles to the south east, in the Berghof, the officers who had gathered around Hitler when Rigby was presented to the Führer, now stood in the same vast room, in the same positions, looking at the same maps. The air felt fusty as before. Outside, sunshine blazed so strongly that the drawn curtains felt warm to the touch.

Hitler appeared infinitely more animated than he had been at any time during the previous few months. His face was now flushed from excitement as much as from drugs. He tapped the map of Normandy with his steel-rimmed spectacles.

'You will recall, gentlemen,' he was saying, 'that among the many reports we received from our agents, one exactly predicted this landing to the day, and even the hour. Corroboration came from a curious source – the valet of the British Ambassador to Turkey. He'd seen the papers in the Embassy safe. But why should they tell their ambassador in Turkey how they propose to invade France? A preposterous idea! This is certainly not the real invasion, gentlemen. But it is a clever attempt to draw our fire.

'I am also sure – as I have said before – that some of our agents in Britain are being paid by the enemy. They take money from both sides. I found this report so unlikely that I did not ask anyone to do any work

191

on it. The whole thing was obviously false.'

'Where do you believe the main landings will be, Mein Führer?' asked Jodl obediently, coming in on his cue.

'Where I have said before, for the reasons you all know so well. In the Calais area.'

Jodl lowered his eyes.

'We have received several requests from OB* West concerning the release of the Panzers for Normandy.'

'So I have heard. But there is no hurry,' Hitler replied. 'I will deal with that matter in a moment.'

The prospect of action had loosened his tongue. His familiar monologue began with reminiscences from the past. Then came criticism of his generals, and sarcasm at the expense of Germany's Intelligence services. Finally, he reached the subject of the Panzers. Rundstedt's arguments for releasing them were put once more, and Hitler nodded his head in agreement.

'Very well, then, let those two divisions go. But, remember, our prime consideration must always be to repulse the *main* invasion, not just subsidiary attacks. For this reason all the other Panzer divisions and the 15th Army will remain where they are. Until I decide otherwise.'

The electric clock on the conference room wall put the time at 15.42 hours.

So the two divisions of Panzers, whose orders to advance nearly twelve hours earlier had been so abruptly cancelled, made ready to move for a second time. But now the roads to the coast were under heavy Allied air attack, and progress was slow, with many halts and diversions. Some units of the 12th SS Panzers did reach Normandy late that evening, but they were seriously diminished in strength and efficiency by casualties and mechanical breakdown. Even so, they bravely managed to mount a limited counter-attack on the following day. But the crucial moment, when their fire power and weight of armour could have proved decisive, had passed. The Allies were ashore, had consolidated their beachheads and were advancing inland while the German Armoured Reserve of five divisions, and the nineteen divisions that comprised the 15th Army remained about 200 miles away, ready to defend Calais.

---

*A spoken abbreviation for Oberfehlshaber, the Commander-in-Chief.

192

To appreciate the decimation that the Panzer divisions could have achieved had Rommel been allowed to place them where he wished, it is only necessary to describe what one isolated but astutely commanded German Mark VI tank achieved a week later, on June 13.

Early that morning, advance units of the British 7th Armoured Division were approaching Caen along a main street with houses on either side. The half-track vehicles contained men of the 4th City of London Yeomanry and the 1st Rifle Brigade.

From a side street, perhaps fifty yards ahead, the German tank suddenly appeared, commanded by a young officer, Michael Wittmann. He instantly appraised the situation and ordered his gunner to open fire. The first shell hit the leading British half-track, which blew up, completely blocking the road, as Wittmann intended it should. The following half-tracks could not force a way past it, nor could they turn speedily because of the houses on either side. It was impossible for them to reverse out of this trap because of the build-up of other vehicles close behind them. The British soldiers aboard them opened fire, but bullets from their rifles and light machine guns could do no more than scratch the paint on the German tank's hull.

Wittmann had them all at his mercy, and he destroyed a total of twenty-five vehicles that morning and held up the advance on Caen indefinitely. Instead of falling within days, another month was to pass before Caen came into Allied control.

If one German tank under a resolute commander could cause such chaos and casualties, and delay the advance for so long, what devastation could have been achieved by ten Panzer Divisions, each containing up to 200 tanks, with other armoured vehicles?


Rigby spent the afternoon preparing himself for the escape attempt he knew he must make before he left for Paris.

With a razor blade he unpicked half an inch of thread from the leather strip at the bottom of his right trouser leg and removed the benzedrine pills and the lethal pill in their tiny waterproof pouches, and put them in his jacket pocket, inside his survival kit. He laid out the clean socks and shirt and pants that the orderly had provided. He did not know when he would be able to change, so he might as well start as fresh as possible. Then he had a bath and shave and lay down on the bed, trying to sleep.

At first, this proved impossible. Images of freedom and captivity churned through his mind. He thought of Elena, and wondered whether she was at that moment thinking of him. He thought of his friends in X-Troop. How many were already on the beaches in Normandy alive – or dead? He thought of his mother in Montreal; of piano lessons and cups of tea with Mr. Werner before the war. He thought of Mannheim and his resolve tightened.

*The pigeons had arrived . . .* it was time to fly.

After some time, he fell asleep, and was awakened by a knock on the door. The orderly came in to put up the blackout screen across the window. He explained that he was doing this earlier than usual, because of news of the enemy landing, and the possibility of air raids.

'*Hear, Oh Israel, the Lord thy God . . . the Lord is One,*' Rigby repeated silently to himself when the man had gone.

As he dressed, he glanced around the room; nothing here would lead anyone to think he had planned to leave. His disappearance must appear to be accidental – or even better, a kidnapping, perhaps by the Resistance. That way, he might give himself some extra time before the search for him began.

He tapped on the door. In the corridor, the orderly was carrying an officer's uniform on a wooden hanger. He opened the door. Rigby called him into his bedroom. If the microphones wre connected, they could record his conversation.

'I may be a bit late in tonight,' Rigby told the orderly. 'Going out with Captain Arngross.'

The orderly smiled knowingly.

'As a matter of fact,' Rigby went on, 'I wish I wasn't. I have a bit of stomach trouble. Thought the captain was the only one to have that! What is the procedure here for seeing the M.O?'

'Inform the orderly officer, sir. Sick parade for officers is at 07.30 hours.'

'Thank you. I will attend that, if you will wake me early.'

'Of course, sir. I will knock on the door at 06.30'.

Rigby waited for Arngross and they walked together to the room where dinner was served.

As they were finishing, Rommel's car arrived, covered with dust, headlamp lenses and windscreen spattered by summer insects, showing the speed at which it had travelled across France. Arngross waited until the Field Marshal had hurried into the castle, then walked with Rigby across the gravel yard towards the Rue d'Audience. A choir was practising the Angelus in the church; Thursday would be the festival of Corpus Christi. Their voices seemed ghostly and remote.

'You're very quiet tonight,' remarked Arngross. 'Hardly ate a thing or said a word at dinner.'

'Got a bit of stomach trouble,' Rigby admitted. 'I suppose it's reaction. I've been through quite a bit these last few days, you know.'

'Of course. I was forgetting,' said Arngross sympathetically. 'Never mind. You should be feeling beter soon.'

They walked in silence along the cobbled street, crossed the main road, turned left and right. Arngross knocked on a wooden door painted dark blue with a metal handle shaped like a human hand. The door opened instantly to allow them inside, and closed as quickly. The hall was barely wide enough for them to stand abreast, and very dark. A smell of garlic and Gitanes and furniture polish hung not unpleasantly on the air.

Madame Pontière, a middle-aged French woman, wearing black, showed them into a back room. Two girls in their twenties, looking like gipsies with garish ear-rings and bright neck scarves and black sweaters too tight for them, sat side by side on a horsehair sofa. Madame Pontière bowed to Rigby and Arngross.

'Antoinette,' she said by way of introduction. 'Hélène.'

The girls smiled mechanically with their reddened lips but not with their eyes.

'You will take wine, Messieurs?' asked Madame Pontière. Without waiting for their reply, she poured red wine into four cloudy glasses on a brass tray. They raised the glasses in a toast.

'To all of us,' said Arngross gallantly. He turned to Rigby. 'And especially to you.'


The duty captain left the teletype room in the Castle at La Roche Guyon, turned both keys in the double locks, and hurried along the corridor to the officer's mess, holding the folded message in his hand.

He expected that the mess would be empty, because all officers were on duty. In the far corner, however, a civilian sat in an armchair, reading *Le Matin*. He lowered the newspaper, and looked at the captain expectantly.

'For you, Herr Mannheim,' said the captain. Mannheim read the teletype message:

MOST SECRET MANNHEIM ARMY GROUP B STOP
IMPERATIVE BRING NIMROD SECURELY TO
PARIS FOR 0730 MEETING JUNE SEVEN STOP
SENIOR REPRESENTATIVES ATTENDING STOP
THIS CANCELS PREVIOUS MEETING FOR
AFTERNOON MEETING SAME DAY MESSAGE
ENDS STOP

'Thank you,' said Mannheim. The message was not unexpected, but he still felt pleased it had arrived. The words 'Senior Representatives' should at least refer to the colonel he had seen in the bunker at Zossen. They might even mean Kaltenbrunner or perhaps Himmler himself. At all events, Mannheim felt that he had secured his own position as a trustworthy agent. They must have their own doubts about Nimrod, or at least about the value of the information he had brought. He folded the message neatly, put it in his wallet. Then he went up to Rigby's room, knocked on the door. There was no answer. The orderly heard the sound and came out of his pantry, polishing a pair of soft leather boots.

'Where's the occupant?' Mannheim asked him.

'Gone out, sir. With Captain Arngross.'

'At this hour? And on this day, with the enemy landing? Where have they gone?'

The orderly smiled uneasily.

'Come on, man,' said Mannheim impatiently.

'There's a house in the village, sir.'

'A house?'

'Some girls who oblige, sir.'

'Where?'

'Go down the Rue d'Audience. Then left and right. Blue front door. Madame Pontière.'

'What time are they due back?'

'Officers are always back here by 23.00 hours, sir. And tonight, they won't be late. Not with the landing.'

'I should hope not.'

Mannheim returned to his room, packed his possessions, rang for his driver.

'We shall be leaving for Paris at midnight,' he told him. 'Check the petrol.'

'Very good, sir.'

Mannheim lit a cigarette. With the blackout curtains in place early on this June night all rooms in the Castle already smelled stale. Typewriters clattered behind office doors. Orderlies hurried along corridors lit by unshaded electric bulbs. He felt suddenly weary of noise and bustle. He opened a side door, walked out between the double blackout screens and stood for a moment in the courtyard, breathing the cool evening air. He wondered how the invasion was proceeding; he wondered about Paris. That brought him to the man he had to take there late that night. Most of all, he wondered what would happen when they arrived.

Arngross was talking to Antoinette; Rigby smiled at Hélène, whose hair and eyes reminded him of Elena. How much did he dare to tell her? All – or anything? Truth or lies? Would he have somehow to buy her trust, or could he rely on her? What if she was a collaborator? Could he bring himself to kill her if that was the only way of ensuring her silence?

Questions chased each other frantically through his mind as he made small talk about the weather, the shortage of good cider, fishing prospects on the river. Tactfully, no-one mentioned the invasion. Finally, after the third glass of wine, Madame Pontière glanced meaningly at the clock on the mantelpiece.

'Messieurs,' she said softly.

Arngross nodded. He led Antoinette up the stairs. Rigby followed with Hélène. Two small bedrooms opened off the landing. In each, a candle guttered on a dressing table. The curtains were drawn. They paused for a moment.

'Where's the lavatory?' asked Rigby suddenly.

'Nervous?' Arngross asked him, grinning.

Antoinette giggled.

'Downstairs,' she said, and went with Arngross into the nearest bedroom.

Rigby ran down the stairs. Madame Pontière had overheard his question and was already holding open the door of the closet for him.

197

Inside he saw the flimsy bolt that turned a disc marked 'Libre' or 'Occupé' on the outside of the door. The room was very narrow, with a small open window. Through this Rigby could see the outline of sheds and buildings. A narrow alley twisted away between them. As he went upstairs and into Hélène's bedroom, he glanced at his watch: 22.55 hours. If the barges came past La Roche Guyon at a quarter to each hour, as they had done on the previous two occasions he had timed them, he must make haste.

'How long have we got?' he asked Hélène, trying to keep all urgency out of his voice.

'As long as you wish, Monsieur. Up to an hour.'

She had already taken off her scarf. Now she pulled her sweater over her head and sat on the edge of the bed, looking absurdly young and strangely defenceless in a white brassiere. Rigby sat down beside her. His heart beat like a drum, not from desire, but from the thought that freedom could lie only minutes away.

'Are you French or German?' he asked her conversationally.

'French, of course. Why do you ask?'

'Because I need your help.'

Hélène looked puzzled.

'How can I help you?' she asked. 'You want to do some special thing?'

'A special thing, yes, but not as you mean it. I have to get out of here.'

'I am displeasing to you?'

She frowned at him.

'No, of course not. Quite the reverse. You are extremely attractive. But you must listen to me. This is serious. I am not a free man. I am virtually a captive. This officer is my escort. My only hope of escape was to suggest that we both came here – because he is in one room and I am here with you. If I can climb out of a back window, I will have a start.'

'But why? You are not a German officer?'

'No,' said Rigby. 'I'm not an officer at all.'

'Who are you, then? You are not French, I think?'

'No,' Rigby admitted. 'I am not French, either. Now tell me something about yourself. Are you Catholic?'

'Yes.'

'So is my mother,' said Rigby. 'And I swear by all she holds holy, by the cross, and everything in which she believes, that what I am telling you is true. I cannot say too much because it is better for you not to know. But I *must* get away. If I don't, they will kill me.'

Hélène looked at him with suspicion and surprise. All this was so far beyond the limited spectrum of her experience that it also lay outside all boundaries of her belief. Rigby saw this, and cursed himself for not realising it before. He must think of a story she could accept. He would tell her the truth; at least, a part of the truth.

'I am from England. I was working with the French Resistance, and was captured outside Bayeux. I am being taken to Paris tomorrow. To the Gestapo.'

'But the officer seems on good terms with you? He toasted you like a friend.'

'He is my guard. They have kept me here in the Castle to find out how much I know about various matters. But now the Gestapo will deal with me. I cannot face that. You must know what it means. Please, will you help me?'

'How can I help you?'

'By staying here in this room. When the officer wants to know where I am, say we spent some time together, then I felt unwell and had to go to the lavatory. As I have already been there, you realised that I was not well. So you waited – and you went on waiting. I told him on the way here I had pains in my stomach, so he won't think anything odd. Not at first, anyway. Nothing will happen to you – if you stick to that story.'

'Is this true, or is it a trap? My father was in the French army. A sergeant. He was a prisoner-of-war in Germany. I have a friend in the Resistance, at Mantes.'

'Then, for his sake, for your father's sake, help me,' said Rigby. 'It *is* true, *all* of it, I swear it is. I have only a little money, but you can have that now, if you wish.'

The girl shook her head.

'No. Visitors pay Madame afterwards. And if you are who you say you are, she would not take the money anyhow. Nor would I. It is little enough I have to do.'

'Believe me, my dear,' said Rigby earnestly. 'It is everything.'

'You mean that, you really mean that?'

Hélène stood up, smiling proudly. Rigby was very close to her. On the impulse, he put his hands on her bare shoulders, drew her to him, and kissed her gently. Her lips were warm, and for a moment he wanted her, not as a whore, but as a girl he could like; someone to whom his heart warmed, who had heeded his plea and would help him, disregarding all risk to herself. Then he released her. There was a time to love and a time to leave. He moved towards the door.

'May God go with you and keep you safe,' said Hélène softly, as he opened it. In the candlelight Rigby could see that her eyes were bright. With tears – or excitement?

'Amen,' said Rigby. 'And I thank you with all my heart.'

He began to walk down the stairs. Madame Pontière heard him and came out of her back room.

'Is everything all right, Monsieur? You want water, a wash?'

'No, thank you. Unfortunately, I have a touch of the gripe.'

The woman made sympathetic noises and retreated into her room. Rigby heard a band play a fanfare; she was listening to the wireless. That should help to obliterate any noise he made. He went into the lavatory, pushed home that bolt and then listened with his ear against the door. Nothing, except the faint sound of the band. He pulled the chain, in case she was also listening, climbed on the lavatory seat, heaved his way up and through the window and jumped down on to the ground outside. It was easier than he had anticipated; the waiting had been far worse than the action.

On either side loomed buildings and backs of houses. Madame Pontiere's wireless chattered; now a studio audience laughed dutifully at the jokes of a French comedian.

Rigby waited until he was certain no-one had heard him jump, for he did not wish a window to be thrown open and hear someone shout a challenge to him. Then he walked cautiously along the alley towards the road. He heard a growl from an unseen dog, the angry cry of a cat he disturbed amid rubbish, but nothing else.

The road was empty. He crossed it quickly, before any sentry or bicycle patrol could appear and order him to halt. He went down the track marked 'Sauf aux Riverains', along which he and Arngross had strolled on the previous day, still walking. A fully dressed running man can look suspicious at dusk; by the same token and at the same time, a walker generally appears harmless.

He reached the river bank and waited under the trees, holding his breath while he listened for the sound of barge or tug engines. There was nothing save the sound of the running river. He cursed the fact that the evening was still so light; he could be seen from half a mile away. The path by the riverside was deserted, and yet somehow he felt uneasy. How often on an exercise in the hills around Aberdovey had he waited just like this, sensing rather than seeing someone else also waiting and watching, just as carefully, just as quietly? He counted thirty. There was still no sign, no sound of anyone. His breathing relaxed. He had been imagining danger when there was none. He was tense and over-wrought.

A German sentry climbed the steps of the platform, stood for a moment in silhouette against the shining expanse of water, spat into the river, turned and walked slowly back up the Rue du Docteur Duval.

Rigby turned his face towards Paris again, straining his ears. In the distance, very faintly, he heard the thrum of an approaching engine. This must be a barge. He checked his watch; 20 minutes to midnight. More confident now, Rigby stepped out from the shelter of the trees.

A voice ten yards away, said in surprise: 'Why, Nimrod, I thought you were – ah – otherwise engaged!'

Mannheim was standing only feet away; he had been walking along the path by the edge of the river. If Rigby had stayed where he was, the man might have passed by without seeing him. He wore a soft felt hat, and kept both hands in the pockets of his raincoat.

'You are not supposed to be out on your own,' Mannheim said reproachfully, as though addressing an invalid who was wilfully disobeying a doctor's orders.

'But I'm not on my own, Herr Mannheim. You're here. And Arngross is just up this road. He is only a few metres behind me.'

The sound of the engine was coming nearer. Within minutes, the barge would be around the bend of the river; and he had still to swim out and meet it in full daylight. *Oh hear, Oh Israel* . . .

'A teletype has just come in about you,' Mannheim went on. 'We have to be in Paris very early tomorrow morning for a meeting. I've told my driver we will leave here at midnight.'

'Why the change in plans?'

Rigby's surprise showed in his voice. At the back of his consciousness, he heard the beat of the engine, thumping like an iron heart, steadily growing louder. In minutes, the barge would be opposite him and then the engine noise would fade and he would have missed his chance. He would have to wait for another hour for the next barge.

And in sixty minutes how many other problems could arise? Who else might find him here?

'I suppose they've just realised how important your information is. How important you are – or maybe they want to question you about some little things.'

'What little things?'

Rigby took a pace towards Mannheim as he asked the question. His throat felt so constricted, he did not recognise his own voice. He heard the question as though someone else was asking it.

Mannheim still stood, hands in his pockets. Was he gripping a gun? Rigby would have to take that chance. Behind him, the drone of the engine was much louder, almost at its peak, but he did not dare to look towards it. Instead, he nodded back towards the track along which he had walked from the main road.

'Ah, Arngross,' he called, as though the captain was approaching, and waved his arm.

'Here's Mannheim, just arrived.'

Mannheim glanced momentarily in the direction of the track.

Rigby hit him then, hard, with the edge of his right hand, across the front of his neck, as he had practised so often in Wales. Mannheim staggered, reeled and fell. As he dropped, the muscles of his fingers tightened in a reflex action. He squeezed the trigger of the pistol he had been holding in the pocket of his raincoat. The bullet scored Rigby's right arm beneath his elbow. He felt a sharp searing pain as though he had burned himself, then numbness and a sudden pumping warmth in his sleeve from his own blood.

He bent down, dragged Mannheim's body to the edge of the river, rolled it down the slope into the water, cursing its weight and his useless arm, hoping, praying that the sentry would not return to the platform and see him. Then he walked down into the water himself and began to swim towards the centre of the river.

The water was bitingly cold. His right arm ached and throbbed, and he felt weak and sick from reaction and loss of blood. Also, the current was far stronger than it had appeared from the bank. The river's chill drove breath from his body and numbed his muscles. The cold seemed to be throttling him. He gasped and gritted his teeth to stop them champing together.

The current steadily carried him down towards the stone platform. He struck out with the strength of despair towards the middle of the river. If the sentry saw him now he was dead, but if he missed the barge he would be as good as dead, for someone must find Mannheim before the next barges were due.

He stopped swimming for a moment and trod water, listening for the approaching grumble of the engine. Thirty yards away; twenty; ten. The bows of the leading barge suddenly loomed up, black as a moving wall, edged with a thin arrow-head of foam. What if someone saw him? Would they raise the alarm, or think he was just a harmless swimmer enjoying an evening swim? It was too late to think of that possibility now.

Feet away from him the barge's propeller thrashed the river until the powerful wash overwhelmed him. He gasped for breath, blinded by the huge rush and weight of water. Then the second barge went past, and the third approached. Only the first had her engine running; she was towing the other two.

Rigby swam now as if in a race, forcing his way through the wash until his outstretched left hand grazed the rough carbuncled metal of the third hull. As this moved past him he saw the huge rudder tower above him, high as a barn door. Two vertical metal supports held it upright. With a last leap, he gripped the nearest one.

The pull of the barge almost dislocated his shoulder. He held on grimly while the wash poured over his head. Then he turned on his back and, body fully extended, let the barge drag him through the water like a piece of driftwood. He drew up his legs beneath him, and managed to place the instep of his right foot on one of the lower braces around the rudder. Now, half standing, some of his weight was released from his arm. He raised his head above the water and looked about him.

The barges were moving in close to the left bank, where trees formed a thick dark screen. To the right, he could see the white cliffs behind the castle, the donjon on top, and the houses perched near the gaping tunnel mouths in the cliff. He wished he were on the other side of the barge so that he would be shielded from anyone on the road beneath the cliff, but he was too weak to move. It was all he could do to hold on where he was.

He glanced at his watch; thank God it was waterproof. Two minutes to midnight. He had perhaps twenty minutes, at the most half an hour, while Arngross desperately searched for him, not wishing – or maybe not daring – to admit to anyone that he had disappeared. Then

Arngross would have to report he was missing. Poor Arngross. Rigby almost felt sorry for him – until he remembered his own predicament.

Arngross opened his bedroom door and walked down the stairs, whistling to himself. Madame Pontière was waiting in the hall. He gave her a folded note. She did not even look at it.

'Delightful girl,' Arngross said insincerely. Madame Pontière bowed slightly.

'And my friend?' he asked her.

'He came down to the toilet, monsieur. Twice. I do not think he is well.'

'Ah. I remember after dinner he said he had some stomach trouble. Probably something he's eaten.'

Arngross knocked on the closet door. The circular celluloid disc on the outside read 'Occupé'.

'You all right in there?'

There was no answer. Arngross turned the handle, but the door was bolted. Perhaps Nimrod had collapsed. Maybe his stomach pains were serious. Arngross examined the disc on the door. In the centre was a square hole so that, in such an emergency, the door could be opened from the outside. He asked Madame Pontière to bring him a screwdriver, inserted the blade and turned the handle. The bolt slid back. He opened the door gently, in case Nimrod had collapsed behind it, but the lavatory was empty.

'He must have gone upstairs again,' said Madame Pontière in a puzzled voice.

'But the door was bolted. You saw it.'

'It is loose, that bolt. If you give the door a bang, it can lock itself.'

Arngross felt immeasurably relieved. For a terrible moment, he thought that Nimrod had deliberately left him. He waited politely for five more minutes, hoping that he would appear, then walked up the stairs and knocked at Hélène's door.

'Yes?' Hélène answered immediately.

'It is time for us to go. My friend all right, eh?'

'Your friend?'

Her voice sounded thin and nervous.

'Is anything the matter?' he asked urgently. 'Where is he?'

There was no reply. Arngross opened the door. Hélène stood by the bed, fully dressed. Her face in the candlelight was very pale. Arngross noted that the bedclothes were rumpled. He glanced underneath the bedstead, in case Nimrod was hiding there as a joke.

'Where the devil is he?'

'He went downstairs, monsieur. He was not well.'

Madame Pontière had come upstairs now. As he looked at them both, a horrible feeling, compounded of panic, resentment and dis-belief that this could be happening to him, started in his stomach and swept through his body. His gut burned like fire.

'Perhaps he was embarrassed and returned to the Castle, monsieur?' suggested Madame Pontière.

Perhaps that was so. Oh, God, make that be true.

'You didn't see or hear him go, either of you?'

'No, monsieur.'

The two women shook their heads gravely.

Arngross ran along the Rue d'Audience to the castle. The choir was still singing in the church; their voices now sounded mocking. He raced up the stairs to Rigby's room. It was empty, the bedclothes neatly turned down. A toothbrush and shaving soap, with razor and flannel cloth were on the wash-stand. A towel was neatly folded on a rail. He must have intended to return, surely? He found the orderly in his pantry.

'Have you seen our visitor?' he asked him breathlessly.

'Before dinner, sir. Said he wasn't feeling too good. He was going out with you and would be late back. Asked me about reporting sick in the morning.'

Something terrible had happened to Nimrod; that was certain. The Resistance must have discovered who he was and had seized him. Those bloody girls and Madame Pontière must have been involved.

Arngross took a deep breath. He could no longer delay what he had to do. He knocked on the office door of the colonel of Intelligence.

'Well?'

The colonel looked up irritably. His eyes were red through reading too many reports: he had been on duty since dawn. What the devil did this fat oaf want now, at such a time?

'I have to report, sir, that Nimrod is not in his room.'

'What? But it is your duty to see he *is* in his room. Where have you been?'

'We went out together, sir. To see some friends in La Roche Guyon.'

'You have only been here a couple of days. What friends have you got here?'

'Two girls, sir.'

'And?'

'Well, I was with one girl, sir. He was with the other. She tells me he said he felt ill.'

'Felt ill?' the colonel repeated slowly, thinking back over his conversations with Nimrod, the Field Marshal and Mannheim. Had he compromised himself in any way? Had he said anything that might now embroil him, or worse, condemn him? He could not be sure, but he thought he had been careful in all his comments.

'Don't just stand there,' he told Arngross irritably. 'Tell the duty officer to turn out the guard to search for this man. Warn every sentry post. Find out whether anyone has seen him pass through alone, or with others. Someone may have kidnapped him. I warned you of that danger. Have the local gendarmes interview these girls. They may have friends in the Resistance.'

'He was in the next room, sir. Close to me as I am to you. Only separated by a thin wall.'

The colonel looked at him balefully, unwilling to admit that the unthinkable could possibly be true; that Nimrod had run away. This could only mean that he was not genuine, but working for the enemy. This, in turn, would mean that his information was totally false. But even as these terrible thoughts crossed his mind, he consoled himself that they could not possibly be true. Too many other sources of information had agreed with Nimrod's news. Thank God for that.

'Damn it, he can't get far,' the colonel said gruffly. 'He hasn't any papers, or a change of clothes, or even a bicycle. My bet is he's been lifted. Order every vehicle to be stopped and searched.'

Arngross turned to go. The colonel called him back.

'And, remember,' he added softly, 'this is entirely your responsibility.'

# Chapter Eighteen

The drone and thump of the barge engine changed its tone slightly. They were turning more strongly to the left. As the vessel swung, Rigby could see a bridge across the river; this must be Bonnières. He would swim ashore here. He did not know how far away the next town might be, or even what it was called, and he could not hold on for much longer with one hand, for the cold water was eating into his bones like acid. The marrow ached and his joints seemed locked together, his whole body rigid. The barge turned even farther to the left, and was now running close inshore, passing an island in the middle of the river.

As the barge came level with the bridge, Rigby released his hold. He sank immediately and then rose sluggishly in his waterlogged clothes. The bridge arched above him, a deeper dark than the darkening sky. For a moment he drifted, turning with the current, weak from his wound and exposure, unable to coordinate his thoughts. Then he saw factory chimneys and knew he must aim in their direction. He began to swim, holding his right arm close to his body. This way, he took a long time to reach the reeds and mud of the river banks. He crawled slowly out of the water and lay down on the grass, sobbing for breath, trembling uncontrollably with cold. He pulled off his jacket painfully and wrung out the water, and did the same with his trousers. Then he rolled up his soaking right shirt sleeve and examined his arm. Mannheim's bullet had sliced his flesh on the edge of a muscle.

The pain was greater now, but the river had washed the wound clean. He tore his pocket handkerchief into three strips, joined them together and bound up his arm. He should have brought a field dressing with him. He would remember that for next time. Next time? This time had not ended yet, and he still had nearly 100 miles to travel in soaking clothes and without any identification papers. Loss of blood made him feel slightly light-headed. He sat shivering, trying to overcome his weakness. He remembered his benzedrine tablets and swallowed one of them. Then he put two Horlicks tablets in his mouth to chew, and tried to concentrate on his next move.

With any luck, the searchers would first examine the roads around La Roche Guyon. He could not possibly have reached this far on foot. But someone was bound to find Mannheim either alive or dead, and then it would be clear that he had taken to the river. The time that the barges came past might be remembered, and the search would widen at once. He had to move as far as he could, as fast as he could.

Rigby searched around the reeds and found a branch about five feet long to serve as a walking stick, and maybe a weapon. If he was challenged for being out after curfew, he decided to say he was German. This would be safer than to pretend he was French, which could only lead to questions, and without any papers he was liable to be arrested.

On the railway line near the river bank, signals changed from red to green. A goods engine pulled a long line of clanking trucks, each covered by shiny black tarpaulins, going north towards Cherbourg. From the slow, heavy puff-puff of the engine, he guessed that it had just started. This meant that the station would be fairly near, and on the left or Paris side of the bridge.

He started to walk up the bank and along the road. His clothes were still wet and clung to his body, rubbing his legs raw. He struck out as briskly as he could to try and generate warmth to dry them. He kept his right hand in his jacket pocket because to swing the arm caused the wound to open. The benzedrine began to have some effect; he felt slightly more cheerful and confident. At least the waiting was behind him.

The houses were set far back from the road, the Avenue de la République. All were in darkness because of the blackout and the pavements were deserted. Soon the houses dwindled and ahead lay the main road to Paris, lined with tall trees on either side. To the left he saw a small tarmac road, perhaps 200 yards long, running between houses. It led to a square roughcast building, festooned with telegraph wires: the station. He walked towards it.

A blue enamelled metal plate with the name *Bonnières* in white letters was nailed to a wall. Near this were two other boards: *Direction-Paris,* and opposite, *Direction-Rouen.* The station seemed neat and well cared for. The door to the ticket office was edged with bricks painted red; the window shutters were pale blue. He decided to find a goods train bound inland for Paris and then change somewhere along the line and come back towards Rouen. That would be safer than trying to jump a train starting from here for Rouen, which would be more likely to be searched. He could not remember exactly where Rouen was, and it was too dark to activate his silk handkerchief map, but at least it was on the way to the coast, in the right direction. He reached the station building and paused. The town, so far as he could judge in the deepening dusk, lay in a valley. A church tower covered in ivy had a weather-cock on top in the shape of a cockerel with an unusually large tail. In front of the station, someone had built an oval flower bed and ringed it with stones. Beyond this was a siding, with lines of trucks and railway carriages. Railway sleepers striped in red and white marked the end of these sidings. An unseen shunting engine hissed steam in the gloom.

As Rigby began to thread his way past the carriages, the engine started to move. Men shouted orders in hoarse voices. There came a clank and crash of metal buffers as trucks ran loose and hit others, behind or ahead. Rigby crawled beneath a stationary carriage as a man came down, expertly coupling up some trucks, uncoupling others with a hook on the end of a pole.

When he had passed, Rigby climbed up on the buffers of the nearest truck. The tarpaulin cover was roped down so tightly he could not raise it with his one good hand. He tried the next one; this was also impossible to loosen, so he opened the door of a brake van. Inside, was a strong smell of axle grease and coal dust, but he sat down thankfully on the gritty floor, back against the wall, and closed his eyes.

He was on the Paris side, he knew. So far, it had been easy enough. Too easy, he told himself. The Skipper would never have let him get away so lightly on an exercise or 'scheme'. Why should he expect to now, when a real enemy was searching for him? He must have made a miscalculation somewhere, he agreed, but the benzedrine made him feel absurdly cheerful and euphoric. Suddenly, he heard voices speaking German and moving down the line. Men were tearing tarpaulins from the trucks. A man was protesting loudly in French.

'There is no-one here, I tell you.'

'How can you be sure?' asked the German. 'A prisoner has made a dash for it. He's dangerous. He must be found.'

The van that had seemed such a safe sanctuary now became a trap. Rigby's self confidence evaporated. He opened the door carefully, jumped down and ran on the tips of his toes – because he made less noise that way – towards the shelter of the station building. From where he stood, he watched half a dozen German soldiers with carbines and torches peer into every truck. Another few minutes and he could have been discovered, defenceless except for a stick.

Several military bicycles were propped against the wall. They must belong to the soldiers, because he had not seen them when he arrived. He had less time than he had realised. Somewhere, something had gone wrong. Perhaps Mannheim had regained consciousness in the cold water and raised the alarm, or maybe Arngross had reported his disappearance. Either way, he was now being hunted, and his pursuers were literally only yards away.

Rigby walked away from the station, as quickly as he could, without appearing to hurry. If anyone saw him he hoped they would think he was a railway worker going home. He reached the main road and then turned left towards Mantes and Paris. He trusted that the Germans would think he had instinctively headed towards the coast.

The main N13 was empty of all traffic. Houses on either side were few and spaced apart, shuttered and dark. Some had a coloured tile on a front gatepost with a warning picture of a barking dog. He hurried past such signs in case the dog did bark. At ten minutes to each hour, he stopped, as he had learned in the Army, and rested for ten minutes, lying flat under a hedge.

Just before dawn, when the effects of the benzedrine had almost disappeared, and the pain of his wound had increased to the point that his whole body seemed tortured, he went into a wood to the right of the road and lay down thankfully on the damp grass. From here, he could see a stretch of road. Several lorries were now on the move, mostly German army vehicles. Once, a convoy of trucks went north in low gear. But in the thick grass he felt secure, for he was sure that no-one could see him from the road.

He must have dozed, because suddenly he was alert. His clothes felt stiff like cardboard on his tired body; his feet had swelled painfully in his sodden shoes. The sun shone brightly through the trees, and in the sunlight an old woman was walking very slowly. She stopped to pick up twigs and small broken branches, putting them carefully into a small canvas bag she carried. She had no teeth and her skin had sunk in on her face. She looked very feeble and poor. Rigby tried to roll under a clump of ferns he had not seen when he lay down, but she noticed the movement, and came towards him, and stood, looking down at him. Her face was totally without expression; he might have been a log. He was at her mercy, in her power. He had nothing to lose now, he thought. His best defence must be truth, or as much of it as she might believe.

'Madame,' he said in French, struggling to stand up. 'I am a member of the Resistance. From Bayeux. I have been wounded.'

He held up his right arm. Blood had seeped through his handkerchief and trickled down to dry on the back of his hand. He felt light-headed and slightly feverish.

'Can you let me have some food? I have money to pay for it.'

'Can you walk?' she asked him.

Rigby nodded.

'Follow me then. About fifty metres behind. But if you see anyone, keep on walking.'

They reached a cottage in the forest without seeing anyone. Three chickens pecked in a dusty patch of earth behind wire netting. He followed her into the only downstairs room. She locked the front door behind him. He sat down on a chair, resting his arms on the table. She took out some pieces of wood from her bag and put them into the stove. She moved slowly, ponderously, beyond any need for haste.

'I can give you some soup and an egg – if the chickens have laid this morning. And a little bread. How much money have you?'

'How much do you want?' Rigby asked, and instantly regretted his reply. Avarice gleamed in her old eyes under their wrinkled lids.

'Ten francs.'

'All right,' he said. This was more than he would have wished, but he was in no position to bargain. He pulled a sodden ten-franc note from the back pocket of his trousers and pushed it towards her across the table. She placed it on a metal plate on top of the stove to dry.

'The Germans give a reward for information about people like you,' she remarked conversationally, as though this was of no concern to either of them.

'You would not take blood money, would you?'

'I am poor. I need any money. How much more have you got?'

'A little more, but I must keep some to get to Bayeux.'

Again he realised too late he had said too much. That damned benzedrine and his loss of blood had loosened his tongue. He should have said, Paris, Lyons, anywhere else. He must be more careful, far more circumspect.

'Another ten francs and I will not tell anyone about you.'

'Let me eat first.'

She went out into the yard, brought back a brown egg, put it into a pan of hot water to boil, stirred some soup in another pot on the stove. He ate quickly.

'Your watch, monsieur. That is worth a great deal.'

'I can't let that go, madame,' Rigby replied. 'Here's ten francs. For your help and your silence.'

He put a second note on the plate. She sat looking at him, and then at the money. Rigby wolfed down the last mouthful of bread, pulled off his jacket and looked at his wound. It was raw and painful, but not septic. He dried the handkerchief on top of the stove and then replaced it. She did not offer him anything else to bind his arm, and he did not wish to ask her. He could not afford to give her any more money. He put on his jacket, still steaming and damp and uncomfortable.

'Thank you,' he said. 'You have quite possibly saved my life.'

She did not reply, but came to the door and stood watching him out of sight. He walked farther into the wood until she could no longer see him, and then carried on for another thirty yards before he turned, unscrewed his jacket button and checked with his compass. He needed to head back through roughly 100 degrees to reach the main road.

He could not walk along the road, because drivers of cars and trucks might see him and remember his appearance. Also, he was more likely to meet German patrols or gendarmes who would ask to see his papers, and he dare not run this risk. He crouched down behind some gorse bushes near the road on a long slow hill rising towards Paris.

German army lorries climbing it could keep a good pace, but French civilian lorries, towing small trailers of logs for their gas producing plants, found the hill a major test of strength. Clouds of black sooty smoke blew out of their exhausts as their engines wheezed and laboured in low gear, making ten miles an hour at the most.

He waited until he saw one of these old French trucks approaching. It was piled with potatoes under a net. As the truck passed Rigby, the driver slowed to walking pace to engage bottom gear for the hill. Rigby ran out behind the vehicle where the driver could not see him. Then he climbed up over the right rear mudguard and sat down on the pile of potatoes. He gripped the net with his good hand as the lorry shuddered on. He thought it safer to sit upright, as though a labourer entitled to be there, rather than to attempt to conceal himself.

About eight kilometres nearer Paris, they passed a large statue at the left of the roadside. It was of Sully, a 16th century duke at the court of Henry of Navarre. He stood in silhouette against the fields, and what was more important to Rigby was that he remembered that Sully had been born near Mantes, so they must be very close to this town. The truck slowed briefly for the driver to disengage bottom gear. The road lay empty in both directions, so Rigby jumped down, raced across it and threw himself flat in the ditch. The lorry moved on, and out of his life.

Rigby crawled through a hedge and lay on the other side at the edge of a field of cows. He would have to wait here until darkness. It would be too risky trying to move into Mantes during daylight hours. After dark, he risked the curfew, but then at least night would be on his side. He took off his jacket, turned the sleeves inside out and spread it on the ground to dry. He broke off some small branches and tore up weeds by the roots. Then he lay down, spread these over himself for conceal-ment, and waited patiently for sleep and dusk.


Captain Arngross stood smartly to attention in the Intelligence colonel's office at La Roche Guyon. His face was pale and strained and his stomach burned as though it had been branded. The innumerable glasses of bismuth and water he had gulped down during the night had been powerless to relieve his agony.

'We have alerted every army unit within a radius of thirty kilo-meters with a full description of Nimrod, sir,' he reported stiffly. 'Nothing to report so far.'

'Depends what you mean by nothing,' retorted the colonel.

'Herr Mannheim would undoubtedly have drowned if two soldiers walking to their billets along the river bank hadn't seen him in the water. He says Nimrod attacked him. One bullet has been fired from his pistol, apparently through his pocket, so he may have hit him, but we just don't know. What we do know is that Nimrod has vanished.

·'I gave you explicit orders that he was to be kept under complete surveillance *at all times*. I made you personally responsible for him. And what did you do? On the evening the enemy lands in France, you

213

take him off to a bawdy-house. And while you are fornicating in one room, he is disappearing from another.'

'I am sure he did not go voluntarily, sir,' protested Arngross.

'So you have already said. But how does that tie up with what Mannheim says? And the whore says he left her voluntarily. Of course, she could be lying, and Mannheim might be mistaken. Either, or. But not both, Arngross. He has gone – and, curiously, on the eve of his interrogation in Paris.

'Here is a man who risked his life to come here from England with information of the highest value – which I may say has been acted on by the OKW under the Führer's own personal orders – and now he has totally disappeared.'

As the colonel paused for breath, there was a discreet knock at the door. An orderly entered with a folder of paper, which he placed on the desk. Instinctively, from long habit, the colonel opened the folder. Arngross stood, still at attention, eyes downcast. He heard the colonel give an exclamation of amazement and then he stood up and crossed the room to a wall map behind his desk. The colonel's face was very grave.

'An American landing craft has been washed up here on the Vire estuary near Gefosse-Fontenay, the area of the 439th "East" battalion,' he began conversationally, as though he had forgotten his previous anger at Arngross. 'A number of dead American naval officers were aboard. One was a beachmaster, responsible for landing arrangements on that particular beach. Under his body our people found a case of papers, waterlogged and stained with blood. They were taken to Division and then on to 84th Corps headquarters to be translated. Do you know what they were?'

'No, sir,' said Arngross.

'Invasion plans. Not only for VII US Corps, to which that landing craft belonged, but also for V US Corps and XXX British Corps. There is no question about it, Normandy *is* the main invasion.

'These papers describe in detail how the Americans plan to link up what they call their Utah and Omaha beach-heads at Carentan, and join the British at Bayeux, so they will then have a vast beach-head. The VIIth plan to go through to the west of the Cotentin peninsula to Coutances to consolidate their position, and then move north to capture Cherbourg.

'This information is so urgent that Corps have not even used a teletype, but have risked sending it by wireless. The original papers are on their way here to Field Marshal Rommel by officer's hand. You-know what this means, don't you?'

Arngross said nothing. His mouth was dry. All blood seemed to have drained from his body. Like a man in a nightmare, he heard the colonel's voice.

'It means we have all been totally deceived as to Allied invasion intentions. They are not concerned with Calais, but with Normandy. We have all been deliberately misled, the Führer, OKW, OB West and ourselves.

'I don't know how these papers tie up with our aerial photographs of the build-up opposite Calais, and what our agents in England have been telling us for months. Maybe Nimrod could tell us – or be made to tell us. No wonder he was so eager to get away. But he cannot have travelled far and he must be found, alive or dead.'

The colonel paused.

'And so far as you and I are concerned in all this,' he added, 'he would be very much better dead.'


When Rigby awoke, dusk dimmed his view of distant woods and shrouded the fields. The evening was chilly and every joint in his body ached. His wound felt raw and tender.

He put on his jacket, still slightly damp, climbed through the hedge, and set out along the road. Only a very few lorries were moving now, with dim, masked headlights. The noise of their engines as they approached gave him ample time to drop into the ditch and wait until they had passed. So at last, weary and cold, he came into the outskirts of Mantes la Jolie. There seemed nothing beautiful about it, so why its name? he wondered. But Mantes would indeed be beautiful if it offered him the chance of escape.

The road was unusually wide, reminding him of roads he had seen in Canada. He followed the sign, 'La Gare,' past a station hotel, the Hôtel de Paris, and along an approach road. A police station was on the left and then the road curved around in front of the station buildings. A subway connected seven platforms. He avoided this, glanced around him to make sure he was unobserved and then climbed over a spiked railing into the goods yard. He could see notices on the platforms indicating that trains from there went to Caen, Ivry or Cherbourg.

The platforms were very wide; one had a strip of grass growing in the centre, like a long lawn, edged with flowers.

He ignored the *Passage interdit au Public* warning and crossed the lines on the parallel sleepers laid between them. He walked purposefully, as though he was on official business and had the right to be there. He was now among trucks and maroon painted carriages, with the distinctive railway smells of smoke and soot and axle grease.

A goods engine shunted somewhere out of sight, with a clash and squeal of buffers. Now and then, a railway worker shouted instructions in French. Rigby traced the Cherbourg line from its platform to a set of points that ran off into the siding. A string of trucks waited near these points; he would have to take the risk they would eventually be connected to a Cherbourg train. He began to walk down the line of trucks, looking for one with a loose tarpaulin.

He paused for a moment – and two hands gripped both his arms from behind and twisted them up sharply against his back. He screamed from the pain of his wound.

'Who are you?' he cried in French.

'Railway police,' a man answered. He shone a masked torch, and seeing the blood on Rigby's hand, released his right arm. 'Who are you?'

Rigby turned. Two stocky men faced him. He could not make out their uniforms because of the poor light, but one held a carbine.

'What are you doing in the goods yard at this hour?'

'Special security detachment,' replied Rigby in German. They were the first words he thought of that sounded vaguely official.

'Tell me another. Your papers?'

The railwayman still spoke in French.

'I don't carry papers for this sort of work.'

'Who are you working with – or for?'

The second man spoke in German.

'You must know if you are German. Security.'

'Security?' The man's disbelief sounded in his voice. 'Come up to the office. There's one in the station now. Been so much sabotage here these last few weeks.'

Holding Rigby by his left arm, they marched him along the tracks, up the slope at the end of the platform, to a concrete hut. The German knocked respectfully on the door. Inside, a light switch clicked. The door opened. All three went into the hut. The light came on as soon as the blackout was secure. A plump man, wearing a grey double-breasted suit too tight for him, went back to his chair behind a heavy railway table. A plate of bread and cheese was on the table with a flagon of cider. He was eating his supper.

'Who's this?' he asked, in German, mouth full, looking with distaste at Rigby.

'We found him walking along the side of the trucks, sir. Seemed to be looking for one with a loose cover,' the German explained. In the light, his uniform was unmistakably SS. Rigby cursed himself for not being more careful before he entered the goods yard. He recalled one of The Skipper's rules: 'Time spent in reconnaissance is seldom wasted.' Why hadn't he acted on that, instead of behaving as though he had every right to be there?

'Says he is with a special security detachment,' the German continued.

'Never heard of it,' replied the plump man.

He turned to Rigby.

'I am a leutnant in the SS Plain clothes duty. Who are you?'

Rigby took a deep breath and drew himself up to his full height, oblivious of his wound and his grotesque, unshaven appearance. One telephone call, and this officer could learn that the authorities in La Roche Guyon were searching for a man of his description. But if he could stop him making that one call, then he might still be in with a chance. He looked with annoyance at the SS soldier and the railwayman who had discovered him.

'Did you hear my question?' the officer asked Rigby sharply.

'Of course I heard it. And it will pay you to speak more civilly, leutnant. I am a colonel attached to the SD.* While these two idiots have been bringing me here, I may tell you that one of the most wanted Allied agents in France is very likely to have got away.'

Rigby held up his wounded arm.

'I have a personal reason for wishing to catch him. He shot me in the elbow.'

Rigby sounded so autocratic and military, his voice had the right harshness of thwarted authority, that the leutnant changed his attitude.

'I heard the army was looking for someone who had escaped custody,' he admitted. 'Thought he was an armed deserter. I didn't

---

* S.D. Sicherheitsdienst, Security Service.

know he was a spy. But I must have proof who you are.'

'I might say the same about you, leutnant,' Rigby retorted. 'I'll prove who I am all right. But get these two men out of here first. This is an "officers only" matter.'

'Leave,' ordered the leutnant. The two others did so, but with reluctance; a slanging match between a colonel and a leutnant would be good to witness.

'Now lock the door,' Rigby told him. 'This is a subject of the highest security.'

'Where are your papers?' the leutnant persisted.

'Do you imagine I carry papers when I am on this sort of work? Might as well go about in big boots and a peaked cap.'

The SS leutnant was not listening. He was looking at Rigby's shabby unshaven appearance; he saw the dried blood on his right hand and the clothes that had been soaked and slept in.

'The man the army is looking for is also thought to be injured – like you,' he said slowly. 'An old woman living in the forest several kilometres south has reported how a man answering to your description claimed he told her he was a member of the French Resistance from Bayeux, and threatened her until she gave him some food. I don't think you are a colonel or anything to do with the SD. I think you are this man.'

'Think what you damn well like,' shouted Rigby angrily. 'But before you drop yourself too far in the mire, leutnant, I order you to telephone Paris. They will explain the whole thing, and save you a lot of embarrassment – at the least.

'Where in Paris?'

'The office, of course. Rue des Saussaies. A personal call to Herr Mannheim. He will vouch for me. He is head of section. You know the number?'

'I should do.'

The leutnant picked up the telephone and asked the operator for the unlisted number. When someone answered in Paris, he turned away from Rigby as though to keep his conversation secret.

'Who are you speaking to?' Rigby asked him. He could not afford to allow him to speak for too long; he could so easily be trapped if he did.

'The duty officer. No-one called Mannheim on that exchange. Never even heard of him.'

'Give me the 'phone,' said Rigby in a resigned voice, and pulled it

218

out of the leutnant's hand before he could object.

'Colonel Rosenberg speaking,' Rigby said briskly, using the first name he could think of, which happened to be his own. 'Can you give me Herr Mannheim's number, if he's not there?'

'I have a special service directory here, sir. If you will wait a moment, I will look it up.'

'Thank you.'

The leutnant picked up a piece of bread and put it in his mouth. Some crumbs stuck to his fingers. He licked them clean.

Rigby held out the telephone to him.

'They want to speak to you.'

'Me?'

The leutnant looked surprised, and still licking his fingers of one hand, stretched out his other hand for the instrument. As he stood, with both arms away from his body, Rigby hit him as hard as he could in the solar plexus. He put all his weight and training behind the blow, all the despair that welled up within him. If this blow failed, he was a dead man.

The leutnant dropped across the desk, and slid clumsily to the floor. Rigby replaced the receiver to cut off the call, then ripped the cord from the wall, and bound it tightly round the German's wrists. He pulled a handkerchief from his pocket and crammed this into his mouth, in case he recovered and tried to call for help.

Rigby picked up the last bit of bread, put it in his own pocket as an iron ration for himself, and took a long draught of the cider. Then he turned off the light, removed the bulb and dropped it into the metal wastepaper basket. The glass shattered instantly. He walked out of the office, locked the door again and pocketed the key.

The two uniformed men were waiting on the platform. Both came to attention as he approached.

'That's settled,' Rigby told them.

'Very sorry about the mistake, sir,' said the German earnestly. 'I didn't realise you were a colonel.'

'You weren't meant to, in these clothes. Now, which is the next goods train to Paris?'

'From this platform, sir. You were actually in the wrong one. You'd have gone to Cherbourg from where we saw you.'

'Thanks. Easy to make a mistake in the dark. When is the Paris train due out?'

'In eight minutes, sir. Next one after that is for Cherbourg.'

'Where are they standing now?'

The man indicated the positions of the waiting trains in the sidings.

'Right. Thank you for putting me right. Now both of you forget you've seen me. There's a very big thing on tonight. We're after one of the most dangerous men in France. If you find anyone else around this station – nab him. Could mean promotion for you both. I'd certainly say a good word for you.'

'Thank you, sir. We heard there was a bit of a scare for someone on the run. Do you think he'll get away?'

'That depends a great deal on you both keeping silent,' replied Rigby gravely, and walked down the platform towards the sidings.

# Chapter Nineteen

The goods train chugged slowly across the flat landscape, as though in no hurry to reach the coast.

Rigby's truck was packed with drums of kerosene. One leaked slightly; the smell became nauseating. He raised one corner of the covering tarpaulin from time to time for fresh air, and to look out at the uninspiring landscape in an attempt to discover exactly where he was. He could see no names of towns on any of the buildings, which were in any case few enough in the featureless expanse of chalky fields. Now and then the train trundled past lakes with islands of rushes and poplar trees; past deserted quarries and small, unattractive houses, miles from any other habitation.

Gradually, the countryside grew lusher and more mellow. The grass appeared greener and richer, with thick hedges and banks. Apple trees were lined up in great orchards. The farmhouses were on a more prosperous scale. Well-fed horses were working in the fields.

He had no idea how far he had travelled, but he knew he could not risk waiting until the train reached its destination, where the trucks would be unloaded. That way, discovery would be virtually certain. He had to leave before then, but where, in daylight? He ate the bread he had taken from the SS leutnant's office and examined his wound. The flesh around the gash was now edged with a fine yellow rim; it was becoming septic. He sucked the wound to try and clean it, then bound his handkerchief once more around his arm.

The train slowed down unexpectedly. Buffers clanged and the shock of sudden braking almost threw Rigby on his back. He carefully lifted one corner of the tarpaulin by two inches. The train was about to stop at a country station with a platform of a peculiar reddish colour. He saw a square, cream-washed building with grey shutters and grey doors. Geraniums grew in boxes at the upper windows. On the facing wall the station's name, *Moult-Argences*, was picked out in white letters on a blue background. There were two other notices: *Direction-Caen* and *Direction-Paris*. He felt reassured that he was travelling in the right direction. Rigby crossed to the other side of the truck and looked along the platform. A workman came out of a small hut half way down it and shouted to the driver.

'What's the matter? You're not due to stop here?'

'We need more water. Pulling about twice the load.'

Two German soldiers now followed the man from the hut, carbines slung over their shoulders. They walked behind him, along the platform to the engine and stood watching while he attached a thick leather sleeve from an overhead supply pipe to the locomotive's water tank.

Rigby calculated – from seeing a similar system replenish engines at Harlech station – that the operation would take several minutes. At such a small station and in the fourth year of war, it was unlikely anyone else would be on duty. This might be as safe a place as any to leave the train.

He lifted the rear of the tarpaulin and climbed out on to the buffers of the truck. Unless someone was standing exactly opposite, they would not see him, for the trucks shielded him.

Rigby regarded with a wry smile a notice that warned against the dangers of crossing the line. For him they were balanced by the dangers of not crossing, of waiting until it was too late to leave.

He dropped down on the line between the rails and crawled as quickly as he could, ducking under each axle, until he was near the rear of the train. He stood up carefully between two long trucks piled with concrete posts. The Paris platform was still empty. Just across the rails he could see a wicket gate and a pedestrian crossing-place that lead to the station yard. He took a deep breath, and walking as casually as he could, as though he crossed here every day, he walked over the line and pushed his way through the gate. He was now hidden from the men on the far platform by the train and the station building.

Washing hung from a line between two apple trees in the little garden. Somewhere in the station house, a baby was crying; he hoped the child would keep the mother occupied so that she did not notice him. On the other side of the yard he could see sidings, where labourers were unloading sacks from open trucks. Some sacks had split and red dust poured out, the colour of blood that had dried in the sun. None of the men seemed to have seen him, or if they had they paid no attention. The station approach was the same colour as the platforms and the dust that spilled from the bags. On the far side was a single storey building, with a red-tiled roof, but shaped like a pagoda. On the wall, yellow and blue tiles spelled out the inscription *Chemin de Fer d'Argences, 1911.*

As Rigby watched, a small goods engine arrived at this building, pulling a row of trucks piled high with red chimney pots and roof tiles and bricks. This must be the dispatch office for a line leading to a pottery or a tile factory. The red dust was probably the factory's raw material.

A labourer uncoupled the engine, which shunted away busily to pull out the empty trucks. Rigby heard the main line goods train on which he had travelled from Mantes start with the great roar of escaping steam and a shudder of wheels slipping on the rails. He could not stay a moment longer in case the soldiers crossed the line and saw him. Shielded by the long line of slowly moving trucks he crossed the station approach. Red dust crunched like broken glass under his feet. Beyond the dispatch office was a strip of waste land covered with bushes and small trees. He headed for this and walked into the thicket for several yards, until he was certain he could not be seen from the station.

He was not sure where Moult-Argences was in relation to Bayeux, or in which direction he should now head, so he took out his map handkerchief and deliberately urinated over the centre of it, to activate the hidden dye. Almost immediately, the outline of roads and railways appeared in dark blue on the soaking silk. The north point was marked and he set the map by his button compass. He was about twenty-five miles from Lisieux and eighty from Bayeux. He wrung out the handkerchief and put it back in his top pocket, concerned at the length and danger of the journey that faced him.

He had no papers, and unshaven and shabby, like a tramp or refugee, he was bound to arouse suspicion if any German soldiers or French gendarmes questioned him. There would probably be many refugees nearer the coast, but they would all be coming south; none would be going north. He dared not risk staying in this clump of trees in case someone had seen him enter it and grew suspicious, but how could he leave in bright daylight? As he stood wondering what to do, he heard the branch line engine begin to rumble towards him from the siding, with its row of empty trucks. This branch line ran through the far side of the little wood. He walked carefully but swiftly towards it. As the last truck came abreast of him, he jumped on a front buffer and sat astride it. The train puffed slowly out over the countryside. For a short distance, the rails ran parallel with the road. Two women pushing prams looked up and waved to the driver. When they saw Rigby, they waved to him, too, thinking him a labourer riding home from work. Rigby waved back. It seemed safer to do that than to ignore them.

Soon the trees and bushes on either side of the track became tinged with red; they must be approaching the tile factory. The engine driver blew the locomotive's steam whistle twice to warn of his arrival, and the track began a wide curve to the right. Rigby jumped off the buffers to the left so that he was shielded by the trucks from the view of anyone in the driver's cab who might look back. He dropped flat beneath the nearest bushes, and the train swung away into a mass of red brick buildings. Tall red chimneys poured out thick, oppressive smoke, and although it was daylight, electric lamps glimmered through a red haze of dust in open-fronted sheds. Piles of red chimney pots and tiles and slates and hollow bricks surrounded the buildings in a vast yard, where horse-drawn carts were being loaded. He had jumped just in time, but it still was unsafe to stand upright because he could be seen by anyone in the factory if they chanced to look in his direction.

He crawled away until he reached a drainage ditch at the edge of a field of cabbages, also unpleasantly tinged with red. He tore off some branches from bushes round about and covered himself with these as camouflage, as he had done outside Mantes la Jolie. Then he lay down to wait until it was dark enough to risk moving.


Teletype machines clattered in the castle at La Roche Guyon; in the Pavillon Henry IV at St. Germain-en-Laye; in the soundproof OKW offices in Berchtesgaden. The brief messages that the machines constantly spewed out with mechanical jerkiness brought no comfort to the grim-faced men who read them.

The 21st Panzer division, based on Lisieux, had reached the outskirts of Caen to find the city so heavily bombed that pedestrians could barely find a way through mountains of debris from ruined houses. Refugees, dazed and bewildered, carrying their pathetic belongings on bicycles or wheelbarrows, were climbing over these mounds of bricks to reach open country. Whoever won the battle, they were the losers.

The Panzer tanks were forced to make a long slow detour around the suburbs. This delayed them and also used up far more of their reserve stocks of fuel than had been anticipated. Allied aircraft concentrated on attacking the division's fuel bowsers, for without petrol the tanks were useless. The 21st divisional commander therefore ordered all available cars to be requisitioned, and fatigue parties crammed them full of jerrycans of petrol in an effort to outwit the pilots.

North of Caen, the divisional commander, General Edgar Feuchtinger, ordered Colonel Hermann von Oppeln-Bronikowski, commanding the 22nd Regiment of Tanks, to take thirty-five tanks to a ridge north of the city and command the approach roads. He hoped that this move would provide sufficient cover for the rest of the division to reach its objective.

General Erich Marcks, the Corps commander, stood next to Feuchtinger when he gave these orders. Marcks had lost a leg on the Russian Front, and at fifty-three was old for active command. But he was a shrewd tactician, and throughout the preceding weeks had resolutely persisted that the invasion would be in Normandy and not in Calais. One evening during the previous week, he had stood with a colleague overlooking the beach at Arromanches. The tide was out, and underwater obstacles, rolls of wire, mines on stakes, stretched in every direction on the damp sand. He had forecast that, despite Army Group 'B's' insistence that the invasion was still some way off, and when it did come Calais would be the landing place, he remained convinced it would be in Normandy — and would begin on the following Monday night.

Both prophecies had proved totally accurate, and this gave added weight to the grave words he now addressed to the colonel.

'Oppeln,' he said quietly. 'The future of Germany may very well rest on your shoulders. If you don't push the British back into the sea, we have lost the war.'

The tanks set off, the exhausts of their Maybach engines bellowing, tracks squealing on the hard road. Cautiously, they climbed a slight incline. No Allied opposition appeared against them. The colonel's spirits rose, but as his tanks reached the top, a distant barrage of guns began to fire at them. The range was so great that the guns were completely out of sight, and it was impossible to calculate where they were. Yet the firing was so accurate that within seconds, six of his tanks were destroyed. To attempt to advance could mean the loss of all. He gave the order to retire.

At La Roche Guyon, General Speidel sat in his office, listening to Wagner on the gramophone. Rommel's adjutant came in to inform the general that the Field Marshal wished to see him. He was surprised at the general's composure.

'How can you play opera, sir, at a time like this?' he asked in amazement.

Speidel smiled.

'Why not?' he asked. 'Surely you do not think that playing a little music is going to stop the invasion now, do you?'

The two men looked at each other; nothing could stop the invasion now.

Rigby slept until late afternoon. When he awoke, his wound was more painful, and his shoulder muscles felt stiff. The field of reddened cabbages stretched away under the afternoon sky; red dust from the pottery covered him.

He sat up slowly, pushed away the covering branches, and chewed Horlicks tablets. He soon had only one left in the tin; he must keep this for dire emergency. As he moved, he became aware that a small hard lump had appeared under his right armpit; the poison in his wound must be spreading. He removed his jacket and retied the handkerchief over the yellowish gash. Then he tore off some cabbage leaves and chewed them. He disliked their strong taste, but they were food of a kind and he was hungry.

When the shadows grew longer he stood up and began to walk along the edge of the field, keeping in the shelter of the hedge. He reached the main road, the N13, the same road along which he had walked (how long ago?) to Mantes La Jolie. He could see very little traffic. A few French trucks pulling trailers piled with logs chugged past him. A middleaged woman pedalled by on a bicycle, and two heavy horses, jingling with harness brasses, drew a farm cart. He crawled through the hedge and began to walk along the road, keeping close to the hedge. Whenever he heard a lorry, he dropped flat until it had passed.

When darkness came, he decided to jump on the back of one of these trucks; he could walk all night and still not reach Bayeux. He waited until one passed him, going more slowly than the others because of the weight it was carrying. As it passed, Rigby breathed a heavy aroma of flour; this must be heading for a bakery. He ran behind the trailer and jumped on it and climbed up clumsily with his one hand. He lay on his stomach across the logs, bracing himself with his good arm against the jolts and bumps of the trailer's flattened springs. The few vehicles still running after dark had minuscule lights; their drivers trusted to the moon. So long as he did not move, no headlights were likely to reveal him. He clung to the logs for more than two hours by his watch and then jumped down. He did not want to push his luck in case he fell asleep, lulled by the rumbling motion and the growl of the exhaust, only to be discovered at some unexpected police check or when the driver reached his destination. He stood motionless against the hedge until the vehicle was out of sight. Then he started to walk.

In the distance, he could now hear a very faint rumbling that reminded him of the constant rumble from a cotton mill during the night shift in Salford, when he was very small. He would lie awake in his bed then, listening to the hum of unseen machinery, the constant clatter of stokers' shovels in the boiler house. It took him some time now to realise that he was hearing the guns fire along the Normandy coast. He might not be within sight of freedom yet, but at least he was within earshot. The thought cheered him. He began to walk more quickly, with more assurance.

The night grew cool. Soon, rain began to fall. He welcomed this at first, because it washed the red gritty dust off his face. Then the rain seeped through his clothes and chilled his skin. He shivered. He knew he was running a temperature. His right armpit ached and throbbed with every beat of his heart, so he pushed his hand into his jacket pocket. His shoes were porous and the leather sodden as wet blotting paper. His trousers and jacket became shapeless; rain plastered his hair to his skull. He plodded on, trying to disregard discomfort, pain, fever, imagining what it would be like when he reached home.

But where *was* home? It could not be Vienna or Frankfurt. Was home his billet in Eastbourne, with Elena married to another man? Or was it the little flat in North London he had not seen for years? Home for him must be wherever he hung his hat – and yet now he did not even own a hat! The absurdity of his situation suddenly became unbearable. He started to laugh, as though it were funny. Here he was, a soldier in shoddy civilian clothes, a German who pretended he was English, alone on one of the main roads of France, miles behind German lines in the fifth year of war, without papers, a weapon or food. All he had was hope. Rain kept falling. He trudged on doggedly.

After another hour, or maybe longer – time now seemed elastic and he could not remember exactly when he had left the tile factory – Rigby reached a fork in the road. Several small houses were huddled on either side of the junction. The main road ran to the right and a secondary road to the left. The local garage stood on the right, with a hand pump and a glass globe. On the tarred wooden wall of a barn was nailed an enamel metal hoarding advertising St. Raphaël. A triangular field at the junction of the roads was piled high with old cars. The fingers of the rain drummed on their rusting roofs. He suddenly felt too wet and weary to walk any further. He must find shelter somewhere, some relief from this chilling rain, from the misery of soaking clothes and shoes. He decided he would creep into one of these cars to shelter. Two hours' sleep and another benzedrine should refresh him and give him energy. His only alternative was to keep walking, in the hope that he might find an empty barn farther along the road where he could sleep. But this meant the risk of arousing a farm watchdog. He had little doubt that by now his description must have been teletyped to German Army units; it would be madness to take any risk he could avoid.

Rigby approached the field cautiously; he had learned from his experience at Mantes. Behind the hedge was a high wooden fence; double gates were chained and padlocked. He found a hole in the fence and crawled through and stood in a graveyard of wrecked cars. Moonlight reflected from silvered headlamps and horns and wide windscreens, all shining in the rain as they had once shone among potted palms and ferns in motor showrooms on the Avenue de la Grande Armée in Paris. The earth was churned into a thick paste of oil and mud. He tripped over a half submerged axle and fell heavily against a car, making a noise like a human gong. He stood for a moment, heart racing, in case anyone challenged him, but no-one came out of any of the houses.

He moved on more cautiously among the cars, trying their doors, but all the locks or hinges had rusted solid. Finally, he came upon an old Delage coupé with horsehair bursting out of its padded canvas hood. The passenger door opened silently. He climbed into the back seat, shut the door gently behind him and huddled down on the damp cord upholstery. There was a strong smell of cat urine, of rotting, soaked cloth and rusting metal. Rigby took off his jacket, wrung it out and spread it over him, and then lay back against a burst quilted corner cushion. He tried to ignore the sour smells and the raw dampness by imagining the elegance of this car years before when it would speed from Paris to Nice along the N7 in the high season. What had happened to those who had travelled so splendidly in it then? Were they now successful collaborators – or had they died in concentration camps? Despite his discomfort and his pain he dozed, to dream of a long straight road, lined by poplars with the sky blue and summery above him.

He awoke, heart pounding, mouth dry. Someone was outside, walking around the car. He heard boots squelch in mud, and then a sniffing and snorting. A guard dog. Rigby did not dare to move. The sniffing increased. Suddenly, the door he had closed so cautiously was ripped open. A torch blinded him. In its blaze he saw the double blued muzzles of a shotgun six inches from his head.

'Got you!' cried a voice triumphantly from the darkness behind the torch. 'Get out, or I'll shoot you now, you thieving bastard.'

Still dazzled by the light, red images flickering before his tired eyes, Rigby crawled slowly over the folded front passenger seat and stood in the darkness, pulling on his sodden jacket. Gradually his eyes grew accustomed to the gloom. An Alsatian dog on a chain choker snarled and strained to reach him. The man who held the chain was in his thirties, heavily built, well fed and bearded. He wore a shabby leather jerkin and an old beret. He kept the shot gun cradled in the crook of his right arm.

'Who are you?' he asked sharply.

'Stéphane Dubillier. I am on the run.'

'From whom? The police?'

'No. The Germans.'

'Why? You do not sound French.'

'I am half English. I was with the Resistance.'

'Why hide here?'

'Because I couldn't walk any further, that's why. I'm wounded.'
Rigby raised his right arm.

'Any papers?'

'No.'

'Armed?'

'No.'

The man ran his left hand over Rigby's pockets.

'So many people come in here at night to steal wheels and tyres to use for their farm carts, and bits and pieces to get their cars going again when the Boche is driven out, that I've had enough. This is my living. Every night, something disappears. Who would go into the butcher's shop to steal a steak or a leg of lamb? No-one. But they all think I'm fair game.

'You will come back to my house. If you try anything on the way, I'll set the dog on you. And if he doesn't deal with you, I'll shoot you. Now – march.'

He pointed his gun at the hole in the fence; they crawled through it to the main road. The rain had stopped; dawn was already lighting the sky. The man opened the door of the house near the petrol pump. Rigby went into a warm kitchen. An oil lamp still burned on a table. The man came in behind him, closed the door. He looked closely at Rigby.

'You're ill,' he said.

'It's my arm and the rain. I've been wet for days.'

'Take your jacket off,' the man told him. 'Hang it over a chair near the fire so it can dry.'

As he spoke, he looped one end of the dog's chain around a hook in the far wall and put the shot gun on the table. He rolled up Rigby's right sleeve and examined his wound. Then he poured a handful of salt into a pan of water, bathed the raw flesh and bound up his arm with a strip of towel.

'Hungry?'

'Yes.'

The man seemed friendly now he was in the house, but there was something about him that Rigby did not like, could not trust. This was an animal reaction, but he heeded it. Why had he suddenly changed from threats to kindness?

'You're in the Resistance, too?' Rigby asked him.

The man shook his head.

230

'No. That is not for me. I am a survivor. When people of the Resistance come here, I give them Calvados. When Germans call, I give them Calvados. When the British and Americans come, I will do the same. They all pass on their way, but I remain. This is my home. It is for them but a staging post. So many people in this village – in this country, in the world – have been brave and patriotic, and where are they now? In cemeteries, my friend.'

He ladled some soup from a pot into a bowl and put it on the table with a spoon and a slice of bread, and poured out a glass of Calvados. Then he motioned to Rigby and sat down to watch him eat.

'Now,' he said. 'How do I know you are who you say you are, and not a thief? You may be telling me lies. I do not wish to get involved with the Germans. Their days in France must be numbered. And when in retreat, soldiers can do terrible things. The Allies have landed all along the coast. They will be here in days.'

'Can I stay here until the British and Americans arrive?' Rigby asked him. 'Then I will be safe.'

'Possibly. You might be able to put in a good word for me with them, eh? But first I must have proof you are who you say you are, and then maybe we can reach an arrangement. As things are, I will run a great risk, keeping you here. I have relations in the Resistance. If they vouch for you, we can discuss the terms on which you could stay. Now, here is a rug. Sleep on the floor.'

He spread the rug in front of the stove. Rigby took off his sodden shoes and socks, put them in front of the stove to dry, and pulled the rug over him. He was still damp and he shivered from time to time with his temperature, but at least he was warm.

It was past nine o'clock next morning when he awoke to hear the clip-clop of hooves outside the house. A cart was arriving. The latch on the front door lifted and a woman came into the house. The man was writing something at the far end of the table. He stood up to greet her. From where Rigby lay, he could only see the woman's back. She was thickly built and wore a blue coat. She spoke rapidly, telling the beareded man her news. Fighting was already reported in the out-skirts of Bayeux. Casualties were heavy, but the Germans were slowly being pushed back. It was a great time for France. Then she noticed Rigby lying under his rug.

'Who's this?' she asked in surprise.

'Says he's half English. In the Resistance. I was going to ask you if

231

you knew anything about him.'

He turned to Rigby.

'Stand up,' he told him.

Rigby stood up, so that he could see her face, and instantly wished that he had not done so. She was the woman who had been washing clothes in the farmyard near Bayeux when the German patrol killed Louis and seized André. The bearded man looked sharply from one to the other.

'I know all about him,' said the woman in a voice heavy with hatred. 'He caused Louis' death, and André's capture. He is a stool-pigeon. The Germans came and took him away in a car and here he is, large as life, while Louis . . .'

She could not continue.

The bearded man crossed the room, gripped Rigby by the neck of his shirt, and pushed him back roughly against the wall.

'Is that true?' he asked gruffly.

'No.'

'But you were with Louis,' the woman insisted. 'He tried to shoot you. I saw it. *He* knew you were a traitor. I was there, close as I am to you now.'

'So that's how you got your wound, eh?'

'No,' shouted Rigby. 'I am a wireless technician. I came from England to sort out some trouble with the sets in his Section.'

'He is a pigeon,' said the woman. 'He went off with the Germans like good friends. They knew his name, Nimrod. They even knew he was coming.'

'If you are a friend of the Germans, then we will hand you back to them, whether they want you or not. You will be no use to me as a card of introduction to the Allies. Let the Boche deal with you. As they will, with a bullet in the back, most likely.'

'They don't want to be bothered with scum like him, any more than we do!' cried the woman. 'You deal with him. You've got a gun.'

She glanced at the shot gun on the table.

'No', replied the bearded man harshly. 'I've played one side off against the other for four years and I've survived. I'm not going to risk losing everything now the war's almost over by shooting some stranger.'

'The Germans are searching for me,' said Rigby despairingly. 'If they find me, I am dead.'

232

'Good,' said the woman.

'Who's running the Section now?' the man asked her.

'Jules. In Bayeux. But we can't involve him. He's too busy. The British are in the outskirts. They'll be here in a few days. Let us deal with him. Here. Now. Before they come. He's got a smooth tongue, this swine. He'll talk his way out of it yet.'

'So we will give him that chance. I'll hand him back to the Boches. Get rid of him that way. It's easier. No comebacks. And they pay a reward.'

The man smiled at the thought. He picked up his shot gun, broke it, took out the cartridges, and locked the gun away in the cupboard.

'There's a detachment two kilometres south. I'll tell them to come and get him.'

'Take him with you.'

'Why? Let them come for him. It's easier for us.'

'Don't leave me here with him, then,' the woman pleaded anxiously.

'I won't, don't worry. You're coming with me. We'll leave the dog with him. He won't get far with Wolf as guard.'

The man removed the chain from the Alsatian's neck. The dog squatted on his haunches, growling, mouth open. His eyes did not leave Rigby's face.

'Wolf is trained to jump at any quick movement,' the bearded man explained. 'He's a one man dog. If he gets his teeth into anything he won't let go until I give the command. And I'll be away for at least half an hour.'

'But why do this when the Allies have landed? The whole war may be over in weeks. What's in this for you? I've had nothing to do with Louis' death. You must believe that. She knows it's true.'

Rigby nodded towards the woman, who turned away her head and walked out of the house without replying.

'She hates you because of Louis,' the man explained almost apologetically. 'She loved him. They had a thing going together. And it's all ended now. For ever. Understand?'

Rigby nodded. He understood, but did not comprehend. He stood in his bare feet watching the man lock the inner door of the room and then pocket the key. He felt that there must be something he could do or say to stop him leaving; some bribe or reward he could promise, to make him change his mind, but his head ached and he was unable to marshal his thoughts.

This cannot be happening to me, he kept telling himself. Surely I am not about to be handed over to the Germans? Not now, so late in the war. Not now, when they'll probably have my description from La Roche Guyon, and kill me rather than be bothered with a prisoner. But somehow he could not translate his thoughts into words, and he stood as though mesmerised while the man prepared to leave. When he returned he would have enemy soldiers with him. Rigby realised he could have only minutes left to live – and he could do nothing or say nothing to make the man change his mind.

The main door had a heavy bolt with a metal tongue that went through a hole in the panel to the outside of the door. The bearded man went out now, closing the door. Rigby heard him slip a padlock on this tongue so that, short of smashing the bolt or the thick country-made staple into which it slid, there was no way of opening it. This meant that there was no way of escape.

He stood listening to their footsteps fade. The horse snorted in its shafts and stamped a hoof on the hard surface of the road. The homely animal noise broke the spell; he began to think, his mind sharpened by his danger.

Even if he could somehow overpower the Alsatian, he still had to unbolt that door, and he had only thirty minutes at the most in which to do so.

Rigby turned towards the dog and felt the metal shape of his survival pack press against his body. Cautiously, he put his hand in his pocket. Immediately, the hair on the dog's back bristled at the movement, as though charged by electricity. The beast bared yellow teeth; saliva drooled expectantly from his mouth. Very slowly, very carefully – because a swift movement could set the dog at his throat – Rigby opened the tin in his pocket and took out his last Horlicks tablet. He dropped this on the floor. The dog sniffed it suspiciously and then began to chew it avidly.

Now Rigby felt in his pocket for his lethal pill, peeled off its protective covering with his thumbnail and rolled the pill across the floor. The dog gulped it down and sat watching Rigby, hoping for something else to eat. Suddenly the animal gave a moan and rolled over on his side. He writhed for a moment, kicking out his legs, arching his back. A little foam frothed around the Alsatian's mouth and then all muscles slackened. Wolf was dead.

Rigby jumped up and wrenched at the front door bolt, but the padlock was far too strong. He ran to the inner door and flung his weight against it, hoping to reach another room, but all the panels were too solid. The window was too narrow for a man of his size. His only way out was through the front door.

He threw his left shoulder against this, but the heavy planks only creaked. He paused, sobbing for breath, forcing his mind to concentrate. He stared at the bolt, trying to think of any way to move it. The only solution would be to cut it. *Cut it.* He remembered the flexible trepanning blade concealed in his left shoe lace. He ripped out the lace, opened a drawer in the dresser, took out two teaspoons and pushed them through the loops at each end of the blade. Using these as handles, he began to saw.

The minuscule teeth bit steadily into the metal bolt. Within minutes he had cut it through completely. Now he put on his shoes, rummaged through the drawers again for a piece of string to use as a shoe-lace, and opened the front door.

All three roads were deserted. A child played with a top outside a house 50 yards away, but he could see no adults. He walked out of the front door, and set off at a brisk pace along the road. As soon as he had passed the pile of old cars and was out of sight of the houses, he began to run. He calculated that any pursurers would assume he would go along the main N13, which was the direct road to the coast, so he chose the minor road. Half a mile from the junction, when he felt it safe to do so, he checked his direction by his button compass and turned right, over fields and through orchards bright with blossom, until he reached the main road.

There might be police checks ahead, but he had to take that chance. He did not know where the other road led, and his one hope of survival lay in reaching Bayeux and an Allied formation before the Germans or Resistance caught up with him.

He ran for five minutes, walked for five, ran for another five, until, with pain growing in his arm, he could run no more. As his speed fell to a slow walk, he approached a farmyard. Outside the metal five bar gate he saw a row of milk churns on a wooden stand. From his time in Wales, he guessed that a cart or lorry would soon arrive to collect them. He would have to be on his way before this happened, but first he must have a drink. He removed the flat lid from the nearest churn and dipped both hands inside to scoop up mouthfuls of rich, creamy milk. In the yard, a dog on a long chain began to bark at him. The yard appeared empty, but someone might come out at any moment to discover why the dog was barking.

Rigby walked on up the road, alongside a high stone wall. Fifty yards ahead, near a green wooden door into the back premises of the farm, a woman's old-fashioned bicycle was propped against the wall. It had string threaded around the edges of the rear mudguard to prevent the rider's skirt being trapped in the spokes. He jumped on the bicycle and then discovered that the rear tyre was punctured. Perhaps this was why it had been left against the wall? He pedalled as hard as he could; even with a flat tyre, it was quicker and easier than walking. Soon, the rubber tore itself to shreds as the rim ground against the hard tarmac, as he covered mile after mile. He had no real idea of distance; only that when he had pedalled for two and a quarter hours by his watch, he decided to stop for a rest. He promised himself he would do so when he reached some trees beyond a series of sharp curves. He could wheel the bicycle off the road and use them for cover.

As Rigby came round the final bend, a man in a German army greatcoat, who had been sitting on the bank under the trees, jumped up and faced him, feet apart, body braced. He held a machine carbine aimed at Rigby's chest.

# Chapter Twenty

One hundred and fifty feet below Whitehall, in a concrete war room beneath a roof supported by red girders eighteen inches thick, a meeting of the British Chiefs of Staff Committee was in session.

The members sat on green upholstered tubular metal chairs around a hollow table covered in black baize. The room had one entrance with two sets of doors, both locked. Between these two doors stood an armed Royal Marines sentry, and beyond the outer doors other armed sentries patrolled the corridor.

Mr. Churchill sat at the head of the table, in a wooden arm chair. Behind him, to his right, was a strategically placed red fire bucket. When he finished a cigar, he tossed the stub into this bucket. The Royal Marines sentries were said to sell them as souvenirs.

The Prime Minister had just given a résumé of the latest reports from Normandy. The greatest, most complicated and crucial invasion in the history of warfare had been successfully launched with extremely light casualties. Progress continued to be encouraging, because the German opposition had been far weaker than many had anticipated. General Montgomery had invited him to visit his head-quarters, and so Mr. Churchill was proposing to go on a tour of inspection in Normandy with General Smuts, the South African Prime Minister, General Sir Alan Brooke, Chief of the Imperial General Staff, the American General Marshall and Admiral King of the United States Navy.

A cheerful mood of optimism gripped everyone in the room. Officers who had sat around this same table discussing military disasters in Dunkirk, in Norway, Hong Kong and Singapore and the Middle East, felt that at last they were within sight of what Churchill had once called the sunlit uplands. And they knew that credit should be given to the handful of men and women who had devised the ingenious, highly sophisticated plans that had helped to deceive the Germans about Allied intentions and objectives. Without these, casualties would have been incomparably higher. If their schemes had failed, this meeting could then have been a postmortem on another military debacle rather than a gathering to mark a glittering success.

Major General Hollis was asked for his assessment of the value of their plans.

Because of these deception measures, the German High Command remained convinced that the main assault was still to come in the Pas de Calais area. Hitler continued to believe that the Normandy invasion was a feint or subsidiary landing, and held back Panzer and other divisions until it was now too late for them to be used to great advantage. There had been one moment of concern when it had seemed that Hitler could change his mind, because detailed Allied plans had been discovered in a wrecked American landing craft, but instant action on the part of the XX Committee had averted this danger.

One of their captive German agents, who had already supplied much checkably accurate (but unimportant) information to the Germans, had sent a special and most urgent warning about these documents. He could not, of course, admit he knew they had been discovered through wireless intercepts, but he explained that false papers were being deliberately issued in the hope of discovery, and if found they should be totally disregarded.

Other captive agents also warned the OKW to beware of plausible ruses by the Allies to convince them that Calais might not be their main target. To back up these warning messages, the Dover coast was subjected to an enormous smoke screen, under which the agents reported that troops were embarking in their thousands for Calais.

Intercepts showed that with so much prior evidence pointing to the importance of Calais, Hitler felt that this sudden and dramatic discovery of dissenting documents was altogether too fortuitous. After all, he reasoned, who would be so foolish as to allow such vital plans to be taken into action by a relatively junior officer, when the risk of death or capture was so great?

After the meeting, Colonel Wingate called into General Hollis's office.

'Any news of Nimrod?' he asked him.

Hollis shook his head.

'Nothing more. As you know, we heard he had landed safely and made contact. And that's all so far.'

'We have made available a sum of money to his mother in Canada,' Wingate continued. 'Just in case he doesn't get back.'

Hollis remembered one of his father's sermons and quoted the Bible with a wry smile: 'Is not this the blood of men who went in jeopardy of their lives?'

'Possibly. But then a lot of men and women are still in grave jeopardy of their lives,' replied Wingate, 'Although none has had anything quite so important at stake. In all the circumstances, it seemed the least we could do.'

'Probably no-one will ever know who he is,' said Hollis. 'Or what he helped to achieve. As Winston said, he is the unknown warrior.'

Rigby jumped off the bicycle and let it roll ahead of him into the bank. The stranger took a pace towards him. He was unsteady on his feet, and despite his army greatcoat, he appeared old to be a soldier. He had obviously been drinking, for his chin was unshaven, his eyes bloodshot. He was thickset and rough, like a gypsy. Several bottles of wine, an ornamental clock, a fur coat and a Zeiss camera lay under the hedge.

'You gave me a fright,' he said accusingly in French. His voice was slurred and thick.

'So did you,' admitted Rigby in the same language. 'Where did you get that coat from?'

'Off a dead Boche. There's all kind of stuff lying about in Bayeux, just for the picking up. Where I got these.'

He waved towards the fur coat and camera and held up two bottles of wine.

'Trade you a bottle for your bike. If you won't, I'll shoot you – and take it.'

He slid back the bolt on the carbine. The barrel wavered ominously.

'Done,' said Rigby.

The man threw him a bottle. Rigby caught it. The cork was already half out of the neck. Rigby removed it with his teeth and drank deeply. The man picked up the bicycle and turned it around.

'You're going in the wrong direction for Bayeux,' Rigby pointed out.

'I know. But I'll be back. I'm going to bury what I've found. Where no-one but me knows where it is. Trust no-one in times like these. No-one at all.'

He gathered together his loot, mounted the machine and pedalled away unsteadily. Rigby stood, listening to the sound of the metal rim die along the road. Curiously, the noise seemed to grow steadily rather than to diminish. With it, he heard cries and shouts as from people in an extremity of terror. Suddenly, the whole sky was filled with the roar of aircraft. A flight of fighter bombers skimmed low above him. As he dropped flat on his face on the road, he saw their white star American markings. Wine trickled uselessly from the opened bottle by his side as he lay. The ground trembled when the bombs exploded. Cone-shaped clouds of black smoke erupted less than thirty yards away. He clasped his hands at the back of his neck, wrists pressed against his ears to protect his eardrums from any closer blast. Again the earth shook, as another stick of bombs fell. Then the noise of the aircraft receded. As Rigby raised himself up on his elbows, a single Spitfire came over, flying fast and so low that he could see the RAF roundels and the wheels folded up beneath the fuselage. Spears of flame flickered from its wings. There was a crisp crackle of cannon, and then this plane was also miles away.

Rigby now heard a distant, receding iron rumble, like tractors on an unseen road. There could be no tractors but there might be tanks. The question was, whose were they? Above the rumble came a distant boom and crack of guns firing and shells exploding. A stream of refugees pushing prams and hand carts laden with mattresses, suitcases, unlikely pieces of furniture, even a parrot in a cage, came towards him, around the bend in the road. A few women among them wept uncontrollably. He was nearer to Bayeux and the battle than he had realised.

No-one spoke to him; no-one appeared even to notice him as he pushed his way through this human tide of despair. He felt safe in the mass anonymity of the crowd, even though he was the only one going north.

By dusk, Rigby reached the outskirts of the town. Four shadowy figures holding machine carbines arose from a ditch at the roadside. He recognised the give-away shape of German helmets, and his heart contracted within him. Surely he would not be shot when he must be only a few hundred yards from safety?

'Why are you in such a hurry?' a soldier asked him.

'You're going the wrong way,' said another. Two carbines pointed at his stomach.

'I'm going back to rescue my mother,' Rigby replied quickly.

'Where does she live?'

'Up in the centre. Near the museum.'

Surely there must be a museum in Bayeux?

'All that area's pretty badly hit. Papers?'

Rigby put a hand in the inside pocket of his jacket and then withdrew it with a shrug.

'I've lost them,' he said, doing his best to appear surprised.

'Lost them?'

The first sentry stepped closer to him.

'Yes. I got shot at by some planes half an hour ago. American and British. It was terrible. I dropped flat on the road. Must have lost them then.'

The sentry paused, irresolute. He should report this to his feldwebel, maybe call in the gendarmes. But what was the use of that now? His feldwebel was dead and the gendarmes had disappeared. Even so, the discipline of years of war did not die easily.

'Let him go,' another soldier shouted from the darkness. 'Haven't we enough trouble without messing around with a Frog who's lost his papers?'

The sentry hesitated. The other soldier was right. What did one Frenchman matter now, when armies were in disarray?

'Get out of it,' the sentry told him.

'Thank you,' said Rigby, and ran before the German could change his mind.

As he came into Bayeux, he slowed to a walk. The Americans or British might already have captured the town, or the Germans could still be in control, at least of the outer streets. The safest thing in all the circumstances was to hole up somewhere and wait under cover until daylight. A disused church loomed to his right, set in a garden thick with thistles. High metal gates were padlocked and chained together; he could be safe here, but the gates would be difficult to climb over, and anyone seeing him walk up the path to the church might think he intended to loot the building. The last thing he could afford now was to call any attention to himself.

He walked on slowly into the Place aux Pommes. Several houses on the edge of the square had received direct hits. Rubble marked where they had stood. Like abrasive fog, dust hung in the air, making him choke. In the early moonlight, old women were raking through rubbish for any belongings that had survived the bombing. A few men piled relics of their homes – a wooden chair, a broken stove – on to hand carts. No-one paid any attention to him; among the homeless, he was only another person without a roof.

Rigby paused, wondering whether to continue straight ahead or to go up one of the narrow streets the stretched away into the darkness. He suddenly became conscious that someone was watching him – but who and where from? He stopped and stood to give an impression of indifference, hands in his pockets, dreading the crack of a rifle. He walked on even more slowly, and then saw a man at the mouth of a small alley that ran behind the houses. The man kept in the shadow; only his face was visible.

'Looking for someone?' he called in German when he realised that Rigby had seen him. His voice was harsh and hostile.

Rigby shook his head.

'*Nein*,' he replied in German – and instantly realised he had made a grave error, possibly a fatal one. He was so used to changing gear in his mind from German to French and back again that he had selected German simply because the question had been put in that tongue.

'A German!' the man shouted excitedly over his shoulder. 'And on his own, the bastard!'

Rigby heard boots race down the alleyway, and the clatter of a firing mechanism. This was no time to stand and attempt to explain who he was – for what explanation could he possibly give with any hope at all they would believe him?

He started to run, zig-zagging across the road, jumping over piles of bricks. An automatic weapon chattered busily behind him. Bullets sprayed the pavement and struck sparks from the brickwork of houses as he dodged from side to side to confuse their aim. The firing stopped. Rigby glanced over his shoulder. In the moonlight a man stood reloading his gun. Others were still running, shouting: 'A German! A German! Kill him!'

Rigby was now in an empty and virtually undamaged street. The houses were shuttered; this part of Bayeux seemed deserted. He had no idea where the street led, but if he could lose himself in the labyrinthine back alleys he felt sure must honeycomb the town, then perhaps he could hide in a celler or empty house. But how to find such a refuge?

Again the gun chattered warningly behind him. Bullets chipped flecks of stone from the front of a house. He heard the tinkle of broken glass as they hit a window. He ran on uphill to a crossroads. The main street ran to left and right across a bridge. Ahead stretched another road lined by shuttered shops. Moonlight glinted greenly on stagnant water beneath the bridge. Left or right were too dangerous for him, because the road was empty and he had no cover. He would be shot within seconds.

Ahead, he had a choice of the street of shops or some stone steps to the left that led down to the river. He ran down these, two at a time. They were steep and without a rail; he had to concentrate or he would trip. At the back of his mind he heard the whistle of a shell high overhead, but descending. Instinctively, he threw himself flat against the wall, head pressed sideways on the damp bricks. The ground trembled as the shell landed. In the street above him the shutters of a house burst open and plaster dust rained down on the pavement. One of his pursuers was shouting, and somewhere a woman screamed in terror. Rigby came out on a towpath by the side of the river. The water was hardly moving, covered with green weed like a lawn. Ahead, the towpath merged into thick grass and nettles; he could not see how far it led, and so he dodged for cover under the curving roof of the bridge.

Half a dozen people were already sheltering there from the shells, huddled together in an extremity of fear. The bridge shuddered as another shell landed. The explosion shook out a handful of old, powdered cement from between bricks above his head. In the darkness, a woman was sobbing. Rigby heard shouts, and running feet on the road above, amplified by the arch of the bridge. Then he heard footsteps coming down the stone steps. He ran on, beneath the bridge, along the side of the river, until he reached a huge mill wheel. Its big wooden blades dripped as they turned. The roar of water pouring through the wooden sluice gates across the river blotted out every other sound. He ran over the top of these gates to the far side of the river, climbed the bank, and was instantly faced by a maze of narrow, twisting alleys behind the main street.

Buildings on either side shook as another shell landed. Loose slates slid to the ground, deadly as hatchet blades. Beyond the silhouette of Hans Andersen rooftops and chimneys, the sky to the north glowed amber. Huge fires were burning somewhere. He came out into the main street and turned left, away from the bridge and the cross roads and his pursuers.

Rigby reached La Rue Saint Jean and saw the iron gates of the Lion d'Or hotel. Behind them, half a dozen palm trees grew around a court-yard, an incongruous sight. He could see no hiding place here, so retraced his steps, past more shuttered shops and grey stone houses. By the side of the Hôtel du Croissant, an archway opened into an alley that in turn widened into a yard. Enormous wooden beams supported the stone arch. To the right stood an ancient petrol pump, its glass bowl marked *S.I.A.M. avec Séparateur d'Air*. He plunged down this alleyway past narrow stone staircases that opened on either side, leading into high, thin stone buildings.

The alley was paved with cobblestones, slippery and steeply cam-bered; once he tripped and nearly fell. At the end of the yard was a stone barn with a pile of old motor tyres and rusting oil drums against its walls. Nettles and willow herb sprouted strongly; the area smelled sour and secret, of cats and drains and rotting rubbish. He cautiously pushed open the door of the barn. It creaked on ancient hinges. The stone walls inside felt foul and slimy to his touch. There were sacks on the floor and some loose stinking straw. An animal had sheltered here quite recently. And another hunted creature is here now, he thought. He closed the barn door, and sat down thankfully, back against the wall, to wait for dawn.


Rigby was dreaming of Elena. They were walking together along a beach, like Eastbourne but yet not Eastbourne; a beach completely deserted, where sunshine gilded a shining sea. But as they walked, the sky grew steadily darker, until heavy clouds completely covered the sun. He heard thunder very close to them, and the beach shook. In the deepening gloom he could no longer see Elena and he kept calling her name: Elena! Elena! She did not answer.

Rigby awoke, heart racing, mouth dry, his right arm stiff and swollen. He glanced at his watch; 7.30 in the morning. The noise of thunder in his dream was the rumble of artillery. Shells were trundling through the sky. The barn walls and the earth floor trembled as they landed. Now and then he heard a roar like a football crowd cheering the home team's goal, and then a crash of falling masonry. He stood up and stretched himself. Rats scurried away into recesses and holes at the movement. The floor of the barn had been soiled by horses and cows. He felt filthy and feverish, and he could no longer bend the elbow of his arm sufficiently to squeeze his hand into his jacket pocket to ease the pain of movement.

He opened the door a few inches. The yard was empty, a dumping ground for rubbish; a burst mattress, the frame of a pram, half-burned newspapers. Rags of washing hung damply from a line. Other openings into decaying buildings had hooks to support doors no longer there. A crest of three stars and a crescent moon was carved above a window. The glass had gone long ago and wire mesh had been nailed across the empty frame to keep out birds that twittered restlessly in the eaves. High up on the walls, green glass insulators supported power cables.

Near the barn door he saw a hand pump. He went out into the fresh cold air and moved its curved metal handle. A trickle of brown rusty water squirted from the nozzle. He pumped until the water came clear and then washed his face and rinsed his mouth. He dried himself on his handkerchief and returned reluctantly to the shelter of the barn. He could not risk being seen in the streets, and possibly questioned or even recognised until he was certain that the Americans or British had arrived, so he waited impatiently, walking up and down in the dank, confined space of the barn.

It was nearly noon when he heard the familiar rumble of tank tracks passing the archway. Now he walked up the alley and stood under the arch, shielded by the petrol pump. On the side of the first tank someone had chalked 'Betty Grable'. He heard men shouting in Cockney slang, and the familiar swear-words, once so tedious, now inexpressibly welcome. An infantry soldier, one of a section running along the pavement in familiar battle order, taking advantage of any cover offered by a buttress or a doorway, dived briefly through the arch to urinate against the wall.

'Where are your mob?' Rigby asked him in English, instinctively falling back into the familiar army idiom.

The man looked at him in amazement.

'Who the bloody hell are you, mate? Didn't see you. Not English, then, are you?'

'Course I am. No. 10 Commando. Over here on special duties.'

'Bloody right in that gear. When did you last get near a razor, tosh?

And you pong like a bleeding polecat.'

'I wish to see the Intelligence officer of your lot. Where's your company HQ?'

'God knows, moosh. Back towards Arromanches somewhere, I reckon. Can't stop. Watch it, mate.'

Then the man was gone, racing down the street, with others like him, rifles across their bodies, heads down, metal boot studs striking sparks from the pavement.

A Jeep bumped after them. A young Signals Corps lieutenant sat by the side of the driver. The big radio set in the back sprouted two thin aerials like quivering whips. The radio speaker chattered constantly; code names, map references, meaningless lists of numbers, questions asked beseechingly and repeated. The Jeep slowed to pass a pile of rubble from a bombed house. Rigby ran alongside and jumped into the back seat.

'What the hell?' cried the lieutenant in surprise.

'No. 10 Commando, sir,' said Rigby. 'Sorry about my appearance, but it is imperative I reach your I.O. as soon as possible.'

'Ten Commando? What the devil are you doing here in those filthy clothes, man?'

'Been working with the Resistance, sir. Was captured but escaped.'

That was the simplest explanation, the one guaranteed to provoke fewest awkward questions.

'Well, hang on. I'll give you a lift. What's the matter with your arm?'

'Flesh wound gone septic, sir.'

Rigby reached the I.O. two hours later when the Jeep returned to company headquarters. He was a harassed captain sitting in the back of a 15 cwt Guy truck surrounded by message forms, transcripts of signals and Sitreps (Situation Reports). Rigby guessed he would never have heard of X-Troop or No. 3 Troop, to give the unit its more conventional title, and stuck to his story that he had been captured when on special duties with the Resistance, had escaped, and now must return to England as urgently as possible for secret reasons.

The I.O. had enough worries; the sooner this man in his filthy clothes got out of his way, the better. He asked him some questions about his unit and its officers, to satisfy himself that Rigby was genuinely a soldier and then issued him with a duplicate AB64, the thin booklet every private soldier received, with details of his Army

246

number, records of vaccinations and inoculation and proficiency tests he had passed.

He also ordered a company clerk to type out a letter of authority, which he signed. Then he wished him well and turned thankfully to his own concerns. The driver of an ambulance packed with wounded going back to the Arromanches beach-head gave Rigby a lift. Rigby waded out to a landing craft about to return across the Channel. An officious corporal refused to allow him aboard, but then he saw an Intelligence Corps sergeant and told him his story. The sergeant over-ruled the corporal, and finally Rigby sank down thankfully on the damp duckboards of the vessel. He felt safe at last.

*'Hear, Oh Israel . . . the Lord is One God. Thank you, Oh, Lord, for listening to thy servant's prayer.'*


Captain Angus came into the office overlooking St. James's Park. The bald-headed major stood at the window, cleaning his pipe with a feather. He was due to go on leave at the end of the week: three days, or seventy-two hours as the Army liked to call it. A leave sounded longer that way.

'Our man's back, sir,' Angus announced, interrupting his thoughts.

'What man?'

'Fellow I bet a hundred to one would never make it.'

'Oh, Nimrod. Rather forgotten about him, poor devil. Been so much else happening. Where is he now?'

'Newhaven. He's just 'phoned from a field hospital. Taken from a landing craft by ambulance.'

'Is he wounded, then?'

'Nick in his arm, that's all. I've spoken to the adjutant. He's given him a rail warrant to get up here. He's also advanced him two pounds. Was a bit doubtful about that, actually, but Rigby hasn't a penny, of course. He had to have *something*. The adjutant wanted to know the authority.'

'You told him?'

'The authority, sir. Nothing else.'

'Then please inform Colonel Wingate that he has returned safely.'


Rigby sat in Colonel Wingate's office near the underground Cabinet

Room beneath Great George Street in London. He wore a new uniform which had been issued to him from army stores at Newhaven. It did not fit particularly well and there had not been time to sew the distinctive Commando shoulder flashes on the top of his sleeves. His wound had been dressed and bandaged.

Colonel Wingate listened intently to his story. Now and then he asked a question or sought amplification of some incident, but for the most part he heard him out in silence.

'Do you think they really believed what I told them, sir?' Rigby asked him when he had finished.

'Our deception plans convinced them totally,' replied Wingate. 'And the Führer still believes – despite all evidence to the contrary – that the main invasion is yet to come at Calais. For this reason, he is holding virtually the whole of the 15th Army out of the battle. There is no doubt that your arrival must have had a considerable psychological effect on his thinking, especially when you assess it in conjunction with all the other corroborative evidence we swamped them with.'

It was too early then to realise just how successful the British deception plans had been, but instead of estimated casualties of seventy per cent, only one man in fifteen had been killed on the first day. Nor was their value limited to the D-Day landings. It lasted for at least six more weeks. On June 6, the Allies landed eight divisions in Normandy, a total of 156,000 troops. At that time, the Germans maintained forty-eight infantry divisions and ten Panzer and Panzer grenadier divisions in France, prepared to repel the invasion.

If the OKW could have calculated correctly when and where this would come, and had been allowed to move their defence forces as Rommel proposed, free of Hitler's veto, these divisions could have driven the Allies back into the Channel, despite Allied air supremacy.

The deception planners, however, had credited the Allies with forty-two totally mythical divisions, all apparently poised to attack the Pas de Calais, about 200 miles east of the Normandy beaches. As a result, only three understrength German divisions were in Normandy. The other divisions were east of the Seine, around Calais, and elsewhere across France, in case of invasion from the west or south.

So the Allied beach-head was successfully secured and not until the third week of July did Hitler finally accept that no major Allied invasion was planned for the Pas de Calais. Six weeks too late, German 15th Army reserves were finally moved in a doomed attempt to contain the advancing Allied armies.

'We were not sure whether you would get back safely,' Wingate continued, 'so it was decided that a sum of money should be made available to your mother in Canada. An account has been set up there in your name in a bank in Montreal. We gave instructions to pay it to your mother if you did not return.'

'I did not do this for money, sir,' replied Rigby rather coldly.

'We are all fully aware of that. But your mother has had a lot of trouble already. We would not have wished her to face further hardship. And what you did was far beyond the normal call of duty expected from any soldier – even a Commando.'

'Thank you, sir. What happens now? Do I report back to X-Troop?'

'We feel it would probably be best if you did not. It is proposed that you be released from the Army and return to civilian life. You can accept demobilisation in any Empire country, you know. If you have no ties here, perhaps you would care to go to Canada to join your mother?'

'It might be a more pleasant trip than my last one,' said Rigby with a smile, remembering the crossing behind the wire in the *Duchess of York*, and his subsequent stay in Sherbrooke.

'I trust so. It is also suggested that you might now become not Rosenberg or even Rigby, but someone else altogether. No-one in your unit knows what you did. And, of course, it is very much in your own interest to keep silent on this matter.'

'I intend to, sir.'

'One more thing. When we thought that our agents on the continent faced the risk of being recognised, because they had lived there before the war or for any other reason, they sometimes had plastic surgery to change their appearance as a precaution before they went back. There was, of course, no need and indeed no time, to do this in your case. But you tell me the Abwehr photographed you in La Roche Guyon, and you could be recognised very easily, even with a new name. It is proposed that you undergo some minor plastic surgery to your face before you leave for Canada. Then you can start a new life in the New World, confident that you are a *completely* new person.'

'You really feel that is necessary, sir?'

'It would be a wise precaution,' replied Wingate gravely. 'An insurance policy, if you like. To make things easy, we have in fact already booked a room for you in the London Clinic.'

249

In the third week of July, the stitches in Rigby's skin were removed, and for the first time he was allowed to see his new face. A nurse gave him a hand mirror; a stranger looked back at him. No-one would recognise him now, he thought, for he could barely recognise himself.

Changing his name yet again had not greatly worried him; several friends in X-Troop had told him long ago that they intended to do this after the war. What concerned him about his new appearance was the uneasy feeling that he had not received a new identity at the same time. Instead, he felt he had no identity whatever. He had put his past behind him, and now would have to make not only a new life for himself, but become a new character, a whole new persona.

At the end of the week, when the puckerings and tucks in Rigby's face had subsided, Captain Angus came to visit him; he brought papers for him to sign regarding his move to Canada. Angus explained that Rigby's passage had been booked in a new name, and he would sail from Southampton to New York in the *Queen Mary*, which was still in use as a troopship. He would be given a rail ticket to travel from New York to Montreal. In the meantime, he could remain in the Clinic until the *Queen Mary* sailed. This would be more convenient than moving to an Army transit camp or an hotel for these few days.

After their meeting, Rigby stood at the window, watching Captain Angus cross Devonshire Place on his way out of his life. He had never imagined leaving the army in such a way, or before the war was over. Now that the moment of departure was upon him, he realised he had been a soldier for longer than he had been anything else, except a schoolboy. He had enjoyed the comradeship as well as the anonymity of uniform. It was ironic, he thought, that for nearly four years he had learned so many different ways of taking life; how to kill silently, swiftly, speedily. And yet, in the end, all this training had been used, not to take life, but to save it. He felt that there must be a moral here, but he could not think what it was.

Captain Angus had advanced several pounds to Rigby from his pay, and on the following morning he took a taxi to Victoria Station. Here he bought a third-class return ticket to Eastbourne. He sat in the corner of his carriage without experiencing any of the elation and anticipation he had assumed he would feel on returning to see Elena. He had dreamed about her; but a dream was not reality, and reality

250

involved another man – her husband.

Rigby had deliberately not written to Elena since his return to England, perhaps because then he was not certain that he would visit her. Her mother's house was not on the telephone, so he had the perfect excuse for not ringing her. Now the moment of meeting could be postponed no longer. Why, he wondered uncomfortably as he watched the countryside flicker past the dirty carriage windows, had he wished to postpone it at all?

At Eastbourne, Rigby walked along the seafront, past the house which still appeared to be X-Troop's company office. He stayed on the other side of the road and glanced with deliberate casualness at the building. Three Commandos came out of the front door. He did not recognise them. They would no doubt be a part of a new draft. He paused for a moment, hoping he might see a familiar face, wondering whether he would make himself known, despite Colonel Wingate's advice, but they were all strangers. He had been away for several weeks, long enough for the pigeons to have arrived for nearly all his contemporaries.

As he approached Elena's house, he felt a sudden nervousness so acute that it dwarfed the fears he had experienced on the other side of the Channel. Instead of ringing the front door bell as he had intended, he walked on beyond the house to the top of the street and paused to light a cigarette. Then he made up his mind. He must ring that bell. It was absurd to feel like this. She might be at home but if she were not, he would leave a note asking her to telephone him at the Clinic. He found himself almost hoping that she was not at home; it would be easier to discuss their future at a distance.

He began to walk down the street more cheerfully now that his mind was made up. A few houses up from Elena's home, he saw her front door open and he paused, pretending to relight his cigarette. A woman came out of the front door and turned, her back to him. Then she turned towards him: Elena.

Rigby was conscious that his heart was beating like a bass drum. Elena walked down the short front path to the pavement. A man followed her, a soldier wearing uniform, but round-shouldered and with a defeated air, looking old, although he was probably still in his twenties. Elena glanced briefly and without interest in Rigby's direction. She saw a strange soldier, walking down the road, smoking a cigarette. The man with her also glanced up the road towards him: the instinctive look of one soldier at another, in case they shared anything in common, apart from uniform; a medal, a cap badge, a shoulder flash.

Rigby recognised him instantly from the photograph in the front room; he was her husband, Jack. He must have been repatriated, perhaps on medical grounds. They began to walk down the road, and as they did so, Elena put her arm through Jack's arm and drew him towards her. Rigby followed, 200 yards behind them. They turned left towards the main part of Eastbourne. He crossed to the other side of Grand Parade, where others were walking, nearer the sea. He leaned for a moment against the railings, and instantly recalled leaning on the wall around the stone platform at La Roche Guyon, watching the barges on the Seine.

The rush of his heart had slowed. He was surprised that now he felt no emotion whatever about Elena. He could call out to her, and introduce himself, and they might try to build something on the foundation he thought had existed, but what value or permanance could it have? Her marriage was real, while his association with her had been brief and transient; already, like his name and his old face, belonging to the past.

Perhaps feeling had died when he had discovered that her husband was alive; perhaps it had all been illusion. For so long he had played a part as an Englishman that maybe his feelings for Elena were part of that self-deception.

And what good could come from trying to continue their association? Not only did he look a different man now, he was a different man, not the Rigby she had known. Rigby; Rosenberg; Dubillier; he had been all three, finally masquerading as Nimrod. Now he was someone else altogether, in name, in face and in his future; a man without a past. He found this difficult enough to accept, so how could he hope that Elena might find it any easier? He remembered the words from Ecclesiastes: 'There is a time to get and a time to lose; a time to keep, and a time to cast away.' This was surely a time to leave. Once more, the pigeons had arrived.

Rigby began to walk more swiftly now, not as though he were following Elena and her husband, but as a man with a purpose, a man with his mind made up. What had been, or what perhaps he had imagined had been, belonged along with so much else to the past, where it should remain.

Rigby reached the station; a train was due out for London in three minutes.

'Ticket, please,' said the collector at the gate. In his left lapel he wore the round silver badge of an ex-Serviceman discharged on medical grounds. The war had already ended for both of them; and not as either had ever imagined it would.

Rigby felt for his ticket in the left pocket of his battledress blouse, then in all his other pockets, but without success.

'Must have lost it,' he said, perplexed.

Perhaps when he had arrived, his mind had been so concerned about Elena that he had absentmindedly given up the whole ticket to the collector then on the gate, and not only half, as he should have done.

'Booking office is over there, mate,' the ticket collector told him. Rigby was about to explain what must have happened, and then shrugged his shoulders; it was only a matter of shillings. He handed a pound note to the ticket clerk behind the booking office window.

'London,' he told him.

'Single or return?' the man asked through the hole in the glass screen.

'Single,' said Rigby.

He picked up the ticket, pocketed his change, and walked out on to the platform.

# *Epilogue*

Some books can take a surprising short time to write, despite their authors' claims to the contrary. Others will spread themselves over a long period, until they almost become part of the writer's life. *The Unknown Soldier* has been one of these.

I first heard about this particular wartime deception many years ago from Major General Sir Leslie Hollis, about whose experiences as Senior Military Assistant Secretary to the War Cabinet and Chiefs of Staff Committee, I wrote *War at the Top*.

At that time, the vital and often crucial role that Allied deception plans played in many Second World War campaigns was still closely shrouded in secrecy. It was therefore impossible to publish more than glancing references to the ingenious ruses devised by so many brilliant and imaginative people under the aegis of Colonel John Bevan and Colonel Ronald Wingate. To illustrate to me the wide range of their plans, and also the extent of one man's selfless courage and patriotism, General Hollis described in the broadest terms how a volunteer of German-Jewish extraction, serving under a British name in the Commandos, had helped to deceive the Germans before the Normandy landings in 1944.

Later, I moved to Wiltshire and came to know Sir Ronald Wingate. By then, much more had been made public about the immense contribution the deception planners had made in victory, and Sir Ronald recalled in some detail this particular episode in which he had played such an important part.

I was then working on another book, Green Beach, which also dealt with individual courage of the highest order. This book described the experiences of Jack Nissen, a British radar expert, who was invited to accompany the Canadians on the Dieppe raid in August, 1942, to evaluate the performance of a German Freya radar station near Pourville. From its code name, Green Beach, I took the title of my book.

Although serving in the RAF, Jack Nissen, a Jew, was to wear the uniform of a Canadian private soldier, and because he had been closely involved with the cavity magnetron valve, which was the key to the supremacy of British radar, it was unthinkable that he should be captured lest he might reveal its secrets. Accordingly, he had to accept a situation unique in warfare. Twelve members of the South Saskatchewan Regiment, to which he was attached, were detailed to guard him – and to kill him if his capture seemed imminent. He thus became the only man in possibly any war to face the guns of the enemy while the guns of his comrades were also trained upon him.

Lord Mountbatten had proposed the original plans for the Dieppe landing, later to be changed by others, and he generously gave me a great deal of help with this book. He had, of course, no knowledge of the grim orders which Nissen had readily accepted, and told me that there had been no need whatever to put Britain's most precious radar secret at risk.

'They could so easily have sent a member of X-Troop,' he said. He then explained how he had formed X-Troop in No. 10 (Inter Allied) Commando from German, Austrian and Hungarian anti-Nazi volunteers, over-whelmingly Jewish, to undertake such hazardous tasks.

Now the recollections of General Hollis and Colonel Wingate immediately fell into place. This was the Commando unit in which The Unknown Warrior had been proud to serve.

So, with Lord Mountbatten's help once more, I began to work on this book as soon as I had finished *Green Beach*. I discovered that, since the war, some former members of X-Troop had reverted to their original German names. Others kept the English names they had taken at Aberdovey or Bradford. Several now have new names and totally new identities. Some I have named; others prefer to remain anonymous, but all are united by courage and comradeship, and the recollection of shared or separate dangers. Of their original total of ninety-one, sixteen were killed and twenty-three wounded. Five were taken prisoner, and four decorated for gallantry.

A shield of secrecy still surrounds X-Troop, and those who served in it. At the Public Record Office, for example, I was informed that the 100 Year Rule prevailed. This meant that no documents could be released for public view until 2042.

Lord Mountbatten introduced me to Sir Michael Cary, then Permanent Under-Secretary at the Ministry of Defence, and permission was granted for me to examine and make use of any relevant documents. Because of Mount-batten's strict orders that the fewest possible details about X-Troop should ever be committed to paper, these records were very sparse. Most entries simply recorded that certain private soldiers had been interviewed at the Great Central Hotel in Marylebone before being posted to Harlech. Their adopted English names were given, and their regiments, usually The Buffs, (the Royal East Kent Regiment), the East Surrey Regiment and The Hampshire Regiment.

I extracted the names of fifteen of these men, with their regiments, and sent this list to the Army Record Centre of the Ministry of Defence, with the request that they provide me with any further information about them and, if possible, their last known addresses. After six weeks of research, the reply from the Record Centre was unequivocal: 'It has not been possible from the particulars furnished to trace any records in respect of their service.'

This showed how well their trail had been concealed, and how efficiently

Mountbatten's specific orders regarding security had been observed. So far as official records are concerned, these men simply did not exist. As Bryan Hilton-Jones wrote in his final report when X-Troop was disbanded, 'The very nature of the unit inevitably involved a great deal of secret and highly complicated administration . . . The men, and their families, had obviously to be guarded against the possibility of identification as Germans either at home or, above all, on capture by the enemy.

'This necessitated the issue of false numbers, names and regiments, false personal histories, false next-of-kin, false mail facilities, etc; and this in turn involved a tortuous procedure whereby all of it was kept secret from the normal Army pay and record offices without disturbing the normal administrative channels. Such extra "tit-bits" as attachment to another unit, overseas service, and the legalisation of the "false" names by A.C.I.* in 1943, simply added to the complications.'

In the spirit of the secrecy that shielded the activities of X-Troop, I have changed some names and paraphrased certain incidents in this book. What no-one can change or diminish is the selfless and inspiring example these young men set to all who wish to live in freedom, or the importance of their contribution to this cause in which they believed so passionately.

What happened to some who served with The Unknown Soldier?

George Lane, who was later awarded the Military Cross, left La Roche Guyon in May, 1944, under escort in an army car. He was blindfolded, as he had been for the journey to the castle, and driven to Paris to spend, in his words, 'some uncomfortable hours at the Hotel Continental with some unpleasant people.' He was then taken to the jail in Fresnes for a full interrogation.

Later that month, Lane was moved to Schloss Spangenberg (Oflag 9/AH), a mediaeval castle near Cassel, where 300 British officers were held prisoners-of-war. On arrival, Lane realised that his false Welsh accent could not conceivably fool them, so he immediately told the senior British officer, Colonel Euan Miller, his real identity, and asked for his advice. He was concerned in case any of the officers would assume he was a German stool-pigeon and deal with him accordingly.

Colonel Miller assured Lane that he would personally check his story, and if he found that it was true, he would then inform the other prisoners.

Lane could not understand how the colonel could possibly verify it, and only after the war did he discover how British prisoners-of-war in some camps had been able to keep in secret touch with the military authorities in London.

Lane told Colonel Miller that he had visited Rommel's headquarters, but he had no idea where it was, because he had been blindfolded on the journey. However, he described the château and the river and the white cliffs with the tower on top. One of the other officers present immediately produced a copy of Charles Morgan's novel *The Voyage*, which contained a vivid description of La Roche Guyon. The news that Rommel's headquarters was located there caused great excitement in the camp. Within hours, this information was passed to London.

*A.C.I. Army Council Institution

256

David Irving, in his biography of Rommel, *The Trail of the Fox*, records that on May 26, 1944, 'a British agent' first reported to London the whereabouts of the Field Marshal's headquarters. Confirmation from other sources was received on July 14.

Three days later, Rommel visited the 1st SS Panzer Corps, and was returning to La Roche Guyon along Route N179 when two RAF Spitfires came in at tree-top height. They opened fire on his car, which overturned. Rommel's driver was mortally injured and Rommel thrown out, fracturing his skull.

After weeks in hospital, he returned to his home at Herrlingen, to convalesce. One morning, two generals called on him to deliver an ultimatum. He was accused of having taken part in the plot against Hitler, and could thus either face trial, with the certainty of a guilty verdict, and all the disgrace and contumely that this would bring, or he could take his own life by swallowing a poison tablet they had brought for this purpose.

In consideration of Rommel's past services to his country, the Führer would then allow him the honour of a state funeral, his widow could draw a Field Marshal's pension, and there would be no reprisals against her or their son, Manfred.

Rommel chose this latter course.

John Coates, after 18 months with No. 10 Commando, served with No. 30 Commando in Sicily, Italy and Corsica, and later with SOE in Yugoslavia and Hungary, and was awarded the DSO. He subsequently joined the Diplomatic Service. Now, as Dr. J.G. Coates, he is Dean of Students and lecturer in Finno-Ugrian Studies at the University of East Anglia, Norwich.

John Envers landed in Normandy on D Day with 41 Royal Marine Commando. Later, he interrogated German personnel in prisoners-of-war and concentration camps. After the war he worked for the Foreign Office, and in 1948 emigrated to Canada. He was with C.B.C. Radio News and subsequently C.B.C. TV news during the 1950s, and since then has been a radio news editor with C.B.C.

Fred Jackson was attached to Field Security in Germany at the end of the war and helped in the arrest of Rudolf Hoess, the former commandant at Auschwitz. Hoess was found hiding in the kitchen of a farmhouse and came out shouting: 'Don't shoot! Don't shoot!'

Many Nazis of his importance had prudently concealed a cyanide suicide pill beneath their tongue for use in such an emergency, but Hoess explained that he had never done this; he was afraid he might accidentally swallow it.

Similarly, this man who admitted killing 10,000 people in one day ('Humanely,' he stressed) would not allow his own blood group number to be tattooed on his arm – an SS requirement – because he thought the tattoo needle could be painful.

After the interrogation was over, Jackson wrote: 'I was drunk for a week. I just could not live with myself. He was the man who had killed my mother.'

Peter Masters landed on D-Day with No. 4 Commando. He was soon promoted to sergeant and then commissioned, and ended his service in Ghana with the Gold Coast Regiment.

After the war, he studied at the Central School of Art and Design in London, and went to the USA as a Fulbright Scholar. He became Art Director of a TV Station and of the U.S. Government's Poverty Programme. He is now Art Director of the U.S. General Services Administration.

Training was so tough that several accidents occurrred. Trefor Matthews, who joined X-Troop in October, 1943, was seriously injured in cliff-climbing. He had been brought up in Caernarvon, where he and Hilton-Jones were boyhood friends.

When Hilton-Jones went to boarding school, they drifted apart, but met again when they both arrived as freshmen at Gonville and Caius College, Cambridge. Matthews was later articled to a chartered accountant in Liverpool.

When war broke out, he initially volunteered for the Red Cross or Royal Army Medical Corps, but they had no vacancies. When he was called up, Matthews registered as a conscientious objector and enlisted in the Non-Combatant Corps. After Dunkirk he decided he must take an active part in the war and transferred to the Royal Corps of Signals and was commissioned. Posted to Eastbourne on a special course, Matthews met Hilton-Jones, who suggested that he should join his Troop.

One Sunday afternoon in March, 1944, at Black Rabbit Rock, Arundel, Sussex, they were testing a new type of light nylon rope to use abseiling down cliffs. The rope broke when Matthews was starting to make his descent. He fell a vertical 90 feet.

Another who was seriously injured in a cliff descent, also using a nylon rope, was Peter Andrew Carson. He had been born in Berlin where his father was a lawyer; his mother was formerly a concert singer.

In 1935, Carson came to England to school. After Munich, he tried to join the Territorial Army, but found this impossible with his German background. In 1940, at the time of Dunkirk, he was interned and sent to Australia. Fifteen months later, Carson returned to Britain to join the Pioneer Corps and later X-Troop.

In March 1944 he was due to take part in a parachute raid on a V-I site in France. The full scale rehearsal for this involved a night descent of the Seven Sisters Cliffs between Eastbourne and Newhaven. Carson was the first man down, and was knotted into the rope. This became entangled at the top when he had been lowered two-thirds of the distance. He was left dangling, with the rope growing tighter around his chest. Just before he lost consciousness, Carson managed to cut the rope but fell 60 feet on to the boulders beneath.

James Monahan, CBE, returned to the BBC, and retired as Controller of their European Services. Shortly after the war he published two volumes of poetry which were very well received. He is now director of the Royal Ballet School.

Paul Streeten, after being wounded in Italy, spent several months in hospital in Egypt and Britain. As a civilian, he returned briefly to Aberdeen University to receive his degree, the examination for which he had taken in the internment camp. He then took a degree with first class honours at Balliol College, Oxford, where he became a Fellow. After holding various important governmental and academic appointments, he is now consultant to the World Bank, and Director of the Centre for Asian Development Studies and Professor at Boston University.

Bryan Hilton-Jones, promoted to major and second-in-command of No. 10 Commando, and later to be awarded the Military Cross, landed in Normandy on D-Day.

He led regular reconnaissance patrols into German forward areas, and returning from one of these was shot and badly wounded in the stomach.

His wife Edwina had only recently given birth to their first child, Gavin, in Bangor. A friend telephoned her to say she had just heard 'Lord Haw-Haw' in Berlin broadcast a list of names of prisoners captured in Normandy, and Hilton-Jones was among them.

In December, 1944, Mrs. Hilton-Jones received a letter from her husband as a POW, and by the same post one from the Red Cross. He had been taken to a German Army hospital in Northern France, where he was considered so seriously wounded that orderlies dug a grave for him. Fortunately, the surgeon at the hospital was an abdominal specialist, and he operated on him despite this gloomy prognosis.

As the Allies advanced, the hospital was evacuated, and the surgeon left Hilton-Jones in charge because he spoke German so well. The Americans reached the hospital and Hilton-Jones was brought back to England. After many months, he was invalided out of the army; it was predicted he would never again be able to eat normal food. But the Skipper confounded them all; within a year, he was not only eating well again, he was actually climbing mountains. As he liked to say, 'Everything's an attitude of mind . . .'

Hilton-Jones went into the Foreign Office, as he had intended before the war but left to join ICI. Later, he and his wife and family moved to Spain, where he and two daughters were killed in a motor accident near Barcelona.

Once, during a time of great danger, George Lane had asked Hilton-Jones what to him was the real meaning of life. Without hesitation, the Skipper replied, 'To do something during my life which will make the world a better place after I have gone.'

The Unknown Soldier, and all who served with him in X-Troop, also lived by these words.

# Acknowledgments

I would like to thank all those who helped me in various ways in connection
with this book, especially:

Mr. Colin Anderson;
Mr. John Barratt, C.V.O;
Mrs. Elizabeth Bauin;
Lt. Col. F.A.D. Betts, M.B.E;
Brigadier Charles Breese, C.B.E;
Mr. Henry Brown, M.B.E;
Mr. L.W. Burnett;
Mr. P.A. Carson;
Sir Michael Cary, K.C.B;
Major-General T.B.L. Churchill, C.B., C.B.E., M.C;
Dr. J.G. Coates, D.S.O;
Mr. John Envers;
Mr. J. Faller-Fritsch;
Mr. A. Firth;
Major-General J.D. Frost, C.B., D.S.O., M.C;
Mr. Manfred Gans;
Mr. Roland Gant;
Mr. H.E.A. Geiser;
Miss Marjorie Goodfellow;
His Honour Judge Brian Grant;
Mrs. Edwina Hilton-Jones;
Major-General Sir Leslie Hollis, K.C.B., K.B.E;
Mr. I. ap G. Hughes;
Captain Lionel Hurd;
Mr. Robert K. Kent;
Mr. George H. Lane, M.C;
Colonel and Mrs. Peter Laycock;
Mrs. Joan M. Leasor;
Mrs. Sheena Lister;

Lord Lovat, D.S.O., M.C., T.D., J.P., D.L;
Mr. Peter Masters;
Mr. Trefor Matthews;
Mr. J.F. McGregor;
Mr. Michael J. Merton;
Mr. James Monahan, C.B.E;
Admiral of the Fleet, the Earl Mountbatten of Burma, K.G., P.C.,
    G.C.B., O.M., G.C.S.I., G.C.I.E., G.C.V.O., D.S.O;
Mr. Harry Nomburg;
Mrs. Barbara Pickering;
Mrs. Margot Pottlitzer;
Dr. Manfred Rommel;
Mr. Lewis Rosenbloom;
Professor Friedrich Ruge;
Mrs. Joan St. George Saunders;
Mr. and Mrs. John Shannon;
Dr. Hans Speidel;
Mr. J.W. Stevens;
Mr. Paul Streeten;
Mr. R.W.A. Suddaby;
Mr. T.G. Swinton;
Mr. Percy Towgood;
Mrs. Jean Whitburn;
Sir Ronald Wingate, Bt. C.B., C.M.G., C.I.E., O.B.E.,
    and Lady Wingate;
The Editor, *Sherbrooke Record,* Sherbrooke, Quebec;
The Librarians and staff at the London Library, Salisbury
    Library and Wilton Library.


Some others who helped me wish to remain anonymous for personal, political or other reasons. My debt to them is no less great.

J.L.

# Bibliography

*The Camouflage Story* : G. Barkas
(Cassell, 1952)
*Von Rundstedt : The Soldier and the Man* by His Chief of Staff Guenther
    Blumentritt
(Odhams Press Ltd., 1952)
*Bodyguard Of Lies* : Anthony Cave Brown
(Harper & Row, USA, 1975)
*Amateur Agent* : Ewan Butler
(George G. Harrap & Co. Ltd., 1963)
*Invasion* - they're coming! : Paul Carell
(George G. Harrap & Co., Ltd., 1962)
*Colonel Henri's Story* : edited by Ian Colvin
(The War Memoirs of Hugo Bleicher, former German Secret Agent)
(William Kimber, 1968)
*Deception In World War II* : Charles Cruickshank
(Oxford University Press, 1979)
*Soldier Of Democracy*
A Biography of Dwight Eisenhower : Kenneth S. Davis
(Doubleday & Co. Inc. 1946)
*The Counterfeit Spy* : Sefton Delmer
(Harper & Row, USA, 1971)
*The Game Of The Foxes* : Ladislas Farago
(McKay, 1971)
*Patton* : Ordeal and Triumph : Ladislas Farago
(Arthur Barker Ltd., 1966)
*S.O.E. in France* : M.R.D. Foot
(HMSO, 1968)
*Panzer Leader* : General Heinz Guderian
(Michael Joseph Ltd., 1952)
*Eva Braun* : Nerin E. Gun
(Leslie Frewin, 1969)

262

*The Other Side Of The Hill* : B.H. Liddell Hart
(Cassell & Co. Ltd., 1948)
*World War II* : Ronald Heiferman
(Octopus Books Ltd., 1973)
*Hitler's Table Talk, 1941-1944*
(Weidenfeld & Nicolson, 1953)
*Canaris* : Heinz Höhne
(Secker & Warburg 1977)
*The Normandy Campaign* : Robert Hung & David Mason
(Leo Cooper, 1976)
*That Drug Danger* : Sir James Hutchison, Bt. DSO, OStJ, LLD, TD.,
    Legion of Honour, Croix de Guerre
(Standard Press, Montrose, 1977)
*The Trail Of The Fox*, The Life of Field-Marshal Erwin Rommel : David
    Irving
(Weidenfeld & Nicolson, 1977)
*Decisive Battles Of World War II: The German View:* Edited by H.A.
    Jacobsen and J. Rohwer
(Andre Deutsch, 1965)
*I Was Monty's Double* : Clifton James
(Rider, 1954)
*The Other Way Round* : Judith Kerr
(Collins, 1975)
*Weapons Of War* : Edited by Andrew Kershaw
(B.P.C. Publishing Ltd., 1973)
*War At The Top* : James Leasor
(Michael Joseph, 1959)
*March Past*, A Memoir by Lord Lovat
(Weidenfeld & Nicolson, 1978)
*The Double-Cross System In The War Of 1938-45* : Sir John Masterman
(Yale University Press, 1972)
*Room 39*, Naval Intelligence in Action 1939-45 : Donald McLachlan
(Weidenfeld & Nicolson, 1968)
*Panzer Battles* : Major-General F.W. von Mellenthin
(Cassell & Co. Ltd., 1955)
*First Time 'D' Day Invasion : June 6th 1944* : Alan Melville
(Skeffington & Son Ltd., 1945)
*The Art Of Blitzkrieg* : Charles Messenger
(Ian Allan Ltd., 1976)
*The Man Who Never Was* : Ewen Montagu
(Evans, 1966)
*Beyond Top Secret U* : Ewen Montagu
(Peter Davies, 1977)
*Peace And War* : A Soldier's Life : Lieut-General Sir Frederick Morgan,
    KCB.
(Hodder & Stoughton, 1961)

*Practice To Deceive* : David Muir
(William Kimber, 1977)
*The Encyclopaedia Of World War II* : Edited by Thomas Parrish
(Secker & Warburg, 1978)
*Instruments Of Darkness* : Alfred Price
(William Kimber, 1967)
*Panzer-Grenadier Division 'Grossdeutschland'* : Bruce Quarrie
(Osprey Publishing Ltd., 1977)
*Rommel in Normandy* : Reminiscences by Friedrich Ruge
(Macdonald & Jane's, 1979)
*The Longest Day* : Cornelius Ryan
(Victor Gollancz Ltd., 1959)
*The Green Beret* : Hilary St. George Saunders
(Michael Joseph, 1949)
*Inside The Third Reich* : Albert Speer
(Weidenfeld & Nicolson, and Macmillan Company, New York, 1970)
*We Defended Normandy* : Lieutenant-General Hans Speidel
(Herbert Jenkins Ltd., 1951)
*Adolf Hitler* : John Toland
(Doubleday & Co., Inc., New York, 1976)
*Lunch With A Stranger* : David E. Walker
(Allan Wingate, 1957)
*The Fatal Decisions* (Six Decisive battles of the Second World War from the
    viewpoint of the vanquished)
With a commentary by Lieutenant-General Siegfried Westphal
(Michael Joseph, 1956)
*Stratagem : Deception And Surprise In War* : Barton Whaley
(Centre for International Studies, Massachusetts Institute of Technology,
    USA, 1969)
*Not In The Limelight* : Sir Ronald Wingate, Bt., CB., CMG., CIE., OBE.
(Hutchinson, 1959)
*Rommel* : Desmond Young
(Collins, 1950)

I have also had access to the secret report 'No. 10 Commando – An
International Experiment' by Major Bryan Hilton-Jones, MC, 1946, and have
consulted the following documents in the Public Record Office : War Diaries
of No. 10 Commando W.O. Class 218, pieces, 40, 56, 70 and 88; W.O. Class
106, pieces 4158, 4195, 4196 and 4197; W.O. Class 193, pieces 390 to 394, and
W.O. Class 32, pieces 10416 and 10417.

J.L.